COURSE 1

Daily Notetaking Guide Workbook

Needham, Massachusetts
Upper Saddle River, New Jersey

ISBN: 0-13-131477-7
1 2 3 4 5 6 7 8 9 10 08 07 06 05 04

Daily Notetaking Guide

Contents

Chapter 7
Data and Graphs

Chapter 8
Tools of Geometry

Chapter 9
Geometry and Measurement

Chapter 10
Integers

Chapter 11
Exploring Probability

Chapter 12
Equations and Inequalities

Lesson 1-1 *(pp. 5–7)*   **Understanding Whole Numbers**

Lesson Objective	**NAEP 2005 Strand**: Number Properties and Operations
▼ Writing and comparing whole numbers	**Topic:** Number Sense
	Local Standards: ______________________________

Vocabulary

The standard form of a number uses __________________________________

____

The expanded form of a number shows __________________________________

____

Trillions Period	Billions Period	Millions Period	Thousands Period	Ones Period
2 , 6	2 3 , 6	8 4 , 6	0 8 , 0	0 0

Example

❶ **Writing a Whole Number in Words** Write $42,046,708,002 in standard form and in words.

Standard form: [________] ← **Use commas to separate the periods.**

Words: First write the number in expanded form.

42,000,000,000   +   46,000,000   +   708,000   +   2

42 [______]   46 [______]   708 [______]   [____]

forty-two billion, forty-six million, seven hundred eight thousand, two

Check Understanding

1. Write the value of $26,236,846,080 in standard form and in words.

Standard form: [________]

Words:

[____]

Example

❷ Comparing and Ordering Whole Numbers

a. Use $<$ or $>$ to complete: 60,201 ▨ 60,102.

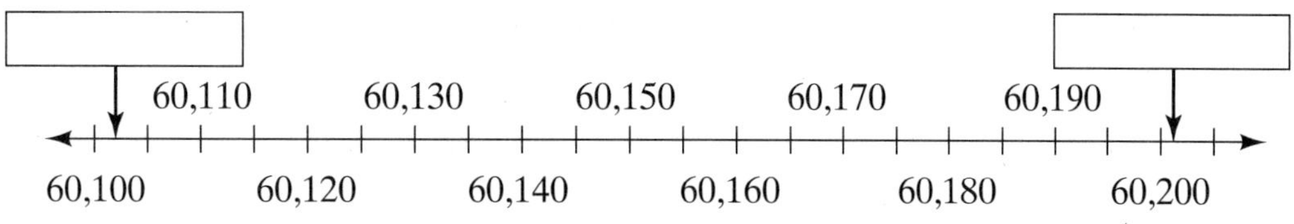

60,201 is to the right of 60,102.

So, 60,201 ☐ 60,102.

b. Write in order from least to greatest: 12,374; 13,341; 12,472.

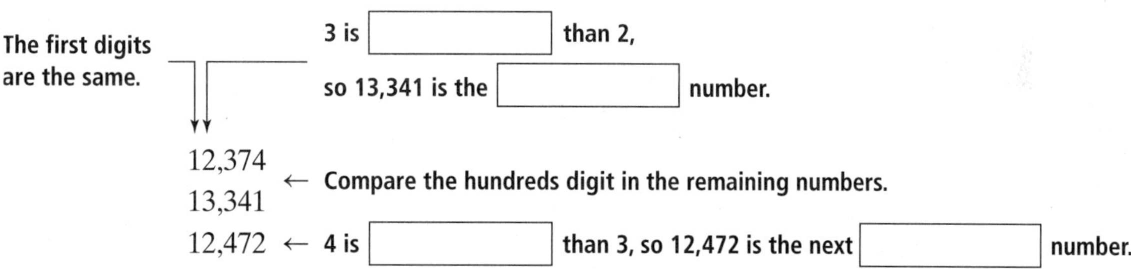

The order from least to greatest is ☐ ; ☐ ; ☐ .

Check Understanding

2. a. Use $<$ or $>$ to complete: 129,631 ☐ 142,832.

b. Write in order from least to greatest: 9,897; 9,987; 9,789.

☐ ; ☐ ; ☐

Lesson 1-2 *(pp. 9–12)*   **Reading and Writing Decimals**

Lesson Objective	**NAEP 2005 Strand:** Number Properties and Operations
▼ Reading and writing decimals	**Topic:** Number Sense
	Local Standards: ________________________________

Example

❶ Writing a Decimal in Expanded Form Write 608.0459 in expanded form.

six hundred	eight	four hundredths	five thousandths	nine ten thousandths

$608.0459 = $ ☐ $+$ ☐ $+$ ☐ $+$ ☐ $+$ ☐

Check Understanding

1. Write each number in expanded form.

  a. 3.1416

  ☐ $+$ ☐ $+$ ☐ $+$ ☐ $+$ ☐

  b. 0.865

  ☐ $+$ ☐ $+$ ☐

  c. 37.5

  ☐ $+$ ☐ $+$ ☐

  d. Reasoning Do you need to include 0.00 in the expanded form of 6.207?
  Explain.

Name_______________________________ Class_______________________________ Date _____________

Examples

❷ Writing a Decimal in Words Write 1.0936 in words.

1.0936 ← **Four decimal places indicate ten-thousandths.**

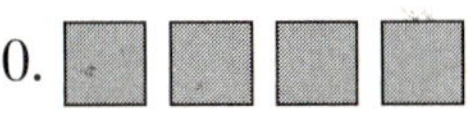 and [   ] ten-thousandths

❸ Writing a Decimal in Standard Form There are four thousand five hundred thirty-six ten-thousandths kilograms in one pound. Write this number in standard form.

[   ] ← **Write the whole number part.**

0. ← **Place the decimal point.**

 ← **Ten-thousandths is** [ ] **places to the right of the decimal point.**

0.[   ] ← **Place 4536.**

Check Understanding

2. Write each decimal in words.

  a. 16,702.3

[   ]

  b. 1,670.234

[   ]

  c. 1.67023

[   ]

3. **a. Olympics** Blaine Wilson scored nine and five hundred eighty-seven thousandths on the pommel horse during the 2000 Olympic Games. Write Blaine's score in standard form.

[   ]

  b. Number Sense In Blaine Wilson's score, which has the greater value, the 5 or the 7? Explain.

[   ]

Lesson 1-3 *(pp. 13–17)*   **Comparing and Ordering Decimals**

Lesson Objectives	**NAEP 2005 Strand:** Number Properties and Operations
▼ Use models	**Topic:** Number Sense
▼ Use place value	**Local Standards:** ________________________

Examples

❶ Using Models to Compare Decimals Draw models for 0.5 and 0.54. Which number is greater?

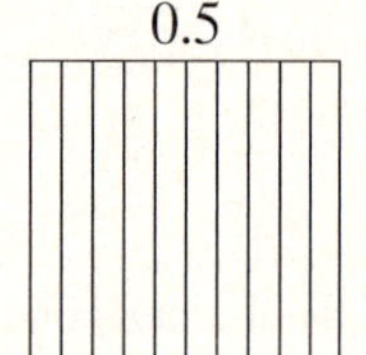
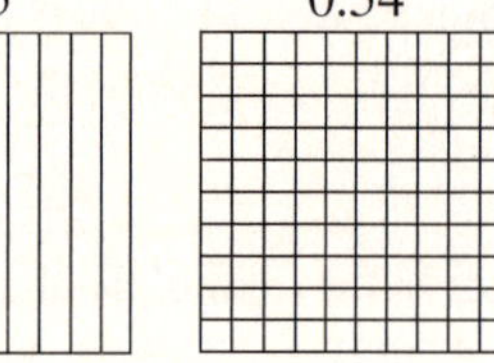

0.5   0.54

A [   ] area is shaded for 0.54 than 0.5, so 0.54 is [   ] than 0.5.

❷ Ordering Decimals on a Number Line Order the decimals 0.34, 0.04, 0.08, and 0.4 on a number line.

All the numbers are between 0 and 0.4. Make a number line showing tenths. Then mark the hundredths. Graph the points.

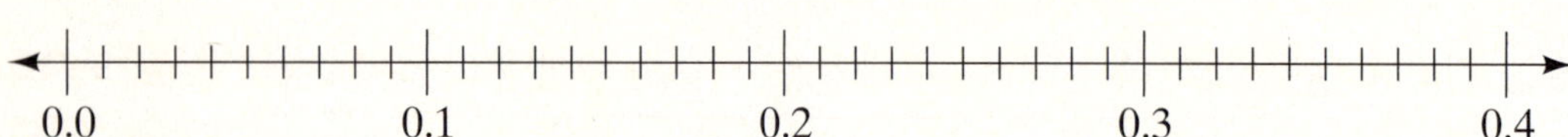

0.0   0.1   0.2   0.3   0.4

❸ Comparing Two Decimals Use <, =, or > to complete the statement: 0.28 ☐ 0.82.

The ones digits are the same.   **The tenths digits are different.**

2 is [   ] than 8.

Compare digits starting with the highest place values.   0.28
0.82

Since the 2 tenths in 0.28 is [   ] than the 8 tenths in 0.82, 0.28 [   ] 0.82.

Check Understanding

❶ Draw models for 0.59 and 0.6. Which number is greater?

[   ] is greater.

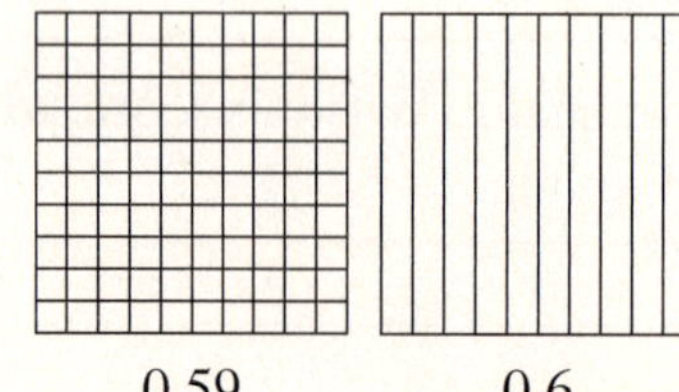

0.59   0.6

Example

❹ **Ordering Decimals** Order 0.8, 0.084, 0.48, and 0.84 from least to greatest. Write zeroes at the end of 0.8, 0.48, and 0.84. Then compare the digits starting with the highest place values.

0 is the [ ] tenths digit, so → 0.800
0.084 is the [ ] decimal.

0.084

0.480 ← 4 is the next [ ] tenths digit, so
0.840

0.480 is the next [ ] decimal.

↑
8 is the [ ] tenths digit, 0 hundredths is less than 4 hundredths, so 0.800 is the third [ ] decimal and 0.840 is the [ ] .

The decimals from least to greatest are [ ], [ ], [ ],
and [ ].

Check Understanding

2. Order the decimals 1.76, 1.87, 1.09, 1.91, 1.67, and 1.3 on a number line.

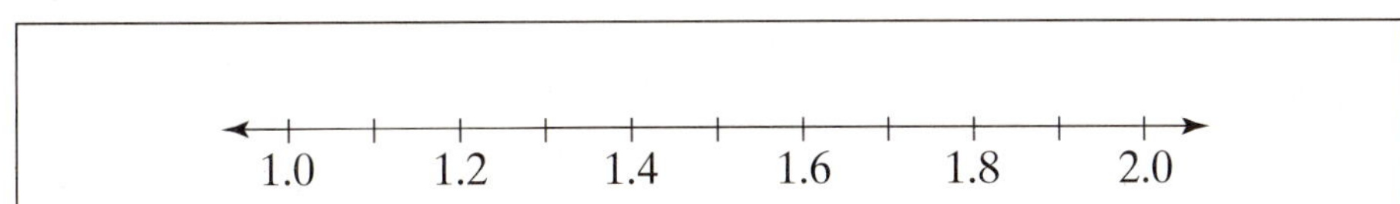

3. Use <, =, or > to complete each statement.

a. 2.37 [ ] 2.7   **b.** 0.56 [ ] 0.543   **c.** 1.650 [ ] 1.65

d. Reasoning Explain how you can use place value to compare 1.679 and 1.697.

4. Order each set of decimals from least to greatest.

a. 2.6, 2.76, 2.076

b. 3.059, 3.64, 3.46

Lesson 1-4 *(pp. 19–23)*

Estimating With Decimals

Lesson Objectives	**NAEP 2005 Strand:** Number Properties and Operations
V1 Estimate by rounding and compatible numbers **V2** Use front-end estimation	**Topic:** Estimation **Local Standards:** ______________________________

Vocabulary

Compatible numbers are ____

____

In front-end estimation, you ____

____

The symbol ≈ means ____

Examples

1 **Estimate by Rounding** Estimate each decimal. First round to the nearest whole number.

a. $15.66 + 4.1$

$$
\begin{array}{r}
15.66 \\
+\ 4.1 \\
\hline
\end{array}
\quad \rightarrow \quad
\begin{array}{r}
\boxed{} \\
+\ \boxed{} \\
\hline
\boxed{}
\end{array}
$$

So $15.66 + 4.1 \approx \boxed{}$.

b. 8.43×6.73

$$
\begin{array}{r}
8.43 \\
\times\ 6.73 \\
\hline
\end{array}
\quad \rightarrow \quad
\begin{array}{r}
\boxed{} \\
\times\ \boxed{} \\
\hline
\boxed{}
\end{array}
$$

So $8.43 \times 6.73 \approx \boxed{}$.

Check Understanding

1. Estimate by first rounding to the nearest whole number.

a. 1.16×32.06

$\boxed{} \times \boxed{} = \boxed{}$

So,

$\boxed{} \times \boxed{} \approx \boxed{}$

b. $5.05 - 1.9$

$\boxed{} - \boxed{} = \boxed{}$

So,

$\boxed{} - \boxed{} \approx \boxed{}$

c. $18.75 + 93.346$

$\boxed{} + \boxed{} = \boxed{}$

So,

$\boxed{} + \boxed{} \approx \boxed{}$

Course 1 Daily Notetaking Guide

Examples

2 **Estimating With Compatible Numbers** Use compatible numbers to estimate $28.75 \div 9.2$.

$28.75 \div 9.2$

$\boxed{} \div \boxed{} = \boxed{}$ ← Use compatible numbers such as $\boxed{}$ and $\boxed{}$.

$28.75 \div 9.2 \approx \boxed{}$.

3 **Using Front-End Estimation** A lemonade costs $1.79, sodas cost $1.29, and water costs $1.49. Use front-end estimation to estimate the total cost of one of each drink.

Step 1 Add the front-end digits, the dollars.

$1.79
  1.29
+ 1.49
$\$\boxed{}$

Step 2 Look at the cents and adjust the estimate.

$\left.\begin{array}{r}\$1.79 \\ 1.29\end{array}\right\} \rightarrow$ about $\$\boxed{}$

$\begin{array}{r}+\quad 1.49 \\ \hline \$3\end{array} \rightarrow$ about $\$\boxed{}$

about $\$\boxed{}$

The total cost is about $\$\boxed{} + \$\boxed{}$, or $\$\boxed{}$.

Check Understanding

2. a. Number Sense In Example 2, why are 30 and 10 compatible numbers?

____

b. Use compatible numbers to estimate $302.1 - 48.79$.

$\boxed{} - \boxed{} = \boxed{}$, so $\boxed{} - \boxed{} \approx \boxed{}$.

3. a. Use front-end estimation to estimate the total cost of one lemonade and two waters in Example 3.

____

b. Reasoning Find an estimate for the total cost of two sodas by rounding to the nearest whole number. Why is front-end estimation a good method when money is involved?

____

Lesson 1-5 *(pp. 25–29)*

Adding and Subtracting Decimals

Lesson Objectives	NAEP 2005 Strand: Number Properties and Operations
1 Add decimals **2** Subtract decimals	**Topic:** Number Operations **Local Standards:** ______________________________

Key Concepts

Properties of Addition

Commutative Property of Addition

Changing the [ ] of the addends does not change the sum.

$3.6 + 7 = $ [ ] $+$ [ ]

Associative Property of Addition

Changing the [ ] of the addends does not change the sum.

$(3.6 + 7) + 3 = 3.6 + $ [ ] $+$ [ ]

Identity Property of Addition

The sum of 0 and any number is [ ].

$3.6 + 0 = 0 + 3.6 = $ [ ]

Example

1 **Finding Decimal Sums** First estimate and then find the sum.

$6.8 + 4.65 + 2.125.$

Estimate $6.8 + 4.65 + 2.125 \approx$ [ ] $+$ [ ] $+$ [ ], or [ ]

Add.

$$
\begin{array}{r}
6.800 \\
4.650 \\
+\ 2.125 \\
\hline
\end{array}
$$

← Line up the decimal points.
← Write zeros so that all decimals have the same number of digits to the right of the decimal point.

Check for Reasonableness

The sum [ ] is reasonable since it is close to [ ].

Check Understanding

1. First estimate and then find the sum $0.84 + 2.0 + 3.32$.

$0.84 + 2.0 + 3.32 \approx$ [ ] $+$ [ ] $+$ [ ], or [ ].

Name_________________________________ Class_________________________________ Date _______________

Examples

❷ Using Properties of Addition Use mental math to find 8.5 + 0.65 + 1.5.

What you think

8.5 and 1.5 are easy to add. Adding 8.5 and 1.5 gives you ⬜.

Adding ⬜ and 0.65 gives you ⬜.

So, 8.5 + 0.65 + 1.5 = ⬜.

Why it works

8.5 + 0.65 + 1.5 = 8.5 + (1.5 + 0.65)   ← [⬜] **Property of Addition**

$\qquad$ = (8.5 + 1.5) + 0.65   ← [⬜] **Property of Addition**

$\qquad$ = ⬜ + 0.65   ← **Add inside the parentheses.**

$\qquad$ = ⬜   ← **Simplify.**

❸ Subtracting Decimals From Whole Numbers First estimate and then find 16 − 8.79.

Estimate 16 − 8.79 ≈ ⬜ − ⬜, or ⬜

Write a decimal point and two zeros.	Rename 6 as 5 and ⬜ tenths.	Rename 10 tenths as 9 tenths and 10 ⬜ .
16.00 + 8.79	$\overset{5\ 10}{1\cancel{6}.\cancel{0}0}$ + 8.79	$\overset{9}{\underset{}{15\ \cancel{\overset{}{16}}\ 10}}$ $\cancel{16}.\cancel{00}$ + 8.79 ← **Add.** ⬜

Check for Reasonableness The difference ⬜ is reasonable since it is close to ⬜ .

Check Understanding

2. Mental Math Use mental math to find each sum.

    a. 8.9 + 0 + 5.0   **b.** 74 + 19 + 1   **c.** 5.92 + 0.4 + 3.08

    ⬜   ⬜   ⬜

3. First estimate and then find the difference.

    a. 98 − 6.8   **b.** 82 − 4.916   **c.** 14.5 − 6.97   **d.** 0.4 − 0.13

    ⬜   ⬜   ⬜   ⬜

    e. Reasoning Use what you know about place value to explain why you should line up the decimal points before adding or subtracting.

    ⬜

Lesson 1-6 *(pp. 30–33)*   **Using a Problem-Solving Plan**

Lesson Objective	**Local Standards:** ______________________
▼ Use a plan to solve problems	

Key Concepts

A Problem-Solving Plan
1. Read and understand the problem.
2. Plan how to solve the problem.
3. Look back and check to see if your answer makes sense.

Example

❶ Seating 46 students and 3 teachers go to camp each day on a bus. The bus has 32 seats, and each seat holds 2 people. If every seat is used, how many seats will have two people?

Read and Understand

Determine what you need to know and what you need to find out. You are asked to find out how many seats on the bus will have [ ] people. You know there are [ ] seats, [ ] students, and [ ] teachers.

Plan and Solve

Choose a strategy.

Before you can find the number of seats with two people, you need to find the total number of passengers.

To find the total number of passengers, you add.

$$\boxed{} + \boxed{} = 49 \text{ passengers}$$

There are [ ] seats and at least one passenger in each seat. Suppose each passenger that gets on the bus chooses an empty seat. Subtract to find the number of people left when all 32 seats have one passenger each.

$$\boxed{} - 32 = \boxed{} \text{ passengers}$$

Since there are [ ] people remaining when each of the 32 seats has one person, there are [ ] seats with 2 people.

Look Back and Check

Think about how you solved the problem.

If 17 seats have two people, then ☐ seats have one person.

This means that there are 17 × ☐ + ☐ , or ☐ people

on the bus. The answer checks.

Check Understanding

1. If 4 additional teachers go to camp on the bus, how many seats will have only one person?

Lesson 1-7 *(pp. 35–39)*   **Multiplying Decimals**

Lesson Objectives	**NAEP 2005 Strand:** Number Properties and Operations
▼ Multiply decimals ▼ Use properties of multiplication	**Topic:** Number Operations **Local Standards:** _________________________

Key Concepts

Properties of Multiplication

Commutative Property of Multiplication

Changing the [ ] of the factors does not change the product.

$4.7 \times 5 -$ [ ] $\times$ [ ]

Associative Property of Multiplication

Changing the [ ] of the factors does not change the product.

$(4.7 \times 5) \times 2 -$ [ ] $\times ($ [ ] $\times$ [ ] $)$

Identity Property of Multiplication

The product of 1 and any number is [ ].

$4.7 \times 1 - 1 \times 4.7 -$ [ ]

Examples

❶ **Multiplying a Whole Number by a Decimal** Find the product 2.73×4.

$2.73 \leftarrow$ [ ] decimal places

$\times \quad 4 \leftarrow +$ [ ] decimal places

[ ][ ].[ ][ ] $\leftarrow$ [ ] decimal places

❷ **Multiplying Decimals** Find the product 0.6×0.42.

$0.42 \leftarrow$ [ ] decimal places

$\times \quad 4 \leftarrow +$ [ ] decimal places

[ ].[ ][ ][ ] $\leftarrow$ [ ] decimal places

Check Understanding

1. Find each product.

a. 6×0.13 **b.** 4.37×5 **c.** $0.3(0.2)$ **d.** $0.9 \cdot 0.14$

e. Number Sense In parts (c) and (d), both factors are less than 1. How does the answer in each part compare to its factors?

Name_____________________________________ Class_____________________________ Date ____________

Examples

❸ Cameron can read 196 words in a minute. Robert reads 1.6 times as fast. How many words can Robert read in a minute?

Estimate $196 \times 1.6 \approx 196 \times 1.5$, or ⬚.

```
      1   9   6  ←  ⬚ decimal places
   ×  1.  6  ←  ⬚ decimal place
   1  1   7   6
   +1  9   6
```
⬚⬚⬚.⬚ ← ⬚ decimal place

Robert can read about ⬚ words in a minute.

Check for Reasonableness ⬚ is reasonable since it is close to ⬚.

❹ Using the Properties of Multiplication Use mental math to find the product $0.25(1.5 \cdot 4)$.

What you think

0.25 and 4 are easy to multiply. Multiplying 0.25 and 4 gives ⬚.

Multiplying 1 and 1.5 gives ⬚. So, $0.25(1.5 \cdot 4) = $ ⬚.

Why it works

$0.25(1.5 \cdot 4) = (1.5 \times 0.25) \times 4$ ← ⬚ **Property of Multiplication**

$= 1.5 \times (0.25 \times 4)$ ← ⬚ **Property of Multiplication**

$= 1.5 \times $ ⬚ ← **Multiply inside the parentheses.**

$= $ ⬚ ← ⬚ **Property of Multiplication**

Check Understanding

2. Find each product.

a. 2.4×3.11

b. $15.1(3.84)$

3. Use mental math to find each product.

a. $2(5 \times 2.3)$

b. $3.1 \times 1 \times 100$

c. $500 \times 0.333(2)$

Lesson 1-8 *(pp. 40–42)*

Multiplying and Dividing Decimals by 10, 100, and 1,000

Lesson Objective	NAEP 2005 Strand: Number Properties and Operations
▼ Multiply and divide by 10, 100, and 1,000	Topic: Number Operations
	Local Standards: ____________________

Example

❶ **Multiplying by 10, 100, or 1,000** Use mental math to find each product.

a. $1,000(5.67) = 5.670.$

← To multiply a decimal by 1,000, move the decimal point ☐ places to the ☐.

= ☐

b. $6.01 \cdot 10 = 6.0.1$

← To multiply a decimal by 10, move the decimal point ☐ place to the ☐.

= ☐

Check Understanding

1. Use mental math to find each product.

a. $100(3.42)$

☐

b. 0.235×10

☐

c. $55.2 \cdot 1,000$

☐

Name_________________________________ Class_________________________________ Date _____________

Example

❷ **Dividing by 10, 100, or 1,000** Use mental math to find each quotient.

a. $7.15 \div 10 = 0.7.15$ ← **To divide a decimal by 10, move the decimal point ☐ place to the ☐ .**

$= $ ☐

b. $267.95 \div 1,000 = 0.267.95$ ← **To divide a decimal by 1000, move the decimal point ☐ places to the ☐ .**

$= $ ☐

Check Understanding

2. Use mental math to find each quotient.

a. $534.2 \div 100$

b. $0.235 \div 10$

c. $55.2 \div 1,000$

d. Number Sense Write a rule to divide by 10,000. Find $7.3 \div 10,000$.

Lesson 1-9 *(pp. 43–47)*

Dividing Decimals

<table>
<tr><td>Lesson Objectives
▼ Divide decimals by whole numbers
▼ Divide decimals by decimals</td><td>NAEP 2005 Strand: Number Properties and Operations
Topic: Number Operations

Local Standards: ______________________</td></tr>
</table>

Vocabulary and Key Concepts

Dividing Decimals

To divide a decimal by a decimal, multiply both the dividend and the divisor by the same number so that the divisor is a whole number.

Example $2.25 \div 0.5 = 22.5 \div 5$

A terminating decimal is __________________________________

____

A repeating decimal is ____________________________________

____

Example

❶ **Dividing by a Whole Number** A class of 27 students held a picnic. They purchased food and drinks for the picnic for a total cost of $93.15. What was the price for each student's meal?

Since you are looking for prices of equal meals, you need to divide.

Estimate $93.15 \div 27 \approx$ ☐ $\div$ ☐ , or ☐ .

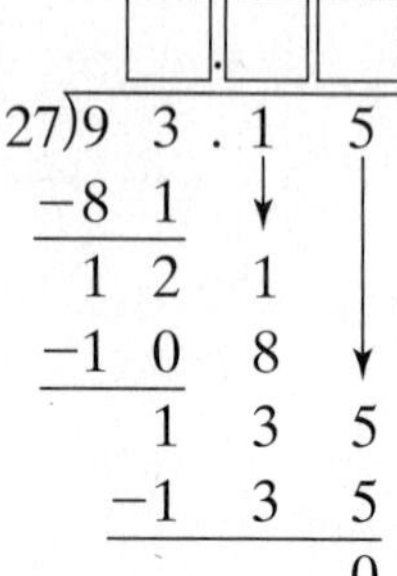

Divide as with whole numbers. Place ← the decimal point in the quotient above the decimal point in the dividend.

Each student's meal cost $ ☐ .

Check for Reasonableness ☐ is reasonable since it is close to ☐ .

Examples

❷ Finding a Decimal Quotient Find the quotient $9 \div 11$. Identify it as a terminating or repeating decimal.

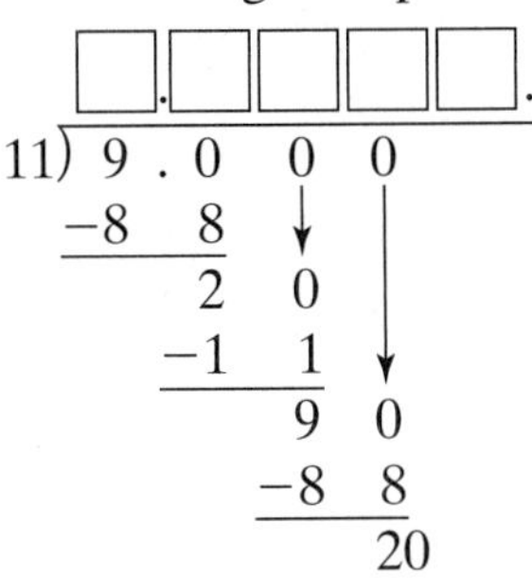

← Insert zeros when needed.

← The steps $20 - \boxed{}$ and $90 - \boxed{}$ will continue without end. So the digits $\boxed{}$ and $\boxed{}$ will keep $\boxed{}$.

Since the $\boxed{}$ repeats, $\boxed{}$ is a $\boxed{}$ decimal.

❸ Dividing a Decimal by a Decimal Find the quotient $9.674 \div 0.7$.

$0.7\overline{)9.674}$ ⟶

← Divide as with whole numbers. Place the decimal point in the quotient above the decimal point in the dividend.

Since the divisor has $\boxed{}$ decimal place, multiply the dividend and the divisor by $\boxed{}$ so that the divisor is a whole number.

Check Understanding

1. Find each quotient. Identify each as a terminating or repeating decimal.

a. $9.12 \div 6$

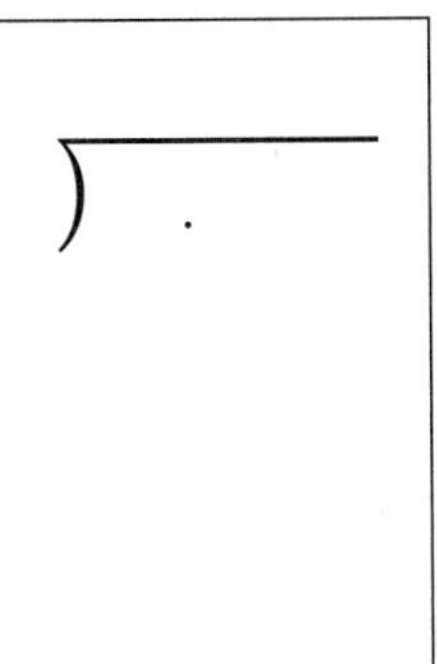

b. $2 \div 3$

c. $0.248 \div 0.04$

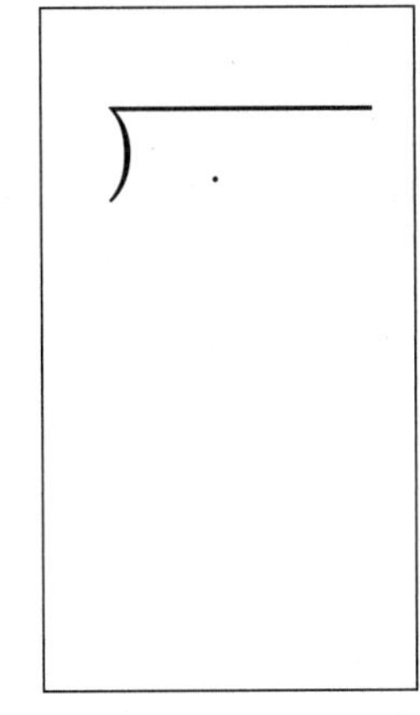

d. $38.125 \div 1.25$

Lesson 1-10 *(pp. 48–51)*

Order of Operations

Lesson Objective	NAEP 2005 Strand: Number Properties and Operations
▼ Use the order of operations	Topic: Properties of Number and Operations
	Local Standards: _________________________________

Vocabulary and Key Concepts

Order of Operations

1. Do all operations within [ ] first.
2. [ ] and [ ] in order from left to right.
3. [ ] and [ ] in order from left to right.

An expression is ____

____

Examples

❶ **Finding the Value of Expressions** Find the value of each expression.

a. $(5.5 + 6.5) \div 6 \times 3$

$(5.5 + 6.5) \div 6 \times 3 = \boxed{} \div 6 \times 3$ ← Add 5.5 and 6.5 within the parentheses.

$= \boxed{} \times 3$ ← Divide 12 by $\boxed{}$.

$= \boxed{}$ ← Multiply.

b. $20 - 5 \times 8 \div 2$

$20 - 5 \times 8 \div 2 = 20 - \boxed{} \div 2$ ← Multiply 5 by $\boxed{}$.

$= 20 - \boxed{}$ ← Divide $\boxed{}$ by 2.

$= \boxed{}$ ← Subtract.

❷ **Writing Expressions** Find the value of $\$3.50 + 8 \times \$.50 - 2 \times \$3.50$.

$\$3.50 + 8 \times \$.50 - 2 \times \$3.50 = \$3.50 + \$\boxed{} - \$\boxed{}$ ← Multiply.

$= \$\boxed{} - \$\boxed{}$ ← Add.

$= \$\boxed{}$ ← Subtract.

Name_________________________________ Class_________________________________ Date _______________

Check Understanding

1. Find the value of each expression.

a. $17 - 4 \times 2.25$

$$\boxed{} - \boxed{} \times \boxed{}$$
$$= \boxed{} - \boxed{}$$
$$= \boxed{}$$

b. $3.4 + 5 \times 2 - 1.7$

$$\boxed{} + \boxed{} \times \boxed{} - \boxed{}$$
$$= \boxed{} + \boxed{} - \boxed{}$$
$$= \boxed{} - \boxed{}$$
$$= \boxed{}$$

c. $(6 + 18) \div 3 \times 2$

$$(\boxed{} + \boxed{}) \div \boxed{} \times \boxed{}$$
$$= \boxed{} \div \boxed{} \times \boxed{}$$
$$= \boxed{} \times \boxed{}$$
$$= \boxed{}$$

d. Reasoning Explain when you might add before multiplying.

2. Find the value of $3 \times \$16.95 - \$10.00 + 4 \times \$1.50$.

Lesson 2-1 *(pp. 63–67)*   **Describing a Pattern**

Lesson Objectives	**NAEP 2005 Strand:** Algebra
▼ Continue a number pattern ▼ Write a rule for a number pattern	**Topic:** Patterns, Relations, and Functions **Local Standards:** _______________________

Vocabulary

Each number in a pattern is called a [ ].

A conjecture is ____

____

Example

❶ Finding Number Patterns Write the next two terms in this number pattern: 5, 12, 19, 26, …

Each term is [ ] **more than the previous term.**

$\rightarrow$ $+7\ +$[ ] $+$[ ] $+$[ ] $+$[ ]

5, 12, 19, 26, [ ] , [ ] , …

$\leftarrow$ Add [ ] to 26 to get the fifth term.
Add [ ] to 33 to get the sixth term.

The fifth and sixth terms are [ ] and [ ].

Check Understanding

1. Write the next two terms in each number pattern.

   a. 1, 11, 21, 31, [ ] , [ ] , …

   b. 56, 48, 40, 32, [ ] , [ ] , …

   c. 29, 36, 43, 50, [ ] , [ ] , …

   d. Reasoning What is the eighth term in the number pattern in Example 1?

   [   ]

Examples

❷ Writing Number Patterns From Rules Write the first six terms in the number pattern described by this rule: *Start with 47 and subtract 3 repeatedly.*

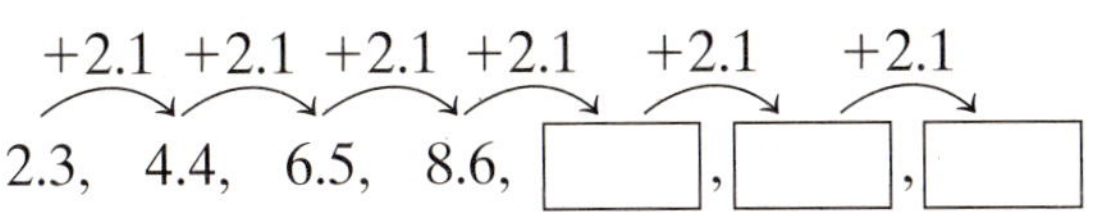

The first term is 47.

−3   ☐   ☐   ☐   ☐   ← **Subtract ☐ from each term to find the next term.**

47, ☐ , ☐ , ☐ , ☐ , ☐

❸ Writing a Rule Write the next three terms. Then write a rule to describe this number pattern: 2.3, 4.4, 6.5, 8.6, …

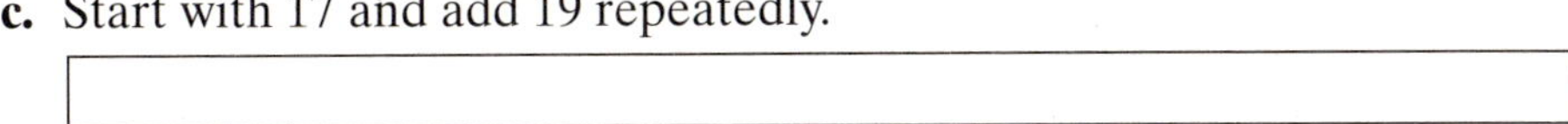

+2.1 +2.1 +2.1 +2.1   +2.1   +2.1

2.3,   4.4,   6.5,   8.6, ☐ , ☐ , ☐   ← **To get from one term to the next, add ☐ .**

The rule is [   ] .

Check Understanding

2. Write the first six terms in each number pattern.

  a. Start with 90 and subtract 15 repeatedly.

  b. Start with 1 and multiply by 3 repeatedly.

  c. Start with 17 and add 19 repeatedly.

3. Write the next three terms and write a rule to describe each number pattern.

  a. 1, 7, 49, 343, …

  b. 10.0, 8.8, 7.6, …

  c. 256, 128, 64, …

Lesson 2-2 *(pp. 68–72)*　　　　　　　　　　　　**Variables and Expressions**

Lesson Objectives	**NAEP 2005 Strand:** Algebra
▼ 1 Use variables	**Topic:** Variables, Expressions, and Operations
▼ 2 Evaluate algebraic expressions	**Local Standards:** _______________________

Vocabulary

A numerical expression is ___________________________________

____

A variable is ____

____

An algebraic expression is a _________________________________

____

To evaluate an algebraic expression is to ____________________

____

Example

❶ From Expressions to Algebra Tiles Draw algebra tiles to model the expression $2x + 3$.

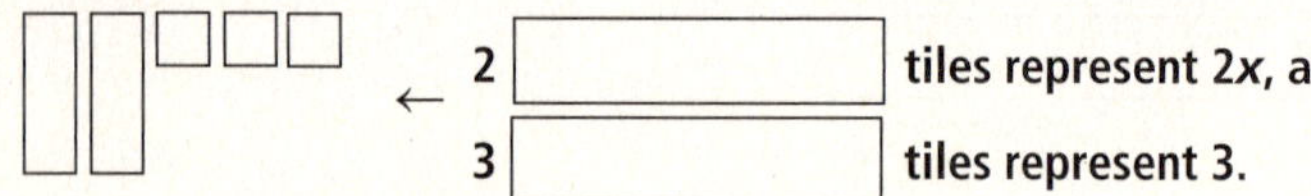

Check Understanding

1. Draw algebra tiles to model each expression.

a. $3x$　　　　　　　　**b.** $x + 2$　　　　　　　　**c.** $4x + 3$

Name_______________________________ Class_______________________________ Date _______________

Examples

② **Evaluate Algebraic Expressions** Evaluate $8x + 2$ for $x = 3$.

$8x + 2 = 8(\boxed{}) + 2$ ← **Replace x with $\boxed{}$.**

$= \boxed{} + 2$ ← **Multiply 8 and 3.**

$= \boxed{}$ ← **Add 24 and 2.**

③ **Canoe Rental** The cost to rent a canoe at the lake is a \$6 basic fee plus \$4 for each hour h the canoe is rented. The expression for the total cost of a canoe rental is $6 + 4h$. Complete the table for the given number of hours.

Hours	Total Cost
h	$6 + 4h$
1	
2	
3	

Substitute each number of hours for h.

← $6 + 4 \times \boxed{}$

← $6 + 4 \times \boxed{}$

← $6 + 4 \times \boxed{}$

Check Understanding

2. Evaluate each expression for $x = 7$.

   a. $3x + 15$ **b.** $5x \div 7$ **c.** $56 - 4x$

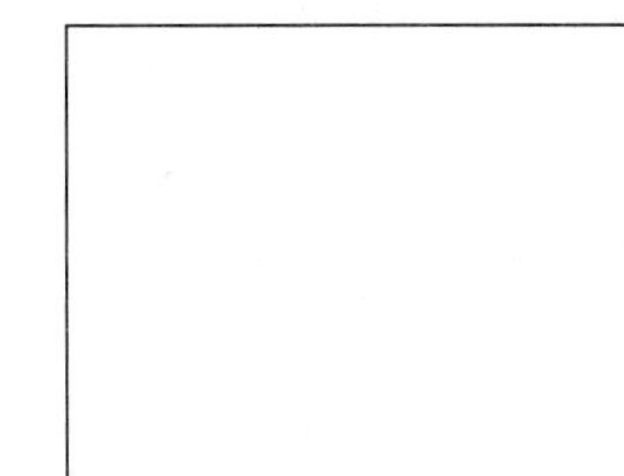

   d. Reasoning Explain how you used the order of operations to evaluate the expression in part (c).

3. In Example 3, how much will it cost to rent a canoe for 6 hours?

Lesson 2-3 *(pp. 74–78)*   **Writing Algebraic Expressions**

Lesson Objectives	**NAEP 2005 Strand:** Algebra
▼ Relate words to algebraic expressions ▼ Use algebraic expressions	**Topic:** Variables, Expressions, and Operations **Local Standards:** _______________________________

Examples

❶ From Words to Expressions Write an expression for each word phrase.

a. 8 less than r

b. the quotient when y is divided by 12

❷ Retail A newspaper advertisement reads, "Buy 3 T-shirts of the same kind, take \$5 off the total price." Let t represent the cost of one T-shirt. Write an algebraic expression that describes the situation.

Total Cost	5
t t t	**Write the cost of 3 T-shirts as** ☐ .

An expression is ☐ − ☐ .

Check Understanding

1. Write an expression for each word phrase.

a. five divided by y

b. six times z

c. m increased by 3.4

2. Space Travel At the end of a space flight, an astronaut's height can temporarily be 2 inches greater than normal. Write an algebraic expression that describes an astronaut's height h after a flight.

Examples

❸ From Patterns to Expressions Write an expression to describe the relationship of the data in the table.

n	■
1	3
4	12
5	15

$1 \times \boxed{} = 3$

$4 \times \boxed{} = 12$ ←

$5 \times \boxed{} = 15$

Multiplying each number in the first column by $\boxed{}$ gives you the number in the second column.

The expression $\boxed{}$, or $\boxed{}$, describes the pattern.

❹ Jobs Harry has been delivering newspapers 2 fewer years than his sister Nancy. Write an expression that represents the number of years Harry has been delivering newspapers.

Let n = the number of years Nancy has been delivering newspapers. ←

You don't know the number of years Nancy has been delivering papers, so choose a variable to represent it.

Since Harry has been delivering newspapers for fewer years than Nancy, he has been delivering papers for $\boxed{}$ years.

Check Understanding

3. Write an expression to describe the relationship of the data in the table.

a.

n	■
2	1
6	3
9	4.5

$\boxed{}$

b.

x	■
2	6
5	9
7	11

$\boxed{}$

4. a. Age Brandon is 28 years younger than his father. Write an expression using Brandon's age to describe his father's age.

$\boxed{}$

b. If Brandon is 13, how old is his father?

$\boxed{}$

Lesson 2-4 *(pp. 80–82)*   Make a Table and Look for a Pattern

Lesson Objective	NAEP 2005 Strand: Algebra
▼ Solve problems by making a table to find a pattern	Topic: Patterns, Relations, and Functions
	Local Standards: ______________________

Example

❶ **Make a Table to Find a Pattern** Each side of a five-sided table seats two people. Find the number of available seats in this chain of six tables.

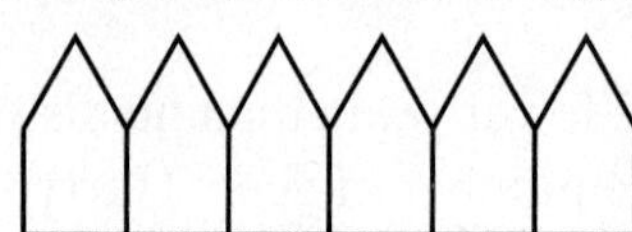

(**Read and Understand**) There are [____] five-sided tables. Each table seats [____] people on each side.

(**Plan and Solve**) To find the number of seats when six tables are pushed together, start by finding the number of seats when there are fewer tables.

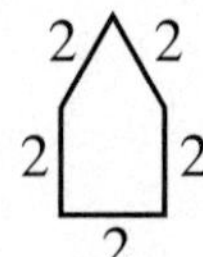   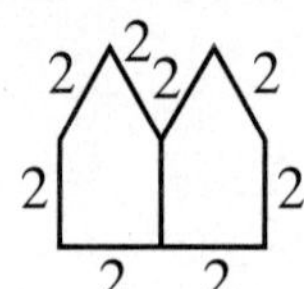   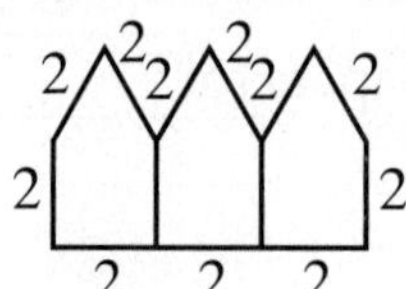

1 table → [____] seats   2 tables → [____] seats   3 tables → [____] seats

Number of Tables	1	2	3	4	5	6
Number of Seats	10	16	22			

← Extend the pattern by adding [__] seats for each new table.

There will be [____] seats available.

(**Look Back and Check**) Six tables pushed together seat 6 × [____], or [____], people on the sides and [____] people on each end, or

36 + [____] + [____] = [____] people.

Name_______________________ Class_______________________ Date _______________

Check Understanding

1. **Number Sense** Is the number of available seats for 20 tables pushed together twice the number of seats for ten tables pushed together? Explain.

Lesson 2-5 *(pp. 80–82)*

Using Number Sense to Solve One-Step Equations

Lesson Objectives	**NAEP 2005 Strand:** Algebra
▼ Use mental math to solve equations	**Topic:** Equations and Inequalities
▼ Estimate solutions	**Local Standards:** _______________________

Vocabulary and Key Concepts

Number Properties

Identity Properties

The sum of 0 and any number is ☐ .

  Algebra $0 + a = $ ☐   **Arithmetic** $0 + 9 = $ ☐

The product of 1 and any number is ☐ .

  Algebra $1 \cdot a = $ ☐   **Arithmetic** $1 \cdot 9 = $ ☐

Commutative Properties

Changing the ☐ of the addends or factors does not change the sum or product.

  Algebra $a + b = $ ☐ $+$ ☐ $a \cdot b = $ ☐ $\cdot$ ☐

  Arithmetic $9 + 6 = $ ☐ $+$ ☐ $9 \cdot 6 = $ ☐ $\cdot$ ☐

Associative Properties

Changing the ☐ of numbers does not change the sum or product.

  Algebra $a + (b + c) = $ ☐ $= $ ☐ $a(bc) = $ ☐ $\cdot$ ☐

  Arithmetic $9 + (6 + 4) = $ ☐ $+$ ☐ $9 \cdot (6 \cdot 4) = $ ☐ $\cdot$ ☐

An equation is ____

An open sentence is ____

A solution of an equation is ____

Examples

❶ Deciding Whether an Equation Is True or False Is the equation $24 - 16 = 8$ *true* or *false*?

$24 - 16 \stackrel{?}{=} 8$ ← **Write the equation.**

☐   ← **Subtract 16 from 24.**

☐ $\stackrel{?}{=} 8$ ← **Compare.**   The equation is ☐ .

Course 1 Daily Notetaking Guide

❷ Using Mental Math Use mental math to solve each equation.

a. $y - 7 = 15$

What you think

[   ] $- 7 = 15$, so the solution is [   ].

b. $d \div 9 = 6$

What you think

[   ] $\div 9 = 6$, so the solution is [   ].

❸ Estimating Solutions Estimate the solution of each equation.

a. $r \div 3 = 67$

Use compatible numbers: It is easy to multiply 3 and 70, and 70 is close to [   ]. Solve $r \div 3 = 70$ to estimate the solution of [   ].

The solution of $r \div 3 = 67$ is about [   ].

b. $b - 29.23 = 41.06$

Round 29.23 and 41.06 to the nearest whole number.

$29.23 \approx$ [   ] $41.06 \approx$ [   ]

Estimate the solution of $b - 29.23 = 41.06$ by solving [   ].

Since [   ] $- 29 = 41$, the solution of $b - 29.23 = 41.06$ is about [   ].

Check Understanding

1. Mental Math Use mental math to solve each equation.

a. $17 - x = 8$

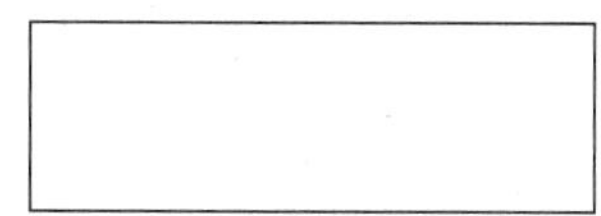

b. $w \div 4 = 20$

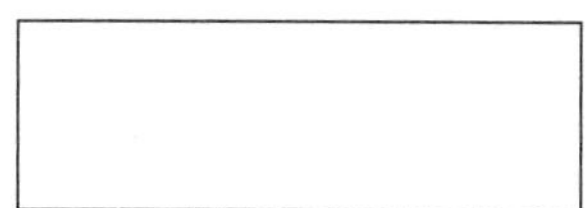

c. $4.7 + c = 5.9$

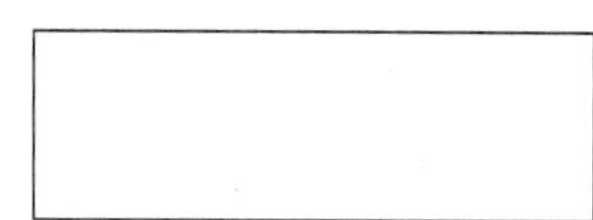

2. Estimation Estimate the solution of each equation.

a. $y - 6.14 = 23.08$

b. $8.2x = 49.3$

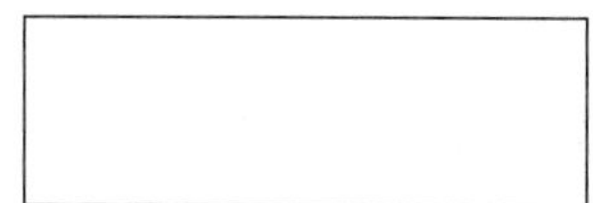

c. $d - 3.8 = 14.1$

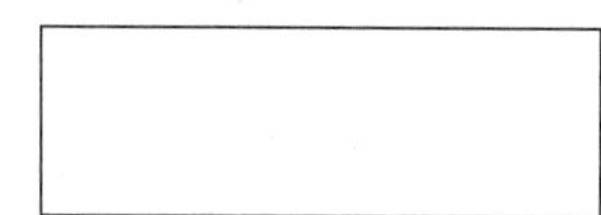

3. Tell whether each equation is *true* or *false*.

a. $7 \times 9 = 63$

b. $4 + 5 = 45$

c. $70 - 39 = 41$

Lesson 2-6 *(pp. 90–94)*   Solving Addition and Subtraction Equations

Lesson Objectives	**NAEP 2005 Strand:** Algebra
▼ Solve equations by subtracting ▼ Solve equations by adding	**Topic:** Equations and Inequalities **Local Standards:** _______________________

Vocabulary and Key Concepts

Subtraction Property of Equality

If you [   ] the same value from each side of an equation, the two sides remain equal.

Arithmetic

$2 \cdot 3 = 6$, so $2 \cdot 3 - 4 = 6 - \boxed{}$.

Algebra

If $a = b$, then $a - c = b - \boxed{}$.

Addition Property of Equality

If you [   ] the same value to each side of an equation, the two sides remain equal.

Arithmetic

$2 \cdot 3 = 6$, so $2 \cdot 3 + 4 = 6 + \boxed{}$.

Algebra

If $a = b$, then $a + c = b + \boxed{}$.

Inverse operations are ____

Example

1 **Solve Equations by Subtracting** Solve $h + 9 = 14$.

Get h alone on one side of the equation.

$$h + 9 = 14$$
$$\underline{\quad -\boxed{} \quad -\boxed{}\quad}$$

← Subtract $\boxed{}$ from each side to undo the $\boxed{}$ and get h by itself.

$$h = \boxed{}$$ ← Simplify.

Check $h + 9 = 14$ ← Check your solution in the original equation.

$\boxed{} + 9 \stackrel{?}{=} 14$ ← Substitute $\boxed{}$ for h.

$\boxed{} = 14 \checkmark$

Check Understanding

1. Solve $w + 4.3 = 9.1$. Check the solution.

[   ]

Examples

❷ Solving Equations by Subtracting Solve $p - 22.3 = 5.08$.

$p - 22.3 +$ [ ] $= 5.08 +$ [ ] ← **Add** [ ] **to undo the** [ ]**.**

$p =$ [ ] ← **Simplify.**

❸ Entertainment The sale price of a CD is $11.49. This is $3.50 less than the regular price of the CD. What is the regular price of the CD?

Words | sale price | is | $3.50 | less than | regular price |

Let [ ] = the regular price.

Equation [ ] = [ ] − [ ]

$r \quad - \quad 3.50 \quad = \quad 11.49$ ← **Write the equation.**

$+$ [ ] $+$ [ ] ← **Add** [ ] **to each side to undo the** [ ]**.**

$r =$ [ ] ← **Simplify.**

The regular price of the CD is [ ].

Check Understanding

2. Solve each equation.

a. $n - 53 = 28$ **b.** $x - 43 = 12$ **c.** $k - 6.4 = 0$

3. A cat has gained 1.8 pounds since its checkup a year ago. It now weighs 11.6 pounds. How much did it weigh at its checkup last year?

4. The temperature dropped 9°F between 7 P.M. and midnight. It was 54°F at midnight. Write an equation to find the temperature at 7 P.M.

Lesson 2-7 *(pp. 95–98)* — Solving Multiplication and Division Equations

Lesson Objectives	NAEP 2005 Strand: Algebra
▼ Solve equations by dividing ▼ Solve equations by multiplying	Topic: Equations and Inequalities Local Standards: _______________________

Key Concepts

Division Property of Equality

If you [____________] each side of an equation by the same nonzero number, the two sides remain equal.

Arithmetic

$4 \times 2 = 8$, so $4 \times 2 \div 2 = 8 \div \boxed{}$.

Algebra

If $a = b$ and $c \neq 0$, then $a \div c = b \div \boxed{}$.

Multiplication Property of Equality

If you [____________] each side of an equation by the same number, the two sides remain equal.

Arithmetic

$6 \div 2 = 3$, so $(6 \div 2) \times 2 = 3 \times \boxed{}$.

Algebra

If $a = b$, then $a \cdot c = b \cdot \boxed{}$.

Example

❶ Solving Equations by Dividing Solve $6x = 144$.

Divide each side by [ ] to undo the

$6x \div \boxed{} = 144 \div \boxed{}$ ← [____________] and get *x* alone on one side.

$x = \boxed{}$ ← Simplify.

Check $6x = 144$ ← Check your solution in the original equation.

$6 \times \boxed{} \stackrel{?}{=} 144$ ← Replace *x* with $\boxed{}$.

$\boxed{} = 144$ ✓

Check Understanding

1. Solve each equation. Then check the solution.

a. $9x = 36$

b. $10y = 27$

c. $0.8p = 32$

Examples

❷ Entertainment The cost of a pay-per-view concert on television is $39.95. Five friends decide to watch the concert together and split the cost equally. What amount will each friend pay?

Use a diagram to help write an equation.

Total Cost				
c	c	c	c	c

Let c = each person's share of the cost of the concert.

The equation $\boxed{}$ = $\boxed{}$ models this situation.

$$5c = 39.95 \qquad \leftarrow \textbf{Write the equation.}$$

$$5c \div \boxed{} = 39.95 \div \boxed{} \quad \leftarrow \textbf{Divide each side by } \boxed{} \textbf{ to undo the } \boxed{}.$$

$$c = \boxed{} \qquad \leftarrow \textbf{Simplify.}$$

Each friend's share is $\boxed{}$.

❸ Solve Equations by Multiplying Solve $x \div 6.3 = 9$.

$$x \div 6.3 \times \boxed{} = 9 \times \boxed{} \quad \leftarrow \textbf{Multiply by } \boxed{} \textbf{ to undo the } \boxed{} \textbf{ and get } x \textbf{ alone.}$$

$$x = \boxed{} \qquad \leftarrow \textbf{Simplify.}$$

Check Understanding

2. Fundraising The Pep Club sells greeting cards for a fundraiser. It receives $.35 profit for each card it sells. The club's total profit is $302.75. Write and solve an equation to find the number of greeting cards the Pep Club sells.

3. Solve each equation. Then check the solution.

a. $n \div 5 = 40$ **b.** $w \div 1.5 = 10$ **c.** $z \div 0.2 = 7.9$

Lesson 2-8 (pp. 99–103)   Exponents

Lesson Objectives	NAEP 2005 Strand: Algebra
▼ Use exponents ❷ Simplify expressions with exponents	Topic: Equations and Inequalities Local Standards: _______________________

Vocabulary and Key Concepts

Order of Operations

1. Do all operations within [   ] first.

2. Do all work with exponents.

3. [   ] and [   ] in order form left to right.

4. [   ] and [   ] in order from left to right.

An [   ] tells you how many times
a number, or [   ], is used as a factor.

$$8 \times 8 \times 8 = 8^3 \leftarrow [\quad]$$
$$\uparrow$$
$$[\quad]$$

A power is ____

Example

❶ **Using Exponents** Write $5 \times 5 \times 5 \times 5$ using an exponent. Name the base and the exponent.

$$5 \times 5 \times 5 \times 5 = 5^{[\;]} \leftarrow 5^4 \text{ means that } [\;] \text{ is used as a factor } [\;] \text{ times.}$$

The base is $[\;]$ and the exponent is $[\;]$.

Check Understanding

1. Write each expression using an exponent. Name the base and the exponent.

   a. 3.94×3.94 **b.** $7 \times 7 \times 7 \times 7$ **c.** $x \cdot x \cdot x$

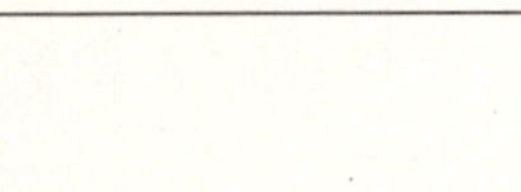   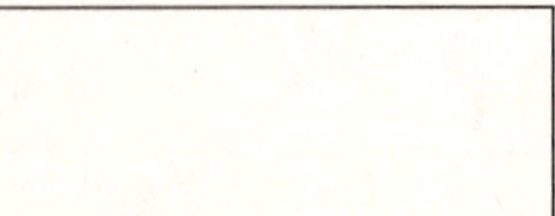

   d. Number Sense Does 5^4 have the same value as 5×4? Explain.

    Course 1 Daily Notetaking Guide

Name_________________________________ Class_________________________________ Date ______________

Examples

❷ **Writing in Expanded Form** Write the number 82,306 in expanded form using powers of 10.

$82,306 = 80,000 + 2,000 + 300 + 6$

$\qquad = 8 \times 10,000 + 2 \times 1,000 + 3 \times 100 + 0 \times 10 + 6 \times 1$

$\qquad = 8 \times \boxed{} + 2 \times \boxed{} + 3 \times \boxed{} + 0 \times \boxed{} + 6 \times 1$

❸ **Simplifying Powers** Simplify each expression.

a. $6^3 = 6 \times 6 \times 6 = \boxed{}$ ← The base $\boxed{}$ is used as a factor $\boxed{}$ times.

b. $3^5 = $  ← Use a calculator without an exponent key.

c. $2.7^4 = $ 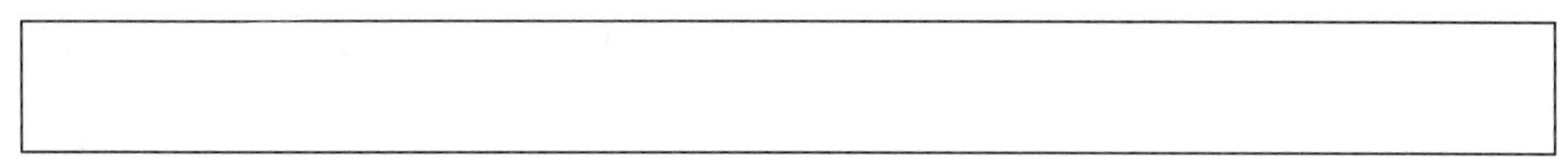 ← Use a calculator with an exponent key.

❹ **Simplifying Expressions** Simplify the expression $24 - (8 - 1.2 \times 5)^2$.

$24 - \left(8 - \boxed{}\right)^2$ ← Simplify 1.2×5 in parentheses first.

$24 - \left(\boxed{}\right)^2$ ← In parentheses, simplify $8 - 6$.

$24 - \boxed{}$ ← Simplify 2^2.

$\boxed{}$ ← Subtract 24 and 4.

Check Understanding

2. Write each number in expanded form using powers of 10.

a. 55,607

b. 380, 254

3. Simplify each expression.

a. 10^5 **b.** 3^9 **c.** 1.1^3

d. $2^3 - 6 \div 3$ **e.** $1 + 11^2 - 20 \div 2$ **f.** $5 + (2 + 1)^2$

Lesson 2-9 *(pp. 105–108)*   The Distributive Property

Lesson Objective	NAEP 2005 Strand: Number Properties and Operations
▼ Use the distributive property	Topics: Number Sense; Number Operations
	Local Standards: _____________________

Key Concepts

The Distributive Property

Arithmetic	**Algebra**
$8 \times (4 + 6) = (8 \times \boxed{}) = (8 \times \boxed{})$	$a(b + c) = \boxed{} + \boxed{}$
$7 \times (6 - 2) = (7 \times \boxed{}) = (7 \times \boxed{})$	$a(b - c) = \boxed{} - \boxed{}$

Example

❶ Evaluating Expressions Use the Distributive Property to simplify 5×47.

What you think

Think of 47 as $40 + 7$.

Then multiply by 5: $5 \times 40 = \boxed{}$ and $5 \times 7 = \boxed{}$.

Now add the two products: $\boxed{} + \boxed{} = \boxed{}$.

Why it works

$5 \times 47 = 5 \times \left(\boxed{} + \boxed{} \right)$ ← Write 47 as $\boxed{} + \boxed{}$.

$\quad = (5 \times 40) + (5 \times 7)$ ← Use the $\boxed{}$ Property.

$\quad = \boxed{} + \boxed{}$ ← Simplify within parentheses.

$\quad = \boxed{}$ ← Add.

Check Understanding

1. Use the Distributive Property to simplify each expression.

a. 3×42

b. 5×68

Example

❷ **Money** A student bought 4 tickets that cost $5.50. What was the total cost of the tickets?

$4 \times 5.50 = 4\left(\boxed{} + \boxed{}\right)$ ← **Write 5.5 as** $\boxed{}$ **+** $\boxed{}$.

$= (4 \times 5.00) + (4 \times 0.50)$ ← **Use the** $\boxed{}$ **Property.**

$= \boxed{} + \boxed{}$ ← **Simplify within parentheses.**

$= \boxed{}$ ← **Add.**

The total cost was $\boxed{}$.

Check Understanding

2. A local video store charges $2.80 for each day a rental is late. What are the late charges if a video is 5 days late?

Lesson 3-1 *(pp. 119–122)*   **Divisibility and Mental Math**

Lesson Objective	**NAEP 2005 Strand:** Number Properties and Operations
▼ Use divisibility tests	**Topic:** Properties of Number and Operations
	Local Standards: _____________________

Vocabulary and Key Concepts

Divisibility of Whole Numbers

A whole number is divisible by

- ☐ if it ends in 0, 2, 4, 6, or 8.
- ☐ if the sum of its digits is divisible by 3.
- ☐ if it ends in a 0 or 5.
- ☐ if the sum of its digits is divisible by 9.
- ☐ if it ends in a 0.

One whole number is ☐ by a second whole number if the

remainder is ☐ when the first number is divided by the second number.

An even number is ____

An odd number is ____

Example

❶ Using Mental Math for Divisibility   Is the first number divisible by the
second? Use mental math.

a. 46 by 3   **b.** 63 by 7

Think Since $3 \times 15 = $ ☐ ,   **Think** Since $7 \times 9 = $ ☐ ,

and $3 \times 16 = $ ☐ ,   63 ☐ divisible by 7.

46 ☐ divisible by 3.

Check Understanding

1. a. Is 64 divisible by 6? ☐   **b.** Is 93 divisible by 3? ☐

  c. Number Sense Since 54 is divisible by 6, explain why 54 is also divisible
  by 2 and 3.

☐

                                    Course 1 Daily Notetaking Guide

Name_________________________________ Class_________________________________ Date _____________

Examples

❷ Divisibility by 2, 5, or 10 Test each number for divisibility by 2, 5, or 10.

a. 580

580 ends with a ⬚.

So, it ⬚ divisible by 2, 5, or 10.

b. 3,042

3,042 ends with a ⬚.

So, it is divisible by ⬚ but not by ⬚ or ⬚.

❸ Divisibility by 3 Test each number for divisibility by 3.

$6 + 5 + 1 + 5 =$ ⬚   ← Find the sum of the digits in 6,516.

$17 \div 3$ has a remainder of ⬚.   ← The sum ⬚ divisible by 3.

So, 6,515 ⬚ divisible by 3.

❹ Divisibility by 9 A baker sells muffins in boxes that contain exactly 9 muffins each. Can the baker place 576 muffins in boxes of 9 with none left over?

If 576 is divisible by 9, then there will be no muffins left over.

$5 + 7 + 6 =$ ⬚   ← Find the sum of the digits in 576.

$18 \div 9 =$ ⬚   ← The sum ⬚ divisible by 9.

So, 576 ⬚ divisible by 9. There ⬚ muffins left over.

Check Understanding

2. Test each number for divisibility.

a. 150 by 2, 5, or 10

b. 325 by 2, 5, or 10

c. 1,021 by 2, 5, or 10

d. 2,112 by 2, 5, or 10

e. 613 by 3

f. 1,770 by 3

g. 882 by 3

h. 225 by 9

j. 1,655 by 9

k. 52,371 by 9

3. Reasoning Explain why a number that is divisible by 9 must also be divisible by 3.

Lesson 3-2 *(pp. 123–126)* **Prime Numbers and Prime Factorization**

Lesson Objectives	**NAEP 2005 Strand:** Number Properties and Operations
▼ Find factors of a number ❷ Find the prime factorization of a number	**Topic:** Properties of Number and Operations **Local Standards:** ______________________________

Vocabulary

A factor is ____

____

A composite number is ____

____

A prime number is ____

____

A prime factorization is ____

____

Example

❶ **Finding Factors** List the factors of each number.

a. 24

1×24 ← **Write factor pairs. Start with 1.**

$2 \times \boxed{}, 3 \times \boxed{}, 4 \times \boxed{}$ ← $\boxed{}, \boxed{},$ **and** $\boxed{}$ **are factors. Skip 5, since 24 is not divisible by 5.**

$6 \times \boxed{}$ ← **Stop when you repeat factors.**

The factors of 24 are $\boxed{}, \boxed{}, \boxed{}, \boxed{}, \boxed{}, \boxed{}, \boxed{},$ and $\boxed{}$.

b. 35

1×35 ← **Write factor pairs. Start with 1.**

$\boxed{} \times 7$ ← **Skip 2, 3, and 4, since 35 is not divisible by 2, 3, or 4.** $\boxed{}$ **is a factor. Skip 6, since 35 is not divisible by 6.**

$7 \times \boxed{}$ ← **Stop when you repeat factors.**

The factors of 35 are $\boxed{}, \boxed{}, \boxed{},$ and $\boxed{}$.

Check Understanding

1. List all the factors of 42.

Name_____________________________ Class_____________________________ Date _____________

Examples

❷ Prime or Composite? Tell whether each number is *prime* or *composite*. Explain.

a. 61 [ ] ; 61 has [ ] factors, [ ] and [ ].

b. 65 [ ] ; 65 is divisible by [ ], so it has more than [ ] factors.

❸ Prime Factorization Find the prime factorization of 90.

Method 1 Using a division ladder

2)90   ← **Divide 90 by the prime number 2. Work down.**

3)[ ]   ← **The result is** [ ] **. Divide by the prime number 3.**

3)[ ]   ← **The result is** [ ] **. Divide by 3 again.**

[ ]   ← **The prime factorization is** [ ] × [ ] × [ ] × [ ].

Method 2 Using a factor tree

$90 = $ [ ] × [ ] → ○ ▭   ← **Since the sum of the digits of 90 is 9, 90 is divisible by 3.**

$30 = $ [ ] × [ ] → ○ ▭   ← **Circle the prime numbers as you find them.**

$10 = $ [ ] × [ ] → ○ ○

The prime factorization of 90 is [ ] × [ ]^2 × [ ].

Check Understanding

2. Tell whether each number is *prime* or *composite*.

a. 39

[ ]

b. 47

[ ]

c. 63

[ ]

3. Find the prime factorization of each number.

a. 36   **b.** 125

[ ]   [ ]

Lesson 3-3 *(pp. 128–131)*　　　　　　　　　**Greatest Common Factor**

Lesson Objective	NAEP 2005 Strand: Number Properties and Operations
▼ Find the greatest common factor	Topic: Number Operations
	Local Standards: ________________________

Vocabulary

A common factor is ____

____

A greatest common factor (GCF) is ____________________________________

____

Example

1 **Using Lists of Factors** List the factors to find the GCF of 48 and 64.

List the factors of 48 and the factors of 64. Then circle the common factors.

Factors of 48: 1, 2, 3, 4, 6, 8, 12, 16, 24, 48

Factors of 64: 1, 2, 4, 8, 16, 32, 64

The greatest common factor (GCF) is ☐.

← **The common factors are**
☐, ☐, ☐, ☐, **and** ☐.

Check Understanding

1. List the factors to find the GCF of each set of numbers.

a. 6, 21　factors of 6: ☐, ☐, ☐, ☐　　　GCF of 6 and 21: ☐
factors of 21: ☐, ☐, ☐, ☐

b. 28, 49　factors of 18: ☐, ☐, ☐, ☐, ☐, ☐　　GCF of 18 and 49: ☐
factors of 49: ☐, ☐, ☐

c. 14, 28　factors of 14: ☐, ☐, ☐, ☐　　　GCF of 14 and 28: ☐
factors of 28: ☐, ☐, ☐, ☐, ☐, ☐

d. **Number Sense** In a stamp club, no more than six people can share equally 18 stamps from one set and 30 stamps from another set. How many stamps from each set will each person receive?

Examples

❷ Using a Division Ladder Use a division ladder to find the GCF of 84 and 90.

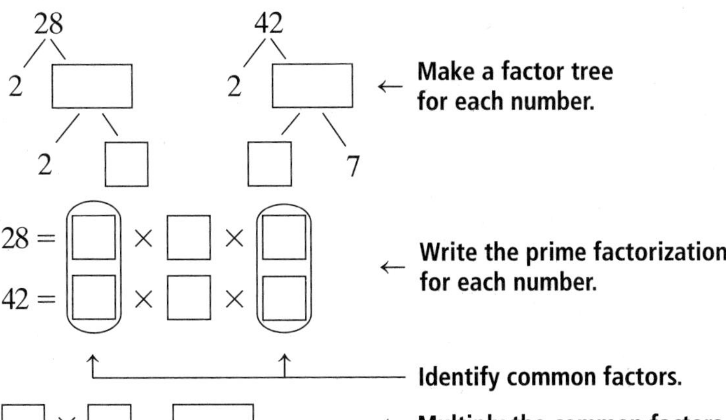

2) 84   90   ← **Divide by** ⬚ **, a common factor of 84 and 90.**

3) ⬚ ⬚   ← **Divide by** ⬚ **, a common factor of 42 and 45.**

⬚ ⬚   ← **14 and 45 have** ⬚ **common factors.**

— **Multiply the common factors:** ⬚ × ⬚ = ⬚ **.**

The GCF of 84 and 90 is ⬚ .

❸ Using Factor Trees Use factor trees to find the GCF of 28 and 42.

28   42

2 ⬚   2 ⬚   ← **Make a factor tree for each number.**

2 ⬚   ⬚ 7

$28 = $ ⬚ × ⬚ × ⬚

$42 = $ ⬚ × ⬚ × ⬚   ← **Write the prime factorization for each number.**

← **Identify common factors.**

⬚ × ⬚ = ⬚   ← **Multiply the common factors.**

The GCF of 28 and 42 is ⬚ .

Check Understanding

2. Use a division ladder to find the GCF of each set of numbers.

a. 24, 54

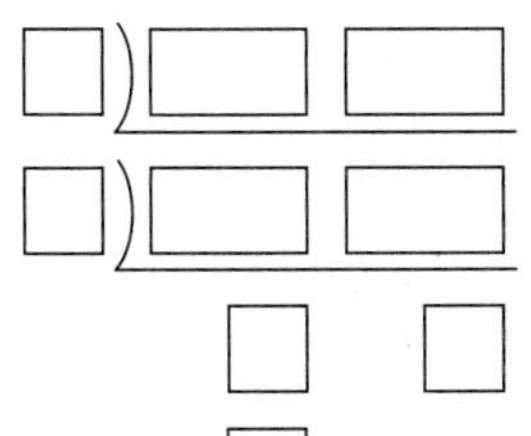

GCF = ⬚

3. Use factor trees to find the GCF of each set of numbers.

a. 12, 32

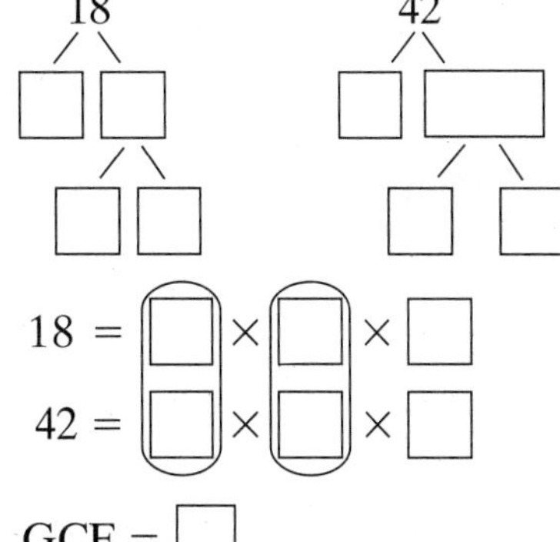

18   42

$18 = $ ⬚ × ⬚ × ⬚

$42 = $ ⬚ × ⬚ × ⬚

GCF = ⬚

Lesson 3-4 *(pp. 134–137)*   Equivalent Fractions

Lesson Objectives	**NAEP 2005 Strand:** Number Properties and Operations
▼ Find equivalent fractions ▼ Write fractions in simplest form	**Topic:** Number Operations **Local Standards:** ________________________________

Vocabulary

Equivalent fractions are ____

____

A fraction is in ⬚⬚⬚⬚⬚⬚ when the only common factor of the
numerator and denominator is 1.

Example

❶ **Equivalent Fractions** Write three fractions equivalent to $\frac{6}{9}$.

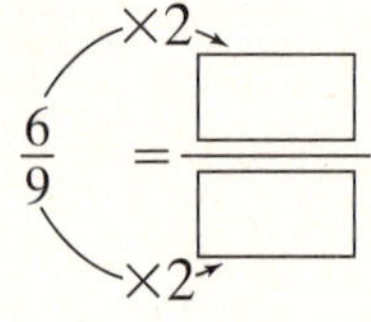

← Multiply the numerator and denominator by 2.

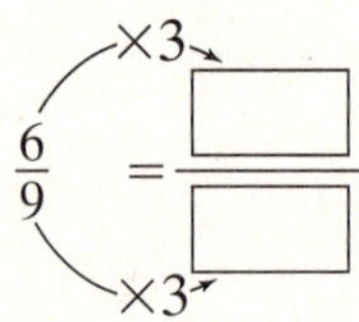

← Multiply the numerator and denominator by 3.

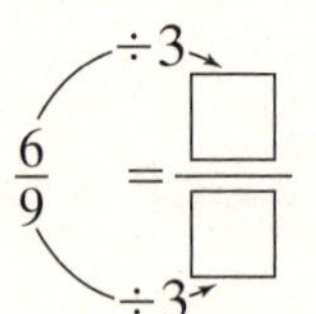

← Divide the numerator and denominator by 3.

So, $\dfrac{\square}{\square} = \dfrac{\square}{\square} = \dfrac{\square}{\square} = \dfrac{\square}{\square}$.

Check Understanding

1. Write three fractions equivalent to each fraction.

a. $\frac{4}{10}$ **b.** $\frac{5}{8}$ **c.** $\frac{2}{6}$

Examples

❷ Fractions in Simplest Form Write $\frac{16}{40}$ in simplest form.

16: ☐ , ☐ , ☐ , ☐ , ☐

40: ☐ , ☐ , ☐ , ☐ , ☐ , ☐ , ☐ , ☐

← List the factors for the numerator and denominator.
Find the greatest common factor.

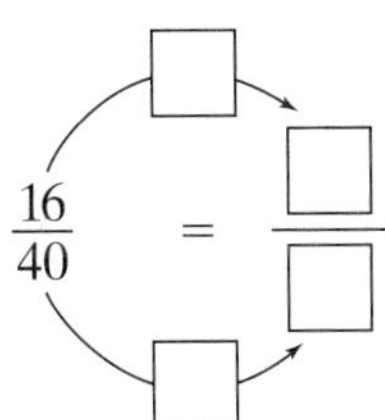

$$\frac{16}{40} = \frac{\square}{\square}$$

← Divide the numerator and denominator bt the GCF.

The fraction $\frac{16}{40}$ written in simplest form is $\dfrac{\square}{\square}$.

❸ A store stocks 12 types of blue pens, 6 types of black pens, and 2 types of red pens. In simplest form, what fraction of the pens are blue?

Add to find the total number of pens: $12 + 6 + 2 =$ ☐ .
Write the fraction.

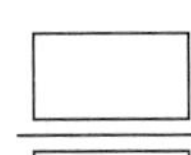

☐ ← number of types of blue pens

☐ ← total number of types of pens

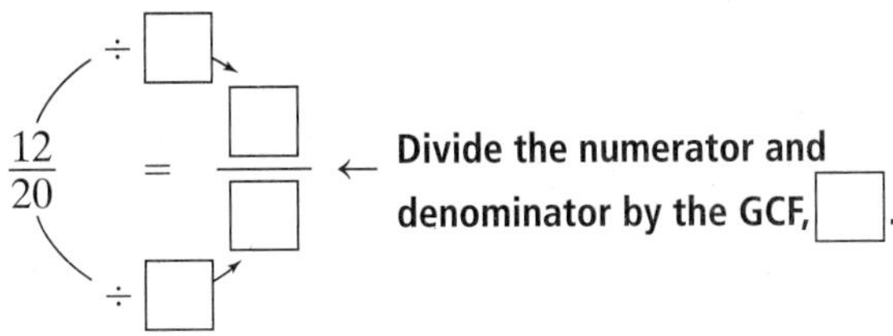

$$\frac{12}{20} = \frac{\square}{\square}$$

← Divide the numerator and denominator by the GCF, ☐ .

So, $\dfrac{\square}{\square}$ of the types of pens are blue pens.

Check Understanding

2. Write each fraction in simplest form.

a. $\frac{24}{32}$

b. $\frac{14}{49}$

c. $\frac{20}{100}$

3. a. In simplest form, what fraction of the types of pens in Example 3 are red pens?

b. Reasoning Which two types of pens together make up $\frac{2}{5}$ of the total pens? Explain your reasoning.

Course 1 Daily Notetaking Guide

Lesson 3-5 *(pp. 139–142)*   Mixed Numbers and Improper Fractions

Lesson Objectives	NAEP 2005 Strand: Number Properties and Operations
▼ Write mixed numbers as improper fractions **▼** Write improper fractions as mixed numbers	**Topic:** Number Operations **Local Standards:** _______________________________

Vocabulary

A proper fraction is ____

____

An improper fraction is ____

____

A mixed number is ____

____

Examples

❶ Writing Mixed Numbers as Improper Fractions Write $4\frac{4}{5}$ as an improper fraction.

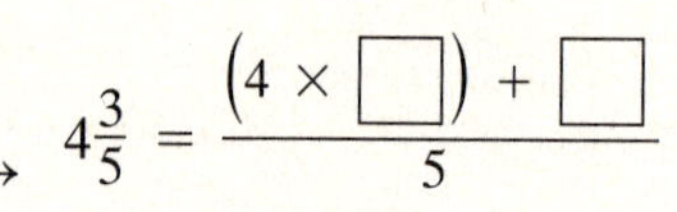

Multiply the whole number by the denominator.
(4 × 5 fifths is 20 fifths) →

$$4\frac{3}{5} = \frac{(4 \times \boxed{}) + \boxed{}}{5}$$ ← **Add the numerator.** **(There are** $\boxed{}$ **more fifths.)**

$$= \frac{\boxed{}}{\boxed{}}$$ ← **Write as an improper fraction.**

❷ A chef needs $2\frac{3}{4}$ quarts of water to make soup. How many cups will the chef need? (*Hint:* 1 cup = $\frac{1}{4}$ quart.)

Change $2\frac{3}{4}$ to an improper fraction.

$$2\frac{3}{4} = \frac{4 \times \boxed{} + \boxed{}}{4} = \frac{\boxed{}}{\boxed{}}$$

Since there are $\boxed{}$ fourths in $2\frac{3}{4}$, the chef will need $\boxed{}$ cups of water.

Example

❸ Writing Improper Fractions as Mixed Numbers Write $\frac{42}{9}$ as a mixed number in simplest form.

Begin by dividing 42 by ☐.

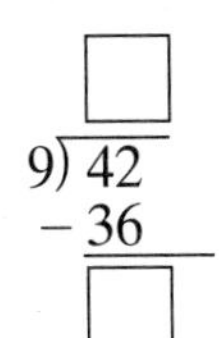

$$\frac{42}{9} = \boxed{\ }\frac{\boxed{\ }}{\boxed{\ }} \quad \leftarrow \textbf{Express the remainder as a fraction.}$$

$$= \boxed{\ }\frac{\boxed{\ }}{\boxed{\ }} \quad \leftarrow \textbf{Simplify.}$$

Check Understanding

1. Write $3\frac{4}{7}$ as an improper fraction.

2. Reasoning What does the denominator in the improper fraction $\frac{7}{1}$ represent?

3. Write each improper fraction as a mixed number in simplest form.

  a. $\frac{40}{9}$ **b.** $\frac{32}{6}$ **c.** $\frac{23}{4}$ **d.** $\frac{30}{18}$

Lesson 3-6 *(pp. 143–146)*   **Least Common Multiple**

Lesson Objective	**NAEP 2005 Strand:** Number Properties and Operations
▼ Find the least common multiple	**Topic:** Number Operations
	Local Standards: ______________________

Vocabulary

A common multiple is ____

____

The least common multiple (LCM) is __________________________________

____

Examples

❶ **Finding the LCM Using Lists of Multiples** List multiples to find the
LCM of 6 and 9.

multiples of 6: ☐ , ☐ , ☐ , ☐ , ☐ , ☐

multiples of 9: ☐ , ☐ , ☐ , ☐

The least common multiple is ☐ .

← **List multiples of each number.**

☐ **and** ☐ **are common multiples.**

❷ **LCM From Prime Factorizations** Use prime factorizations to find the
LCM of 6, 9, and 15.

Write the prime factorizations for 6, 9, and 15. Then circle each different
factor where it appears the greatest number of times.

$6 = $ ☐ $\times$ ☐   ← **2 appears** ☐ .

$9 = $ ☐ $\times$ ☐   ← **3 appears** ☐ .

$15 = $ ☐ $\times$ ☐   ← **5 appears** ☐ .

☐ $\times$ ☐ $\times$ ☐ $\times$ ☐ $= $ ☐   ← **Multiply the circled factors.**

The LCM of 6, 9, and 15 is ☐ .

Example

❸ Find the LCM of 20, 30, and 45.

Method 1

Use the prime factorizations of 20, 30, and 45 to find the LCM.

$20 = \square \times \square \times \square$ ← **2 appears** $\boxed{}$ **. 5 appears** $\boxed{}$ **.**

$30 = \square \times \square \times \square$ ← **Don't circle 2 or 5 again.**

$45 = \square \times \square \times \square$ ← $\boxed{}$ **appears twice.**

$\square \times \square \times \square \times \square \times \square = \boxed{}$ ← **Multiply the circled factors.**

The LCM of 20, 30, and 45 is $\boxed{}$.

Method 2

The greatest number is $\boxed{}$. List the multiples of 45 until
you find one that is also a multiple of 20 and 30.

                   90 is a multiple of 30, but not of $\boxed{}$ **.**

$45, \boxed{}, \boxed{}, \boxed{}$ ← **180! That's a multiple of both** $\boxed{}$ **and** $\boxed{}$ **.**

So, the LCM of 20, 30, and 45 is $\boxed{}$.

Check Understanding

1. **a.** List multiples to find the LCM of 10 and 12.

    multiples of 10: $\boxed{}, \boxed{}, \boxed{}, \boxed{}, \boxed{}, \boxed{}$

    multiples of 12: $\boxed{}, \boxed{}, \boxed{}, \boxed{}, \boxed{}$

    The LCM of 10 and 12 is $\boxed{}$.

    b. Number Sense Name the first five common multiples of 4 and 6.

2. Use prime factorizations to find the LCM of 25, 35, and 50.

3. Find the LCM of 6, 9, and 10. Explain which method from Example 3 you
chose and why.

Lesson 3-7 *(pp. 148–152)*   Comparing and Ordering Fractions

Lesson Objectives	NAEP 2005 Strand: Number Properties and Operations
✔ Compare fractions ✔ Order fractions	Topic: Number Sense Local Standards: _______________________

Vocabulary

The least common denominator is (LCD) ____

____

Example

❶ **Comparing Fractions** Compare $\frac{5}{8}$ and $\frac{7}{10}$. Use $<$, $=$, or $>$.

Method 1 Multiply denominators to find a common denominator. Use 8×10, or 80, as a common denominator.

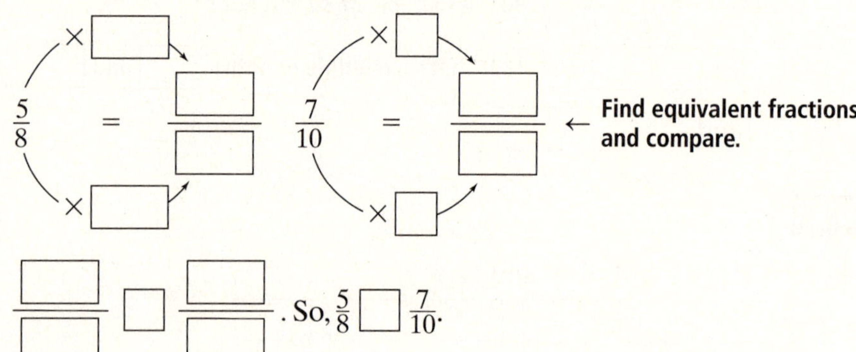

So, $\frac{5}{8}\ \square\ \frac{7}{10}$.

Method 2 Use the least common denominator. The least common multiple of 8 and 10 is $\boxed{}$.

$$\frac{5}{8} = \frac{\boxed{}}{\boxed{}} \qquad \frac{7}{10} = \frac{\boxed{}}{\boxed{}}$$

← Find equivalent fractions and compare.

So, $\frac{5}{8}\ \square\ \frac{7}{10}$.

Check Understanding

1. Compare each pair of fractions. Use $<$, $=$, or $>$.

a. $\frac{6}{8}\ \square\ \frac{7}{9}$ **b.** $\frac{6}{10}\ \square\ \frac{9}{15}$ **c.** $\frac{2}{3}\ \square\ \frac{5}{8}$

d. Number Sense Use the common denominator 60 to compare $\frac{2}{3}$ and $\frac{3}{5}$. How many minutes are in $\frac{2}{3}$ of an hour? In $\frac{3}{5}$ of an hour? Which is greater?

Examples

❷ Comparing Mixed Numbers If you need a piece of lumber that is $4\frac{3}{16}$ feet long, is a $4\frac{1}{4}$-foot piece long enough?

Since the whole numbers are the same, compare $\frac{3}{16}$ and $\frac{1}{4}$.

$$\frac{3}{16} = \frac{3}{16} \qquad \frac{1}{4} = \frac{\boxed{}}{\boxed{}}$$ ← **Find equivalent fractions. Use the LCD 16.**

$$\frac{3}{16}\ \boxed{}\ \frac{4}{16},\text{ so, } 4\frac{3}{16}\ \boxed{}\ 4\frac{3}{16}.$$ ← **Compare fractions and mixed numbers.**

The $4\frac{1}{4}$-foot piece $\boxed{}$ long enough.

❸ Ordering Fractions Order from least to greatest: $\frac{3}{5}, \frac{7}{10},$ and $\frac{4}{7}$.

Any multiple of 10 is also a multiple of $\boxed{}$. So, you can multiply $10 \times \boxed{}$ to find a common multiple. A common multiple of 5, 10, and 7 is $\boxed{}$.

$$\frac{3}{5} = \frac{\boxed{}}{\boxed{}} \qquad \frac{7}{10} = \frac{\boxed{}}{\boxed{}} \qquad \frac{4}{7} = \frac{\boxed{}}{\boxed{}}$$ ← **Write equivalent fractions.**

$$40\ \boxed{}\ 42\ \boxed{}\ 49$$ ← **Arrange the numerators in order.**

$$\frac{40}{70}\ \boxed{}\ \frac{42}{70}\ \boxed{}\ \frac{49}{70}$$

So, $\frac{4}{7}\ \boxed{}\ \frac{3}{5}\ \boxed{}\ \frac{7}{10}$.

Check Understanding

2. Compare each pair of mixed numbers using $<, =,$ or $>$.

a. $4\frac{2}{5}\ \boxed{}\ 4\frac{3}{7}$ **b.** $1\frac{2}{3}\ \boxed{}\ 1\frac{6}{11}$ **c.** $2\frac{12}{21}\ \boxed{}\ 2\frac{4}{7}$

d. Number Sense In Example 2, would a $4\frac{5}{8}$-foot piece be wide enough? Explain.

$$\boxed{}$$

3. Order $2\frac{5}{6}, 2\frac{4}{5},$ and $2\frac{2}{3}$ from least to greatest.

$$\boxed{}$$

Lesson 3-8 *(pp. 153–156)*

Fractions and Decimals

<table>
<tr><td>Lesson Objectives
▼ Write decimals as fractions
▼ Write fractions as decimals</td><td>NAEP 2005 Strand: Number Properties and Operations
Topic: Number Sense

Local Standards: _______________________</td></tr>
</table>

Example

1 Writing Decimals as Fractions Write 0.028 as a fraction in simplest form.

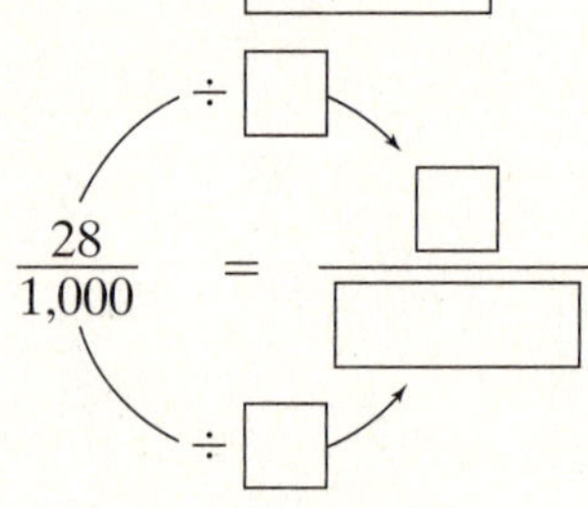

$0.028 = \dfrac{28}{\boxed{}}$ ← **Use the place value of 8 to write a fraction.**

$\dfrac{28}{1,000} = \dfrac{\boxed{}}{\boxed{}}$ ← **Simplify. The GCF of 28 and 1,000 is** $\boxed{}$.

So, $0.028 = \boxed{}$.

Check Understanding

1. Write each decimal as a fraction or mixed number in simplest form.

a. 0.6

b. 0.35

c. 5.08

d. 7.405

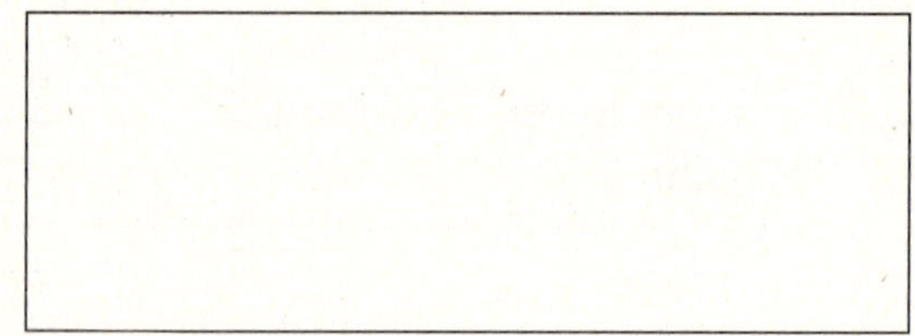

e. Reasoning How does saying or writing the decimal in words help you to write the decimal as a fraction?

Examples

❷ Writing a Fraction as a Decimal You need at least $\frac{3}{4}$ pound of dried apricots for a recipe. You find a bag that contains 0.8 pound. Is this enough?

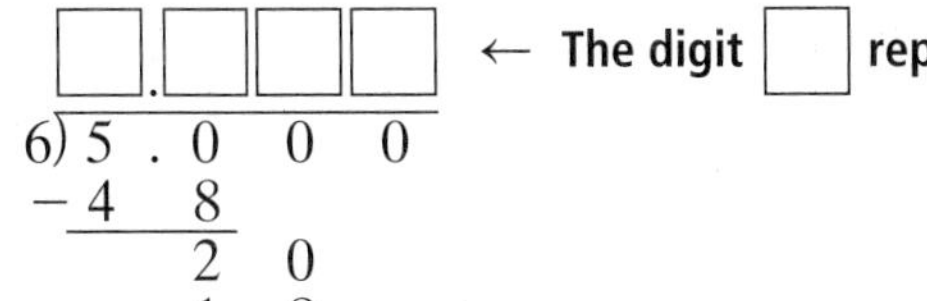

To write $\frac{3}{4}$ as a decimal, divide 3 by 4.

Since ☐☐ 0.8, there ☐ enough in the 0.8-pound bag.

❸ Repeating Decimals Write $\frac{5}{6}$ as a decimal.

Method 1 Divide.

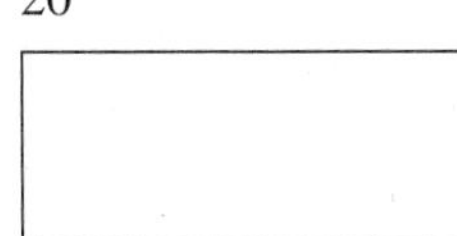

$\frac{5}{6}$ = ☐

Method 2 Use a calculator.

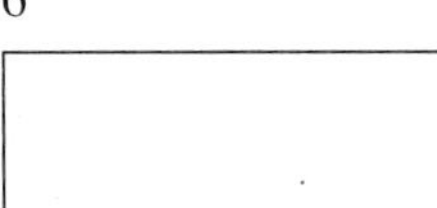

The calculator rounds the last digit in the display to 3. Look for the repeating digits 333...

$\frac{5}{6}$ = ☐

Check Understanding

2. Write each fraction as a decimal. Use a bar to show repeating digits.

a. $\frac{9}{20}$ **b.** $\frac{1}{6}$ **c.** $\frac{5}{9}$ **d.** $\frac{4}{3}$

3. Reasoning Explain how to write $2\frac{3}{4}$ as a decimal.

4. Number Sense Examine the fractions $\frac{2}{3}$, $\frac{3}{3}$, $\frac{4}{3}$, and $\frac{6}{3}$. Explain when a denominator of 3 will result in a repeating decimal.

Lesson 3-9 *(pp. 157–160)*   Try, Check, and Revise

Lesson Objective	
▼ Solve problems by trying, checking, and revising	**Local Standards:** _______________________

Example

❶ There are exactly 50 coins in a bank. Their total value is $9.50. The coins are either quarters or dimes. How many dimes are there?

(Read and Understand) There are quarters and dimes in the bank. The total value of the coins is [   ]. You need to find how many of the 50 coins are [   ].

(Plan and Solve) To help determine how many coins are dimes, try, check, and revise a reasonable combination of numbers.

Try Since there are 50 coins in the bank, try 40 dimes and 10 quarters.

You can organize your data in a table.

Dimes	Quarters	Total Value		
40 × $.10 = [ ]	10 × $.25 = [ ]	[ ] + [ ] = [ ]		

Check With 10 dimes, the total value of [   ] is too low. Since [   ] is too low, increase the number of coins with greater value.

Revise Increase the number of [   ]. Keep a total of 50 coins.

Dimes	Quarters	Total Value		
30 × $.10 = [ ]	20 × $.25 = [ ]	[ ] + [ ] = [ ]		
10 × $.10 = [ ]	40 × $.25 = [ ]	[ ] + [ ] = [ ]		

Name_________________________________ Class_______________________________ Date ______________

You can see that the total value for 30 dimes is too [ ], and the total value for 10 dimes is too [ ]. But the total values are close to $9.50. Revise once more. Try 20 dimes.

Dimes	Quarters	Total Value
20 × $.10 = [ ]	30 × $.25 = [ ]	[ ] + [ ] = [ ]

(**Look Back and Check**) With [ ] dimes and [ ] quarters, the number of coins is equal to [ ] and the total value is [ ].

Check Understanding

1. If the total value of the 50 coins is $12.00, how many dimes are there?

Lesson 4-1 *(pp. 171–174)*　　　　　　　　**Estimating Sums and Differences**

Lesson Objective ▼ Estimate sums and differences	**NAEP 2005 Strand:** Number Properties and Operations **Topic:** Estimation **Local Standards:** _______________________________

Vocabulary

A benchmark is ____

____

Description	Examples	Benchmark
Numerator is close to 0. Denominator is not close to 0.	$\dfrac{1}{8}, \dfrac{3}{16}, \dfrac{2}{25}, \dfrac{9}{100}$	
Numerator is about one half of denominator.	$\dfrac{3}{8}, \dfrac{9}{16}, \dfrac{11}{25}, \dfrac{52}{100}$	
Numerator is about one half of denominator.	$\dfrac{7}{8}, \dfrac{14}{16}, \dfrac{23}{25}, \dfrac{95}{100}$	

Example

❶ **Estimating Sums and Differences** Estimate each sum or difference.
Use the benchmarks $0, \frac{1}{2},$ and 1.

a. $\dfrac{5}{6} + \dfrac{4}{7}$

$\dfrac{5}{6} + \dfrac{4}{7} \approx \boxed{} + \dfrac{\boxed{}}{\boxed{}}$ ← Replace each fraction with a benchmark. →

$= \boxed{}\dfrac{\boxed{}}{\boxed{}}$ ← Simplify. →

b. $\dfrac{7}{8} - \dfrac{1}{9}$

$\dfrac{7}{8} - \dfrac{1}{9} \approx \boxed{} - \boxed{}$

$= \boxed{}$

Check Understanding

1. Estimate each sum or difference.

a. $\dfrac{5}{6} + \dfrac{3}{7}$

$\dfrac{5}{6} + \dfrac{3}{7} \approx \boxed{} + \dfrac{\boxed{}}{\boxed{}}$

$= \boxed{}\dfrac{\boxed{}}{\boxed{}}$

b. $\dfrac{12}{13} - \dfrac{2}{25}$

$\dfrac{12}{13} - \dfrac{2}{25} \approx \boxed{} - \boxed{}$

$= \boxed{}$

　　　　　　　　Course 1 Daily Notetaking Guide

Example

❷ **Estimating With Mixed Numbers** Steven is $13\frac{11}{12}$ years old. Chloe is $9\frac{1}{4}$ years old. Estimate how many years older Steven is than Chloe.

Estimate $13\frac{11}{12} - 9\frac{1}{4}$.

$13\frac{11}{12} \approx \boxed{}$ ← **Since $\frac{11}{12} > \frac{1}{2}$, round to** $\boxed{}$.

$9\frac{1}{4} \approx \boxed{}$ ← **Since $\frac{1}{4} < \frac{1}{2}$, round to** $\boxed{}$.

$\boxed{} - \boxed{} = \boxed{}$ ← **Estimate by finding the difference.**

Steven is about $\boxed{}$ years older than Chloe.

Check Understanding

2. **Travel** It takes $3\frac{3}{4}$ hours to drive to the beach. It takes $8\frac{1}{2}$ hours to drive to the mountains. Estimate the difference in driving times.

$3\frac{3}{4} \approx \boxed{}$

$8\frac{1}{2} \approx \boxed{}$

Lesson 4-2 *(pp. 175–178)*   Fractions With Like Denominators

Lesson Objectives	NAEP 2005 Strand: Number Properties and Operations
▼ Add fractions ▼ Subtract fractions	Topic: Number Operations Local Standards: ________________________________

Examples

❶ Adding With Like Denominators Find $\frac{2}{9} + \frac{4}{9}$.

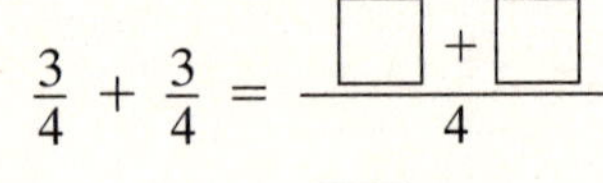

← The fractions have like denominators.
Add the numerators. The denominator stays the same.

← Simplify the numerator.

← Divide the numerator and denominator by the GCF, ☐.

❷ Sums Greater Than 1 Find $\frac{3}{4} + \frac{3}{4}$.

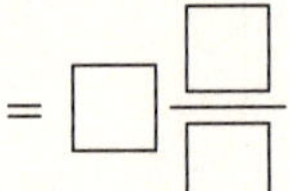

← Add the numerators. The denominator remains the same.

← Simplify the numerator.

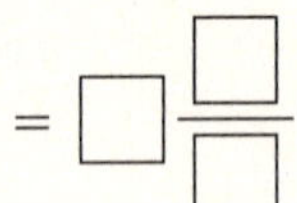

← Write as a mixed number.

← Divide the numerator and denominator by the GCF, ☐.

                              Course 1 Daily Notetaking Guide

❸ Subtracting With Like Denominators Find $\frac{7}{8} - \frac{1}{8}$.

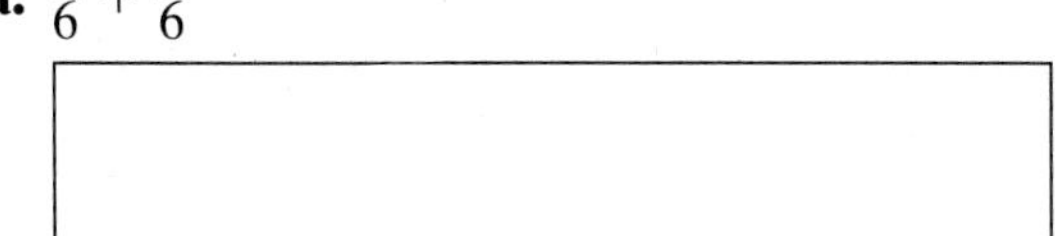

← Subtract the numerators. The denominator remains the same.

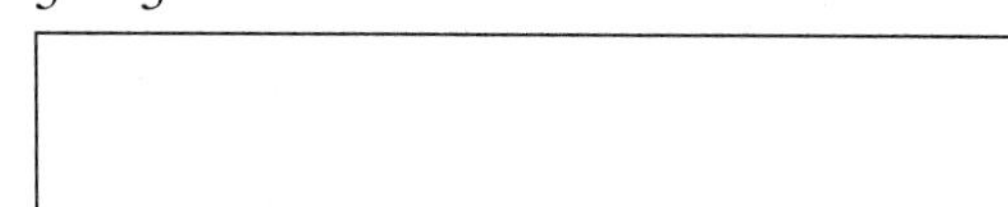

← Simplify the numerator.

← Write the fraction in simplest form.

Check Understanding

1. Find each sum.

a. $\frac{1}{6} + \frac{4}{6}$

b. $\frac{2}{5} + \frac{1}{5}$

c. $\frac{5}{16} + \frac{13}{16}$

d. $\frac{11}{20} + \frac{17}{20}$

e. Number Sense Explain how you could recognize when your answer needs to be written in simplest form.

2. Find each difference.

a. $\frac{3}{5} - \frac{2}{5}$

b. $\frac{3}{4} - \frac{1}{4}$

c. Suppose you are building a tree house. A board is $\frac{11}{12}$ yard. You need $\frac{7}{12}$ yard of the board for a brace. How much is left after you cut off the piece you need?

Lesson 4-3 *(pp. 180–184)*   Fractions With Unlike Denominators

Lesson Objectives	**NAEP 2005 Strand:** Number Properties and Operations
▼ Add fractions	**Topic:** Number Operations
❷ Subtract fractions	**Local Standards:** ___________________________

Example

❶ **Adding Fractions With Unlike Denominators** Find $\frac{1}{3} + \frac{1}{2}$.

Method 1 Model $\frac{1}{3} + \frac{1}{2}$.

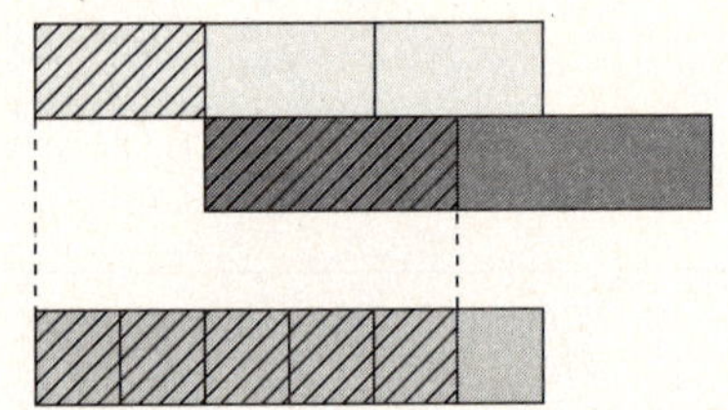

← **Use the fraction model for** $\dfrac{\Box}{\Box}$.

← **Use the fraction model for** $\dfrac{\Box}{\Box}$.

$$\frac{1}{3} + \frac{1}{2} = \frac{\Box}{\Box}$$

Method 2 Use a common denominator.

$$\frac{1}{3} \rightarrow \frac{1 \times \Box}{3 \times \Box} \rightarrow \frac{\Box}{\Box}$$

$$+\frac{1}{2} \rightarrow \frac{1 \times \Box}{2 \times \Box} \rightarrow +\frac{\Box}{\Box}$$

$$\frac{\Box}{\Box}$$

← **The LCD is** $\Box$. **Write the fractions with the same denominator.**

← **Add the numerators.**

Check Understanding

1. Find $\frac{3}{5} + \frac{1}{10}$. Use a model or a common denominator.

Name_________________________________ Class_________________________________ Date _____________

Examples

❷ Subtracting Fractions Using a Model Find $\frac{5}{8} - \frac{1}{6}$.

Model $\frac{5}{8} - \frac{1}{6}$.

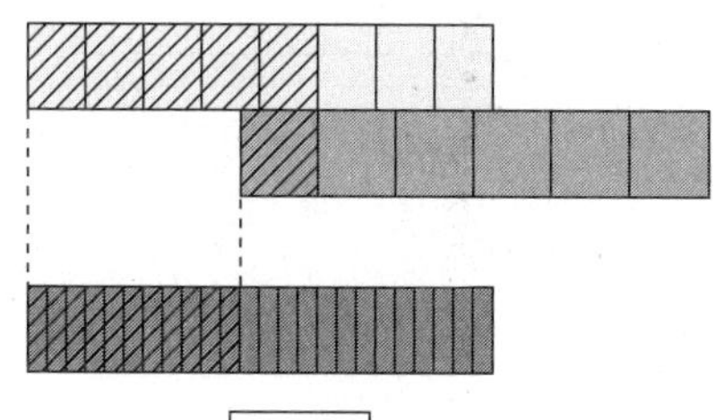

← Use the fraction model for $\dfrac{\square}{\square}$.

← Use the fraction model for $\dfrac{\square}{\square}$.

$\dfrac{5}{8} - \dfrac{1}{6} = \dfrac{\square}{\square}$

❸ Subtracting Fractions Using the LCD If Laura skates $\frac{1}{4}$ mi more, she'll have skated $\frac{9}{10}$ mi. How far has Laura skated so far?

Subtract $\dfrac{\square}{\square}$ from $\dfrac{\square}{\square}$ to find how far Laura has skated.

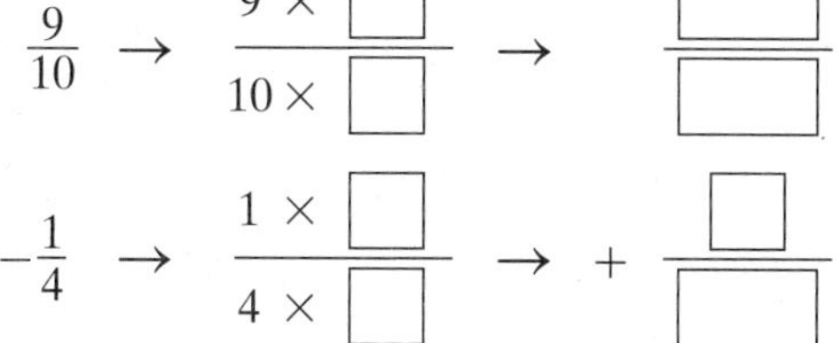

$$\frac{9}{10} \rightarrow \frac{9 \times \square}{10 \times \square} \rightarrow \frac{\square}{\square}$$

The LCD is $\boxed{}$. Write the fractions with the same denominator.

$$-\frac{1}{4} \rightarrow \frac{1 \times \square}{4 \times \square} \rightarrow + \frac{\square}{\square}$$

$$\frac{\square}{\square}$$

← Subtract the numerators.

Laura has skated $\dfrac{\square}{\square}$ mi so far.

Check Understanding

2. Find $\frac{3}{4} - \frac{5}{8}$. Use a model or a common denominator.

3. Suppose you have $\frac{3}{5}$ yard of felt. You use $\frac{1}{2}$ yard of the felt for a display. How much felt do you have left?

Lesson 4-4 *(pp. 185–189)*   **Adding Mixed Numbers**

Lesson Objectives	**NAEP 2005 Strand:** Number Properties and Operations
▼ Add mixed numbers ▼ Add mixed numbers by renaming	**Topic:** Number Operations **Local Standards:** ______________________________

Examples

❶ Adding Mixed Numbers Mentally Use mental math to find $3\frac{1}{9} + 5\frac{3}{9}$.

$3 + 5 = \boxed{}$ ← **Add the whole numbers.**

$\dfrac{1}{9} + \dfrac{3}{9} = \dfrac{\boxed{}}{\boxed{}}$ ← **Add the fractions.**

$8 + \dfrac{4}{9} = \boxed{}\dfrac{\boxed{}}{\boxed{}}$ ← **Combine the two parts.**

❷ Adding Mixed Numbers A mother cat weighs $14\frac{5}{8}$ lb. Her kitten weighs $1\frac{1}{2}$ lb. How much do they weigh together?

Find $14\frac{5}{8} + 1\frac{1}{2}$.

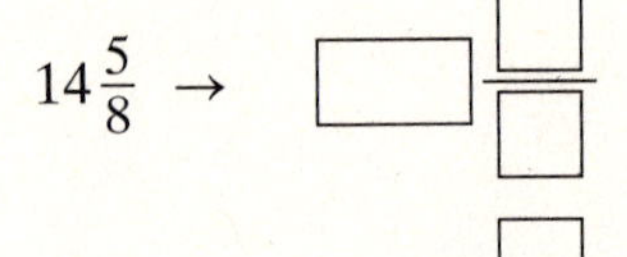

$14\frac{5}{8} \rightarrow \boxed{}\dfrac{\boxed{}}{\boxed{}}$

← **The LCD is** $\boxed{}$ **. Write the fractions with the same denominator.**

$+\, 1\frac{1}{2} \rightarrow +\, \boxed{}\dfrac{\boxed{}}{\boxed{}}$

$\boxed{}\dfrac{\boxed{}}{\boxed{}}$ ← **Add the whole numbers. Then add the fractions.**

$= 15 + \boxed{}\dfrac{\boxed{}}{\boxed{}}$ ← **Rename** $\dfrac{9}{8}$ **as** $\boxed{}\dfrac{\boxed{}}{\boxed{}}$ **.**

$= \boxed{}\dfrac{\boxed{}}{\boxed{}}$ ← **Add the whole numbers.**

The mother cat and kitten together weigh $\boxed{}\dfrac{\boxed{}}{\boxed{}}$ lb.

Name_______________________________ Class_______________________________ Date _____________

❸ Juggling Tyler juggled $1\frac{1}{3}$ h during the school week. He juggled for $2\frac{1}{4}$ h over the weekend. How many hours did he juggle in all that week?

Find ▢$\frac{▢}{▢}$ + ▢$\frac{▢}{▢}$.

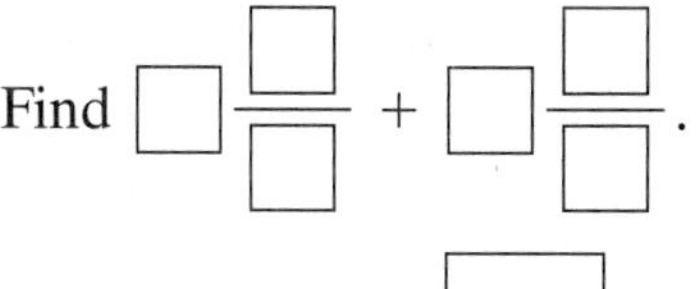

$1\frac{1}{3}$ →

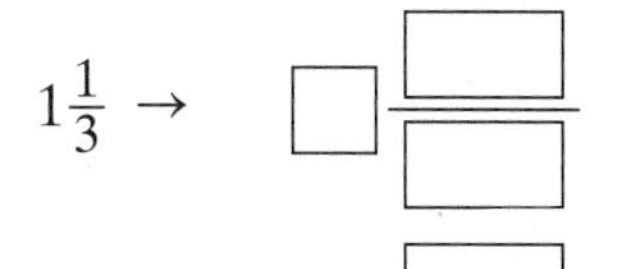

← The LCD is ▢ . Write the fractions with the same denominator.

$+ 2\frac{1}{4}$ → +

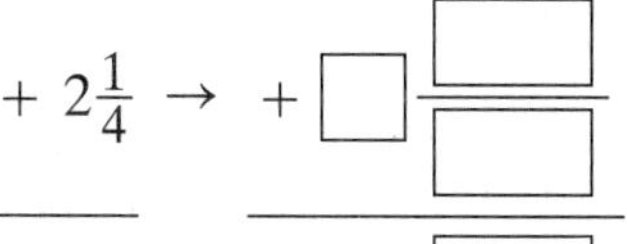

← Add the whole numbers. Then add the fractions.

Tyler juggled for a total of ▢$\frac{▢}{▢}$ hours.

Check Understanding

1. **Reasoning** In Example 1, does it matter whether you add the whole numbers of the fractions first to get the correct answer? Explain.

2. Find each sum.

   a. $3\frac{5}{6} + 5\frac{11}{12}$

   b. $12\frac{3}{8} + 6\frac{3}{4}$

   c. $7\frac{3}{5} + 13\frac{2}{3}$

3. Some students spent $2\frac{1}{3}$ hours on Friday and $3\frac{4}{5}$ hours on Saturday working on a science project. How long did the students work?

4. **Number Sense** One recipe used $1\frac{3}{4}$ cups of milk. Another recipe uses $1\frac{1}{2}$ cups of milk. You have 3 cups of milk at home. Do you have enough milk to make both recipes? Explain.

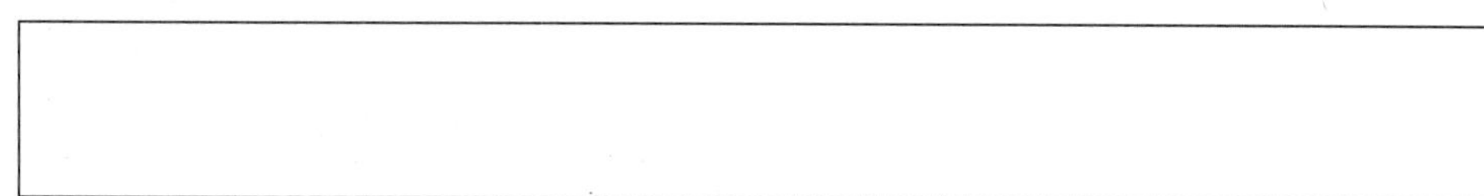

Lesson 4-5 *(pp. 190–194)* **Subtracting Mixed Numbers**

Lesson Objectives	NAEP 2005 Strand: Number Properties and Operations
▼ Subtracting mixed numbers ▼ Subtracting mixed numbers by renaming	Topic: Number Operations Local Standards: ____________________________

Examples

① Subtracting Mixed Numbers A black bear is about $5\frac{1}{4}$ ft long. An Alaskan brown bear is about $7\frac{1}{2}$ ft long. How much longer is an Alaskan brown bear than a black bear?

To calculate the difference in lengths, find 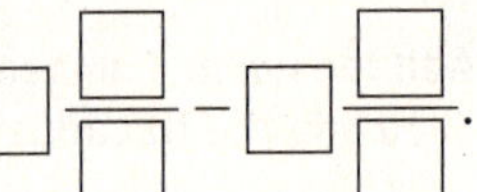.

$7\frac{1}{2} \rightarrow 7\dfrac{\square}{\square}$ ← The LCD is $\square$.

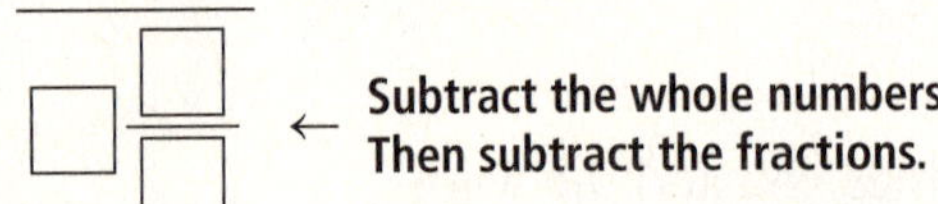

$-5\frac{1}{4} \rightarrow -5\ \dfrac{1}{4}$

$\dfrac{\square}{\square}$ ← Subtract the whole numbers. Then subtract the fractions.

An Alaskan brown bear is $\square\dfrac{\square}{\square}$ ft longer than a black bear.

② Renaming Whole Numbers Find $9 - 1\frac{2}{3}$.

Write 9 as a mixed number. Use 3 for the denominator since you must subtract $\frac{2}{3}$.

$9 \rightarrow \square\dfrac{\square}{\square}$ ← Rename 9 as $8 + 1 = 8 + \dfrac{\square}{\square}$, or $\square\dfrac{\square}{\square}$.

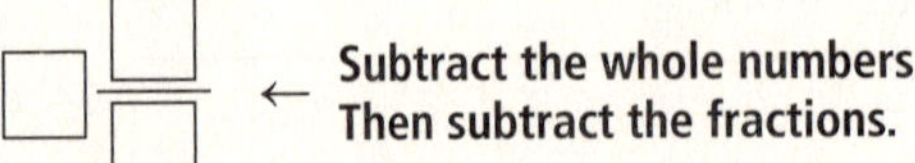

$-1\frac{2}{3} \rightarrow -1\ \dfrac{2}{3}$

$\square\dfrac{\square}{\square}$ ← Subtract the whole numbers. Then subtract the fractions.

Check Understanding

1. Reasoning In Example 1, could you use 8 as the common denominator? Explain your answer.

Name_________________________________ Class_________________________________ Date _____________

Example

❸ Renaming Mixed Numbers A two-week-old panda bear weighed $\frac{3}{4}$ pound. At age one month, the cub weighed $2\frac{3}{10}$ pounds. How many pounds did it gain?

To answer the question, find $\boxed{}\ \frac{\boxed{}}{\boxed{}} - \frac{\boxed{}}{\boxed{}}$. Since $\frac{3}{10} < \frac{3}{4}$, rename $2\frac{3}{10}$.

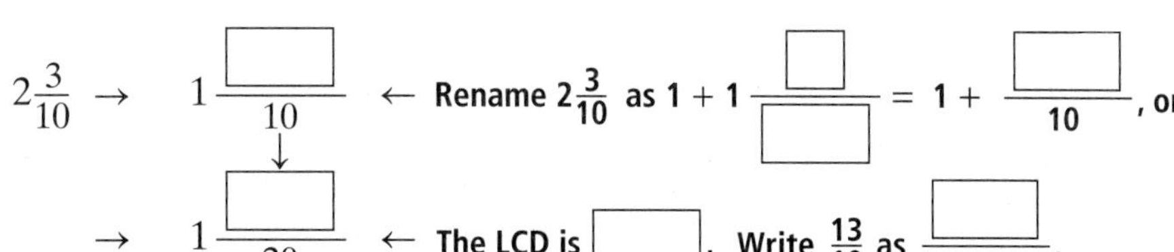

$$2\frac{3}{10} \rightarrow \quad 1\frac{\boxed{}}{10} \quad \leftarrow \text{Rename } 2\frac{3}{10} \text{ as } 1 + 1\frac{\boxed{}}{\boxed{}} = 1 + \frac{\boxed{}}{10}, \text{ or } \boxed{}\frac{\boxed{}}{\boxed{}}.$$

$$\rightarrow \quad 1\frac{\boxed{}}{20} \quad \leftarrow \text{The LCD is } \boxed{}. \text{ Write } \frac{13}{10} \text{ as } \frac{\boxed{}}{20}.$$

$$-\frac{3}{4} \rightarrow \quad -\frac{\boxed{}}{20} \quad \leftarrow \text{The LCD is } \boxed{}. \text{ Write } \frac{3}{4} \text{ as } \frac{\boxed{}}{20}.$$

$$\boxed{}\frac{\boxed{}}{\boxed{}} \quad \leftarrow \text{Subtract.}$$

The panda bear gained $\boxed{}\ \frac{\boxed{}}{\boxed{}}$ pounds.

Check Understanding

2. A supporting wedge for a window is $2\frac{3}{16}$ inches wide and $2\frac{7}{8}$ inches long. How much longer is the wedge than it is wide?

3. Find each difference.

a. $5 - 3\frac{2}{3}$

b. $10 - 4\frac{1}{4}$

4. Number Sense How can you use benchmarks to tell whether you will have to rename before subtracting?

Lesson 4-6 *(pp. 196–199)*

Equations With Fractions

Lesson Objectives	NAEP 2005 Strand: Algebra
▼ Use mental math to solve equations ▼ Solve equations with fractions	**Topic:** Equations and Inequalities **Local Standards:** ________________________

Examples

1 Using Mental Math in Equations Solve $12\frac{7}{9} = x + 3\frac{4}{9}$ using mental math.

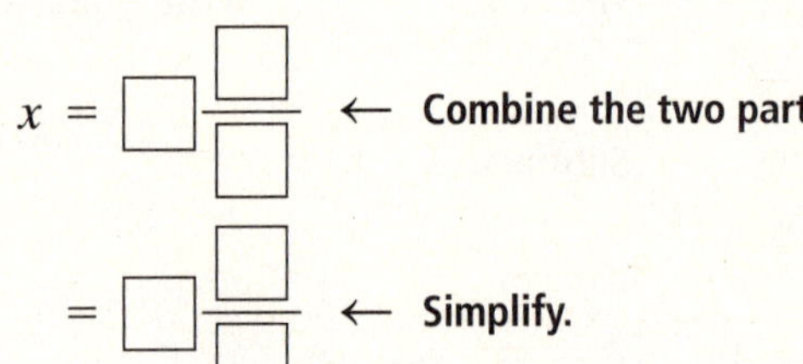

$$\boxed{} + 3 = 12$$

$$\frac{\boxed{}}{\boxed{}} + \frac{4}{9} = \frac{7}{9}$$

← Use mental math to find the missing whole number and the missing fraction.

$$x = \boxed{}\frac{\boxed{}}{\boxed{}}$$ ← Combine the two parts.

$$= \boxed{}\frac{\boxed{}}{\boxed{}}$$ ← Simplify.

2 Solving Equations With Fractions Solve $x - \frac{1}{8} = \frac{3}{4}$.

$$x - \frac{1}{8} = \frac{3}{4}$$

$$+ \frac{\boxed{}}{\boxed{}} \qquad + \frac{\boxed{}}{\boxed{}}$$ ← Add $\frac{\boxed{}}{\boxed{}}$ to each side.

$$x + 0 = \frac{3}{4} + \frac{1}{8}$$ ← Write the sum.

$$x = \frac{\boxed{}}{8} + \frac{1}{8}$$ ← The LCD is $\boxed{}$. Write $\frac{3}{4}$ as $\frac{\boxed{}}{8}$.

$$x = \frac{\boxed{}}{\boxed{}}$$ ← Simplify.

Check Understanding

1. Solve each equation using mental math.

a. $5\frac{5}{6} - x = 2\frac{1}{6}$

b. $14\frac{1}{4} + x = 25\frac{1}{2}$

c. $x - 1\frac{3}{8} = 1\frac{3}{8}$

Example

❸ An empty container weighs $\frac{1}{12}$ lb. The same container full of chopped fruit weighs $\frac{7}{8}$ lb. How much does the fruit weigh?

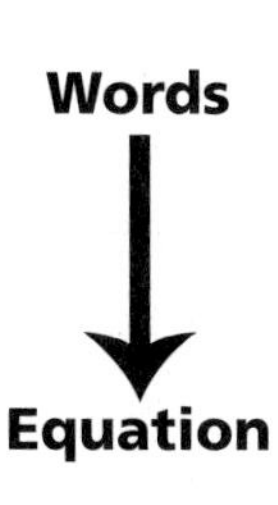

Words

| weight of empty container | + | weight of fruit | = | weight of full container |

Let $\boxed{}$ = the weight of the fruit.

Equation

$$\frac{\boxed{}}{\boxed{}} \quad + \quad \boxed{} \quad = \quad \frac{\boxed{}}{\boxed{}}$$

$$\frac{1}{12} \quad + \quad f \quad = \quad \frac{7}{8}$$

$$-\frac{\boxed{}}{\boxed{}} \qquad -\frac{\boxed{}}{\boxed{}} \qquad \leftarrow \text{ Subtract } \frac{\boxed{}}{\boxed{}} \text{ from each side.}$$

$$f = \frac{7}{8} - \frac{1}{12} \qquad \leftarrow \text{ Write the difference.}$$

$$= \frac{\boxed{}}{24} - \frac{\boxed{}}{24} \qquad \leftarrow \text{ The LCD is } \boxed{}\text{. Write each fraction with a denominator of } \boxed{}\text{.}$$

$$= \frac{\boxed{}}{\boxed{}} \qquad \leftarrow \text{ Subtract.}$$

The weight of the fruit is $\dfrac{\boxed{}}{\boxed{}}$ lb.

Check Understanding

2. Solve each equation.

a. $n + \frac{1}{3} = \frac{11}{12}$

b. $\frac{2}{5} + a = \frac{13}{20}$

3. You drive a nail that is $2\frac{3}{8}$ inches long through a wooden block. The nail extends beyond the board by $\frac{5}{8}$ inches. How thick is the wooden block?

Lesson 4-7 *(pp. 201–205)*   **Measuring Elapsed Time**

Lesson Objectives	NAEP 2005 Strand: Measurement
▼ Add and subtract measures of time	**Topic:** Systems of Measurement
▼ Read and use schedules	**Local Standards:** ______________________

Key Concepts

Units of Time

second (s)		day	1 day = [ ] h
minute (min)	1 min = [ ] s	week (wk)	1 wk = [ ] days
hour (h)	1 h = [ ] min	year (yr)	1 yr = [ ] wk

Examples

❶ **Writing Equivalent Times** How many minutes are equivalent to 1 h 45 min?

1 hour 45 minutes = [ ] min + 45 min   ← **One hour is equivalent to** [ ] **minutes.**

= [ ] min   ← **Simplify.**

❷ **Calculating Elapsed Time** Find the elapsed time between 7:25 A.M. and 9:05 A.M.

To find the elapsed time, subtract [ ] from [ ].

9:05 → 9 h 5 min   →   8 h [ ] min   ← **Rename 9 h 5 min as 8 h** [ ] **min.**
7:25 → 7 h 25 min → − 7 h   25 min
                        [ ] h [ ] min   ← **Subtract.**

The elapsed time is [ ] h [ ] min.

Check Understanding

1. How many days are equivalent to 4 weeks 3 days?

Examples

❸ Find the elapsed time between 10:15 a.m. and 2:25 p.m. Since 2:25 p.m. is later than 10:15 a.m., you need to add ☐ hours to 2:25.

2:25 → 2 h 25 min   ← **Add** ☐ **to the later time.**

+ ☐ h

☐ h 25 min

14:25 → 14 h 25 min

10:15 → − 10 h 15 min   ← **Subtract the** ☐ **time.**

☐ h ☐ min   ← **Subtract.**

The elapsed time is ☐ .

❹ Reading and Using a Schedule You arrive at the Glenmont bus stop at 8:00 A.M. and buy a ticket for the next bus.

a. How long will you wait for the next bus?

The bus runs every ☐ minutes. You arrived ☐ minutes after the 7:55 A.M. bus, so you will wait ☐ − ☐ ,

or ☐ minutes.

b. What time will you arrive at the Reedville bus stop?

The next bus will leave at ☐ A.M. Using the first run,

the elapsed time of the bus ride is ☐ A.M. − ☐ A.M.,

or ☐ min. So, you will arrive at 8:10 + ☐ min, or ☐ A.M.

Buses Run Every 15 min Monday–Friday	
LEAVE	ARRIVE
Glenmont	Reedville
7:40 A.M.	8:15 A.M.
7:55 A.M.	8:30 A.M.
. . .	. . .
9:55 A.M.	10:30 A.M.

Check Understanding

2. Find the elapsed time between 7:25 A.M. and 8:12 A.M.

3. a. Find the elapsed time between 10:00 A.M. and 7:15 P.M.

b. Reasoning Explain why you add 12 in Example 2.

4. It is a 5-minute walk from the bus stop in Reedville to a gym. Which bus should you take from Glenmont to get to the gym by 6:00 P.M.?

Name_______________________________ Class_______________________________ Date_______________

Lesson 4-8 *(pp. 206–208)*   Draw a Diagram

Lesson Objective	**NAEP 2005 Strand:** Geometry
▼ Draw a diagram	**Topic:** Relationships Among Geometric Figures
	Local Standards: ___________________________

Example

❶ **Sports** A school is hosting a soccer tournament. The field is 110 yards long and 80 yards wide. It will be divided into mini soccer fields that are 25 yards long and 20 yards wide. How many mini-fields will fit on the large field? *Hint:* Not all the space will be used.

Read and Understand The field is ☐ yards by ☐ yards. Each mini soccer field is ☐ yards by ☐ yards. You are asked to find how many mini soccer fields will fit on the field.

Plan and Solve To help decide, first *draw a diagram* of the field. Then show how many mini soccer fields that are ☐ yards by ☐ yards fit on the field.

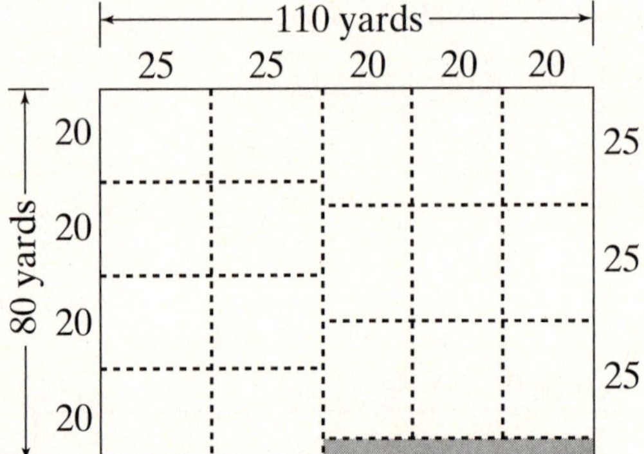

To use the entire length of the field, mark off ☐ mini soccer fields with the long side along the length of the field and ☐ mini soccer fields along the width of the field. Then mark off ☐ more mini soccer fields with the short side along the length of the field and ☐ along the width of the field. Since $2 \times 4 = $ ☐ and $3 \times 3 = $ ☐, you can fit ☐ + ☐ = ☐ mini soccer fields on the field.

                                    Course 1 Daily Notetaking Guide

Name_________________________________ Class_________________________________ Date ______________

Look Back and Check Check the answer by dividing the area of the field by the area of a mini soccer field. Use the formula area = [   ] × [   ].

$$\frac{\text{area of the field}}{\text{area of mini soccer field}} \rightarrow \frac{[\quad] \text{ yards} \times [\quad] \text{ yards}}{[\quad] \text{ yards} \times [\quad] \text{ yards}}$$

$$\rightarrow \frac{[\quad] \text{ square yards}}{[\quad] \text{ square yards}} = 17.6$$

[   ] mini soccer fields is a reasonable answer.

Check Understanding

1. A gymnastics floor exercise mat is 14 yards by 14 yards. How many floor exercise mats are needed to cover a soccer field?

Lesson 5-1 *(pp. 219–223)*

Multiplying Fractions

Lesson Objectives	NAEP 2005 Strand: Number Properties and Operations
▼ Multiply two fractions ▼ Multiply fractions by whole numbers	Topic: Number Operations Local Standards: _________________________

Key Concepts

Multiplying Fractions

Arithmetic

$$\frac{3}{4} \times \frac{1}{2} = \frac{3 \times 1}{4 \times 2} = \frac{3}{8}$$

Algebra

$$\frac{a}{b} \cdot \frac{d}{c} = \frac{ac}{bd}, \text{ where } b \text{ and } d \text{ are not zero.}$$

Examples

❶ Modeling Fraction Multiplication Draw a model to find the product $\frac{1}{3} \times \frac{5}{8}$.

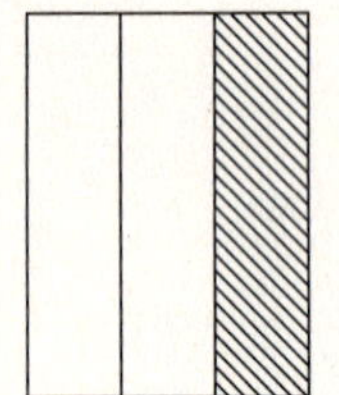

← Divide a rectangle in thirds. Shade one of the thirds.

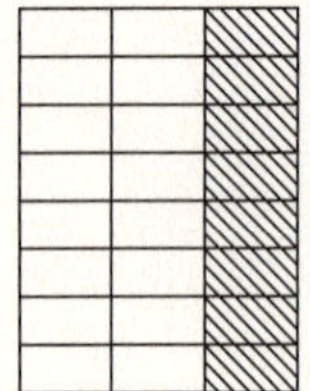

← Divide each third into eighths. Shade five of the eighths.

$$\frac{1}{3} \times \frac{5}{8} = \frac{\boxed{}}{\boxed{}}$$

❷ Multiplying Two Fractions Find the product $\frac{5}{6} \cdot \frac{3}{8}$.

$$\frac{5}{6} \cdot \frac{3}{8} = \frac{5 \cdot \boxed{}}{\boxed{} \cdot 8}$$ ← Multiply the numerators.

← Multiply the denominators.

$$= \frac{\boxed{}}{\boxed{}}$$ ← Find the two products.

$$= \frac{\boxed{}}{\boxed{}}$$ ← Simplify.

❸ Multiplying Fractions by Whole Numbers There are 30 students in Shari's homeroom. Of these students, $\frac{2}{5}$ worked at the school fair. How many students in Shari's homeroom worked at the school fair?

Find $\frac{2}{5}$ of 30, which means $\frac{2}{5}$ ☐ 30.

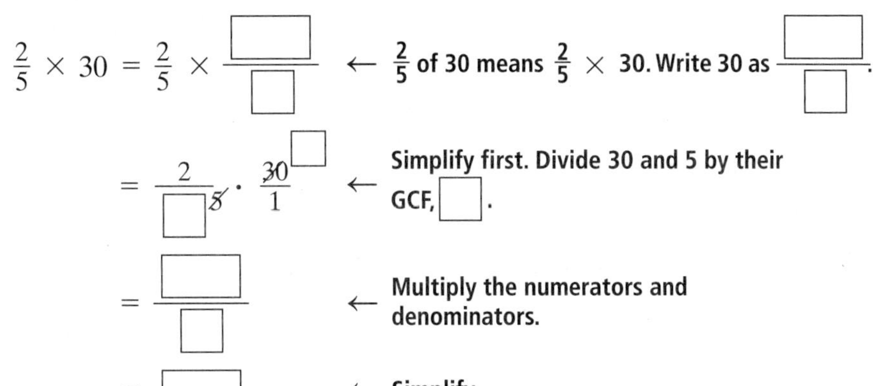

$$\frac{2}{5} \times 30 = \frac{2}{5} \times \frac{\boxed{}}{\boxed{}} \qquad \leftarrow \frac{2}{5} \text{ of 30 means } \frac{2}{5} \times 30. \text{ Write 30 as } \frac{\boxed{}}{\boxed{}}.$$

$$= \frac{2}{\boxed{}\cancel{5}} \cdot \frac{\overset{\boxed{}}{\cancel{30}}}{1} \qquad \leftarrow \text{Simplify first. Divide 30 and 5 by their GCF, } \boxed{}.$$

$$= \frac{\boxed{}}{\boxed{}} \qquad \leftarrow \text{Multiply the numerators and denominators.}$$

$$= \boxed{} \qquad \leftarrow \text{Simplify.}$$

$\boxed{}$ students in Shari's homeroom worked at the school fair.

Check Understanding

1. Use a model to find the product $\frac{1}{3} \times \frac{2}{5}$.

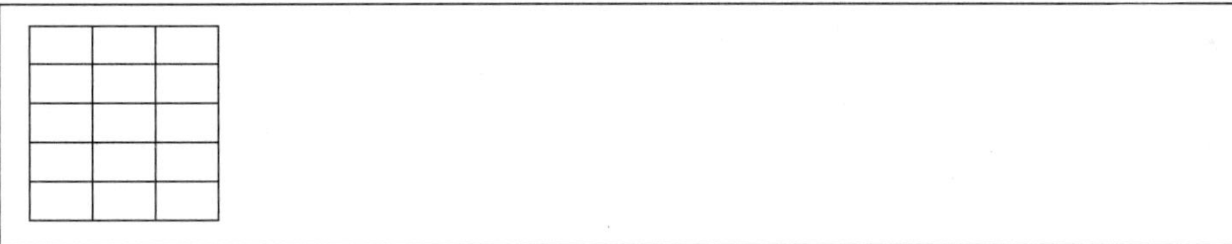

2. a. Find $\frac{3}{5} \cdot \frac{1}{4}$.

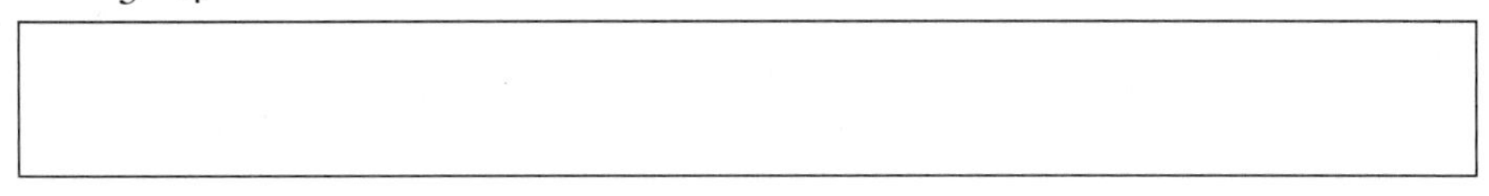

b. Reasoning How is adding $\frac{3}{8}$ and $\frac{5}{8}$ different from multiplying the two fractions?

3. Find each product.

    a. $\frac{4}{5}$ of 7

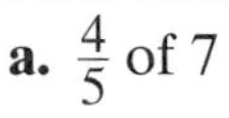

    b. $24 \cdot \frac{5}{9}$

Lesson 5-2 *(pp. 224–228)*   **Multiplying Mixed Numbers**

Lesson Objectives	**NAEP 2005 Strand:** Number Properties and Operations
▼ Estimate products of mixed numbers ▼ Multiply mixed numbers	**Topic:** Number Operations **Local Standards:** _________________________________

Example

❶ **Estimating Products** The pages of a book are $5\frac{1}{9}$ inches wide and $8\frac{3}{4}$ inches long. Estimate the area of a page in square inches.

Step 1 Round the length and width to the nearest whole numbers.

Step 2 Multiply and estimate the area.

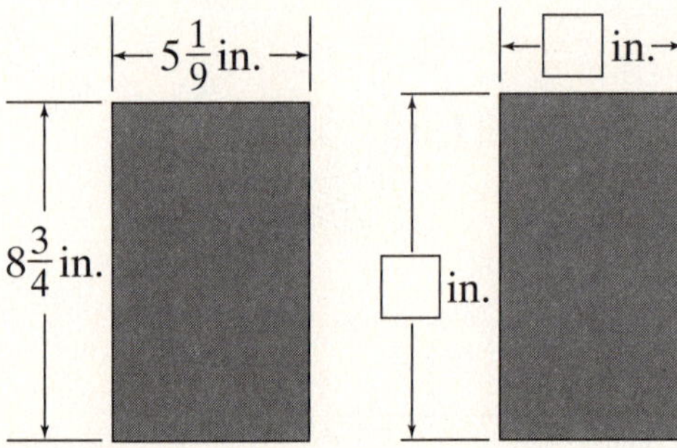

$$\text{Area} = \text{length} \times \text{width}$$
$$\approx \boxed{} \times \boxed{}$$
$$= \boxed{}$$

The area of a page is about $\boxed{}$ square inches.

Check Understanding

1. Estimate each product.

a. $5\frac{5}{6} \times 6\frac{4}{9}$

b. $7\frac{11}{16} \cdot 7\frac{1}{5}$

c. $12\frac{1}{2} \times 10\frac{2}{3}$

d. Reasoning Suppose you want to estimate the product of $82\frac{5}{7}$ and $\frac{1}{8}$.

Explain why $80 \cdot \frac{1}{8}$ is a better estimate than $83 \cdot 0$.

Name_________________________________ Class_________________________________ Date _______________

Examples

❷ Multiplying Using Improper Fractions Find the product $3\frac{3}{8} \times 1\frac{5}{9}$.

Estimate $3\frac{3}{8} \times 1\frac{5}{9} \approx \boxed{} \times \boxed{}$, or $\boxed{}$.

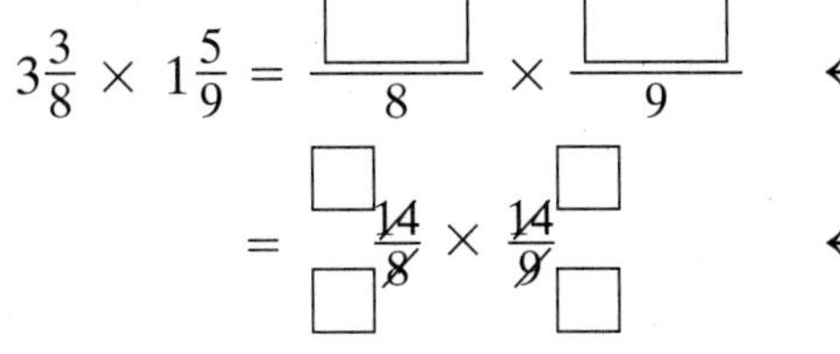

$$3\frac{3}{8} \times 1\frac{5}{9} = \frac{\boxed{}}{8} \times \frac{\boxed{}}{9} \qquad \leftarrow \text{Write the mixed numbers as improper fractions.}$$

$$= \frac{\boxed{}}{\boxed{}}\frac{14}{8} \times \frac{14}{9}\frac{\boxed{}}{\boxed{}} \qquad \begin{array}{l}\leftarrow \text{Divide 27 and 9 by their GCF, } \boxed{}. \\ \leftarrow \text{Divide 8 and 14 by their GCF, } \boxed{}.\end{array}$$

$$= \frac{\boxed{}}{\boxed{}}, \text{ or } \boxed{}\frac{\boxed{}}{\boxed{}} \qquad \leftarrow \begin{array}{l}\text{Multiply the numerators and denominators.} \\ \text{Then write as a mixed number.}\end{array}$$

Check for Reasonableness $\boxed{}\dfrac{\boxed{}}{\boxed{}}$ is near the estimate of $\boxed{}$.

❸ A gear on a machine makes $2\frac{2}{3}$ turns in one minute. How many turns does this gear make in $4\frac{1}{2}$ minutes?

$$\boxed{\begin{array}{c}\text{total number} \\ \text{of turns}\end{array}} = 2\frac{2}{3} \times \boxed{\text{number of minutes}}$$

$$= 2\frac{2}{3} \times 4\frac{1}{2}$$

$$= \frac{\boxed{}}{3} \times \frac{\boxed{}}{2} \qquad \leftarrow \text{Write the mixed numbers as improper fractions.}$$

$$= \frac{\boxed{}}{\boxed{}}\frac{8}{3} \times \frac{9}{2}\frac{\boxed{}}{\boxed{}} \qquad \begin{array}{l}\leftarrow \text{Divide 8 and 2 by their GCF, } \boxed{}. \\ \leftarrow \text{Divide 3 and 9 by their GCF, } \boxed{}.\end{array}$$

$$= \frac{\boxed{}}{\boxed{}}, \text{ or } \boxed{} \qquad \leftarrow \begin{array}{l}\text{Multiply the numerators and} \\ \text{denominators.}\end{array}$$

The gear makes $\boxed{}$ turns in $4\frac{1}{2}$ minutes.

Check Understanding

2. Find $1\frac{1}{4} \times 2\frac{3}{4}$.

3. How many turns can the gear in Example 3 make in $5\frac{1}{4}$ minutes?

Lesson 5-3 *(pp. 230–234)*   **Dividing Fractions**

Lesson Objectives	**NAEP 2005 Strand:** Number Properties and Operations
▼ Divide fractions by whole numbers	**Topic:** Number Operations
▼ Divide fractions by fractions	**Local Standards:** ______________________________

Vocabulary and Key Concepts

Dividing Fractions

Arithmetic

$$\frac{3}{5} \div \frac{1}{3} = \frac{3}{5} \times \frac{3}{1}$$

Algebra

$$\frac{a}{b} \div \frac{c}{d} = \frac{a}{b} \times \frac{d}{c} \text{, where } b, c, \text{ and } d \text{ are not 0.}$$

Two numbers are [________] if their product is 1.

Example

① **Writing a Reciprocal** Write the reciprocal of each number.

a. $\frac{4}{9}$

The reciprocal is $\frac{\square}{\square}$.

Check $\frac{4}{9} \times \dfrac{\square}{\square} = \dfrac{\square}{\square}$ or 1.

b. 5

Write 5 as $\frac{5}{1}$. The reciprocal is $\frac{\square}{\square}$.

Check $\frac{5}{1} \times \dfrac{\square}{\square} = \dfrac{\square}{\square}$ or 1.

Check Understanding

1. Write the reciprocal of each number.

a. $\frac{3}{4}$ **b.** 7   **c.** $\frac{8}{7}$

Name_______________________________ Class_______________________________ Date ______________

Examples

❷ Using Reciprocals to Divide by a Fraction Find $4 \div \frac{6}{7}$.

$4 \div \frac{6}{7} = 4 \times \dfrac{\square}{\square}$ ← Multiply 4 by $\dfrac{\square}{\square}$, the reciprocal of $\frac{6}{7}$.

$= \frac{4}{1} \times \dfrac{\square}{\square}$ ← Write 4 as $\frac{4}{1}$.

$= \dfrac{\overset{\square}{\cancel{4}}}{1} \times \dfrac{7}{\underset{\square}{\cancel{6}}}$ ← Divide 4 and 6 by their GCF, $\square$.

$= \dfrac{\boxed{}}{\boxed{}}$ ← Multiply.

$= \square\dfrac{\square}{\square}$ ← Write as a mixed number.

❸ Dividing a Fraction by a Fraction Find $\frac{3}{8} \div \frac{7}{12}$.

$\frac{3}{8} \div \frac{7}{12} = \frac{3}{8} \times \frac{12}{7}$ ← Multiply by $\dfrac{\boxed{}}{\square}$, the reciprocal of $\frac{7}{12}$.

$= \dfrac{3}{\underset{\square}{\cancel{8}}} \times \dfrac{\overset{\square}{\cancel{12}}}{7}$ ← Divide 8 and 12 by their GCF, $\square$.

$= \dfrac{\boxed{}}{\boxed{}}$ ← Multiply.

Check Understanding

2. Find each quotient.

a. $8 \div \frac{3}{4}$

b. $7 \div \frac{2}{9}$

c. $\frac{5}{8} \div \frac{5}{6}$

d. $\frac{8}{15} \div \frac{2}{3}$

e. $\frac{3}{8} \div 12$

f. $\frac{11}{15} \div 110$

3. Your art teacher must cut $\frac{5}{6}$ yard of fabric into five equal pieces for his students. How much fabric does each student get?

Lesson 5-4 *(pp. 236–240)*   **Dividing Mixed Numbers**

Lesson Objectives ▼ Estimate quotients of mixed numbers ▼ Divide mixed numbers	**NAEP 2005 Strand:** Number Properties and Operations **Topic:** Number Operations **Local Standards:** _____________________

Examples

① **Estimating Quotients** Paulo wants to put a row of decorative tiles along a wall. The wall is $72\frac{3}{8}$ inches wide. Each tile is $3\frac{3}{4}$ inches wide. Estimate the number of tiles he will need. Draw a diagram to model the situation.

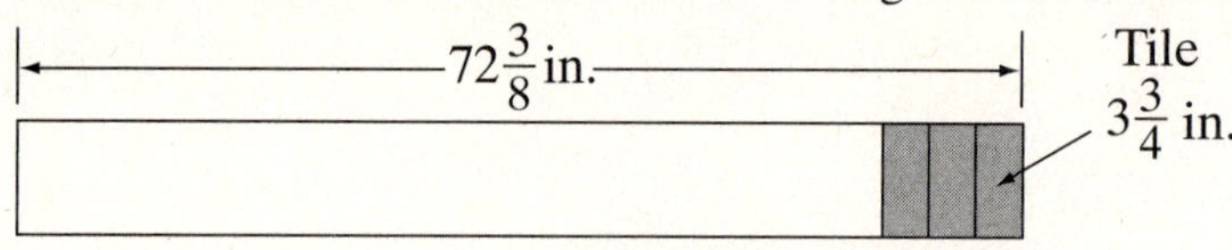

$72\frac{3}{8} \div 3\frac{3}{4}$ ← **Round each mixed number to the nearest whole number.**

$\boxed{} \div \boxed{} = 18$ ← **Divide.**

Paulo needs about $\boxed{}$ tiles.

② **Dividing Mixed Numbers** Shaleen has enough oatmeal to make 5 batches of cookies. She wants to distribute $3\frac{1}{3}$ cups of raisins equally among each batch. What amount of raisins should she put into each batch?

$\boxed{} \div \boxed{}$ ← **You need to divide the cups of raisins by the number of batches.**

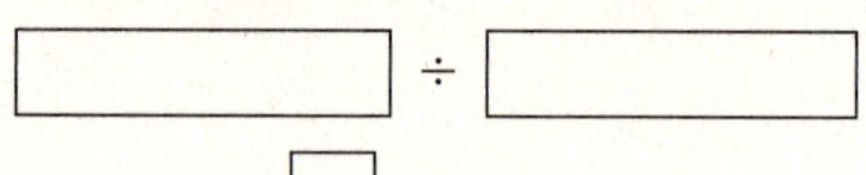
$\boxed{}\dfrac{\boxed{}}{\boxed{}} \div \boxed{} = \dfrac{10}{3} \div \dfrac{5}{1}$ ← **Substitute. Then write the numbers as improper fractions.**

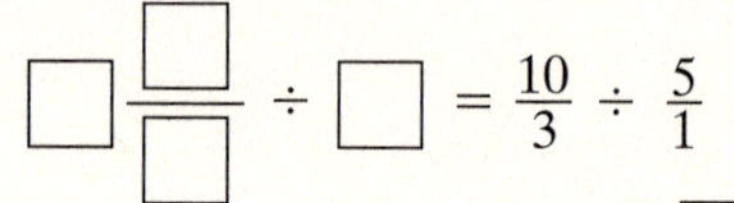
$= \dfrac{10}{3} \times \dfrac{\boxed{}}{\boxed{}}$ ← **Multiply by $\dfrac{\boxed{}}{\boxed{}}$, the reciprocal of 5.**

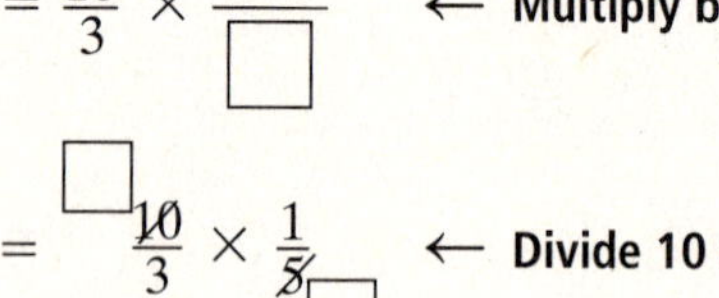
$= \dfrac{\boxed{}}{3} \times \dfrac{1}{\boxed{}}$ ← **Divide 10 and 5 by their GCF, $\boxed{}$.**

$= \dfrac{\boxed{}}{\boxed{}}$ ← **Multiply.**

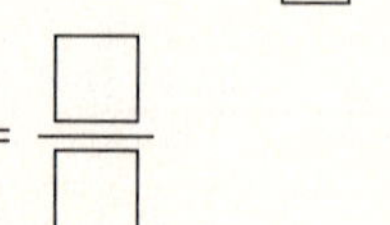
Each batch of cookies gets $\dfrac{\boxed{}}{\boxed{}}$ cups of raisins.

Check for Reasonableness When you estimate $3\frac{1}{3} \div 5$, the result is $3 \div 5$,

or $\dfrac{\boxed{}}{\boxed{}}$ cup. So, $\dfrac{\boxed{}}{\boxed{}}$ cup is a reasonable answer.

❸ **Dividing Mixed Numbers** Find $6\frac{1}{4} \div 1\frac{7}{8}$.

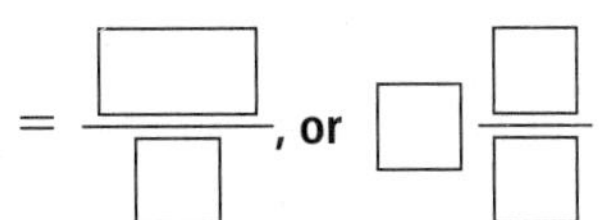

$6\frac{1}{4} \div 1\frac{7}{8} = \frac{25}{4} \div \frac{15}{8}$ ← Write the numbers as improper fractions.

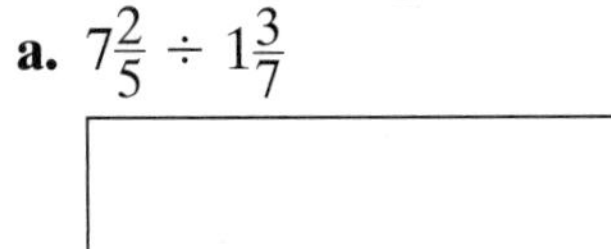

$= \frac{25}{4} \times \dfrac{\square}{\square}$ ← Multiply by $\dfrac{\square}{\square}$, the reciprocal of $\frac{15}{8}$.

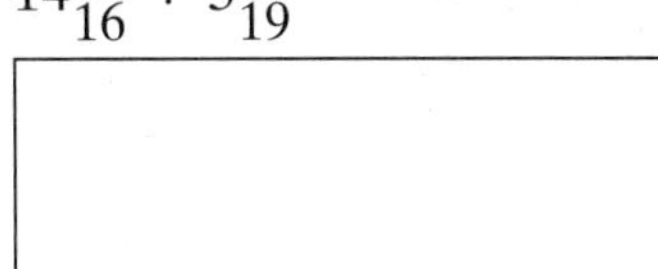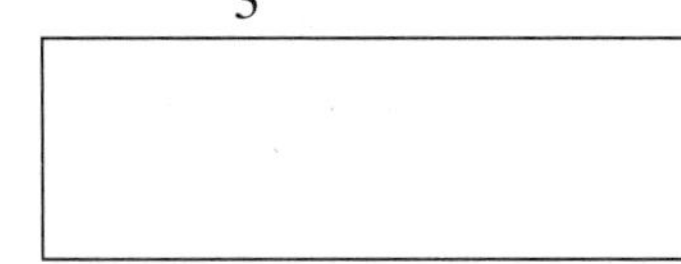

$= \frac{25}{4} \times \frac{8}{15}$ ← Divide 25 and 15 by their GCF, $\square$.

Divide 4 and 8 by their GCF, $\square$.

$= \dfrac{\square}{\square}$, or $\square\dfrac{\square}{\square}$ ← Multiply and simplify.

Check Understanding

1. Estimate each quotient.

  a. $7\frac{2}{5} \div 1\frac{3}{7}$

  b. $14\frac{9}{16} \div 3\frac{8}{19}$

  c. $100 \div 9\frac{2}{3}$

  d. Estimation Suppose the tiles are $5\frac{6}{7}$ inches wide in Example 1. Estimate the number of tiles needed to cover the $72\frac{3}{8}$-inch wall.

2. Suppose Shaleen has $1\frac{2}{3}$ cups of raisins in Example 2. How many cups of raisins should go into each batch to make 5 batches of cookies?

3. Find each quotient.

  a. $7 \div 1\frac{1}{6}$

  b. $6\frac{5}{6} \div 3\frac{1}{3}$

  c. $8\frac{3}{4} \div 2\frac{1}{2}$

  d. Number Sense How can you tell that $2\frac{1}{3} \div 3\frac{1}{2}$ will be less than 1?

Lesson 5-5 *(pp. 242–245)*   Solving Function Equations by Multiplying

Lesson Objective	NAEP 2005 Strand: Algebra
▼ Solve fraction equations	Topic: Equations and Inequalities
	Local Standards: _____________________________

Examples

❶ Solving Equations by Multiplying Solve $\frac{c}{3} = 14$.

$$\frac{c}{3} = 14$$

$$\boxed{} \cdot \frac{c}{3} = \boxed{} \cdot 14 \quad \leftarrow \text{ Multiply each side by } \boxed{}.$$

$$\frac{\boxed{}}{1} \cdot \frac{c}{\boxed{}} = \boxed{} \quad \leftarrow \text{ Write 3 as } \frac{3}{1}. \text{ Simplify.}$$

$$\frac{\boxed{}}{1} = \boxed{} \quad \leftarrow \text{ Multiply the numerators and the denominators.}$$

$$c = \boxed{} \quad \leftarrow \text{ Simplify.}$$

❷ Using Reciprocals to Solve Equations Solve $\frac{3}{4}m = 24$. Check the solution.

$$\frac{3}{4}m = 24$$

$$\frac{\boxed{}}{\boxed{}} \cdot \left(\frac{3}{4}m \right) = \frac{\boxed{}}{\boxed{}} \cdot (24) \quad \leftarrow \text{ Multiply each side by } \frac{\boxed{}}{\boxed{}}, \text{ the reciprocal of } \frac{3}{4}.$$

$$\boxed{} \cdot m = \boxed{} \quad \leftarrow \text{ Multiply.}$$

$$m = \boxed{} \quad \leftarrow \text{ Simplify.}$$

Check

$$\frac{3}{4}m = 24 \quad \leftarrow \text{ Start with the original equation.}$$

$$\frac{3}{4}\left(\boxed{} \right) \overset{?}{=} 24 \quad \leftarrow \text{ Replace } m \text{ with } \boxed{}.$$

$$\boxed{} = 24 \checkmark \quad \leftarrow \text{ The solution checks.}$$

❸ Writing and Solving Equations Mai Li worked $7\frac{1}{2}$ hours and earned $150. What amount did she earn per hour?

Words $\boxed{\text{hours worked}} \times \boxed{\text{earnings per hour}} = \boxed{\text{amount earned}}$

Let $\boxed{m}$ = earnings per hour.

Equation $\boxed{} \times \boxed{} = \boxed{}$

$$7\frac{1}{2}m = 150 \quad \leftarrow \text{ Write the equation.}$$

$$\frac{\boxed{}}{\boxed{}}m = \frac{150}{1} \quad \leftarrow \begin{array}{l}\text{Write } 7\frac{1}{2} \text{ as an improper fraction.}\\ \text{Write 150 as } \frac{150}{1}.\end{array}$$

$$\frac{\boxed{}}{\boxed{}} \cdot \left(\frac{15}{2}m\right) = \frac{\boxed{}}{\boxed{}} \cdot \frac{150}{1} \quad \leftarrow \begin{array}{l}\text{Multiply each side by } \frac{\boxed{}}{\boxed{}}, \text{ the}\\ \text{reciprocal of } \frac{15}{2}.\end{array}$$

$$m = \frac{2}{\cancel{15}} \cdot \frac{\cancel{150}^{\boxed{}}}{1} \quad \leftarrow \text{ Multiply.}$$

$$m = \boxed{} \quad \leftarrow \text{ Simplify.}$$

Mai Li earned $\boxed{}$ per hour.

Check Understanding

1. Solve $\frac{x}{2} = 15$.

2. Solve each equation. Check the solution.

a. $\frac{9}{10}x = 18$ **b.** $\frac{4}{5}x = 20$ **c.** $\frac{7}{8}x = 42$

3. Beth needs boards that are $\frac{3}{4}$ foot long. She has a board that is 8 feet long. How many $\frac{3}{4}$-foot sections can she cut from it?

Lesson 5-6 *(pp. 246–249)*   Solving a Simpler Problem

Lesson Objective	**NAEP 2005 Strand:** Number Properties and Operations
▼ Solve a simpler problem	**Topic:** Number Operations
	Local Standards: ___________________________

Example

❶ You and your friends are going to bake 48 loaves of bread for a bake sale. You need $1\frac{1}{4}$ cups of flour for each loaf. A bag of flour contains $18\frac{3}{4}$ cups. How many bags do you need for all the loaves?

Read and Understand

You are making 48 loaves of bread, each of which uses $1\frac{1}{4}$ cups of flour. The flour comes in bags that contain $18\frac{3}{4}$ cups. You must determine the number of bags of flour you need.

Plan and Solve

To help you decide how many bags are needed, solve a simpler problem. Replace $1\frac{1}{4}$ with 1 and $18\frac{3}{4}$ with 19.

Simpler Problem You are making 48 loaves of bread. Each loaf uses 1 cup of flour. A bag of flour contains 19 cups of flour. How many bags do you need for all the loaves?

Step 1 To make all the loaves of bread, you need

$48 \times 1 = \boxed{}$ cups

Step 2 To get 48 cups of flour, you need

$48 \div 19 \approx \boxed{}\,\dfrac{\boxed{}}{\boxed{}}$ bags

So, you need about $\boxed{}\,\dfrac{\boxed{}}{\boxed{}}$ bags of flour for 48 loaves.

Now solve the original problem, using the same steps.

Step 1 Multiply to find the total number of cups of flour needed to make 48 loaves.

$$48 \times 1\tfrac{1}{4} = 48 \times \dfrac{\boxed{}}{4}$$

$$= \dfrac{\boxed{}}{1} \cdot \dfrac{5}{\boxed{}}$$

$$= \boxed{} \text{ cups}$$

Step 2 Divide to find the number of bags needed.

$$60 \div 18\tfrac{3}{4} = 60 \div \dfrac{\boxed{}}{4}$$

$$= \dfrac{\boxed{}}{1} \cdot \dfrac{4}{\boxed{}}$$

$$= \dfrac{\boxed{}}{\boxed{}}$$

$$= \boxed{}\dfrac{\boxed{}}{\boxed{}} \text{ bags}$$

You will need $\boxed{}\dfrac{\boxed{}}{\boxed{}}$ bags of flour to bake 48 loaves of bread.

(**Look Back and Check**)

Using mental math, you can see it takes $\boxed{}$ cups of flour to make $\boxed{}$ loaves. Therefore, to make 4×12 loaves you need $\boxed{}$ cups of flour. Each bag holds a little less than 20 cups, which means it will take a little more than $\boxed{}$ bags of flour to bake 48 loaves of bread. The answer checks.

Check Understanding

1. Each of 12 people from Company A gives a business card to each of 17 people from Company B. Each person from Company B gives a card to each person from Company A. How many cards are given?

Lesson 5-7 *(pp. 250–253)*

The Customary System

Lesson Objective	**NAEP 2005 Strand:** Measurement
▼ Choose appropriate units of measurement	**Topic:** Systems of Measurement
	Local Standards: ____________________

Example

❶ Choosing a Unit of Length Choose an appropriate customary unit of measure to describe the length of an automobile.

The unit [   ] is too large and [   ] is too small.
Use [   ].

Check Understanding

1. Choose an appropriate unit for each length. Explain.

   a. length of a pencil

   b. length of an adult whale

   c. Reasoning Explain why inches are not an appropriate unit of measure for the distance from your home to school.

Name________________________ Class________________________ Date ____________

Examples

❷ Choosing a Unit of Weight Choose an appropriate customary unit of measure to describe the weight of a bag of popcorn.

The customary units that describe weight are ⬚ , ⬚ , and ⬚ .

The weight of a bag of popcorn is best described in ⬚ .

❸ Choosing a Unit of Capacity Choose an appropriate customary unit of measure to describe the capacity of a household bucket.

The customary units that describe capacity are ⬚ , ⬚ , ⬚ , ⬚ , and ⬚ .

The capacity of a household bucket is best described in ⬚ .

Check Understanding

2. Choose an appropriate unit for each weight. Explain.
  a. weight of a refrigerator

  b. weight of an ice cube

3. Choose an appropriate unit for each capacity. Explain.
  a. gasoline in a tanker truck

  b. water in a bathtub

  c. serving of yogurt

  d. bottle of cough syrup

Lesson 5-8 *(pp. 254–257)*   Changing Units in the Customary System

Lesson Objectives	NAEP 2005 Strand: Measurement
▼ Change units ▼ Compute with units	Topic: Systems of Measurement Local Standards: _______________________

Example

❶ Changing Units of Length Complete each statement.

a. 111 in. = ▨ ft

$$111 \text{ in.} = \left(111 \div \boxed{}\right) \text{ ft} \qquad \leftarrow \textbf{ Divide 111 by } \boxed{}.$$

$$= \left(111 \times \frac{\boxed{}}{\boxed{}}\right) \text{ ft} \qquad \leftarrow \textbf{ Multiply by } \frac{\boxed{}}{\boxed{}}, \textbf{ the reciprocal of 12.}$$

$$= \frac{\boxed{}}{\boxed{}} \text{ ft, or } \boxed{}\frac{\boxed{}}{\boxed{}} \text{ ft}$$

b. 14 ft = ▨ yd

$$14 \text{ ft} = (14 \div 3)\,\text{yd} \qquad \leftarrow \textbf{ Divide 14 by 3.}$$

$$= \left(14 \times \frac{\boxed{}}{\boxed{}}\right)\text{yd} \qquad \leftarrow \textbf{ Multiply by } \frac{\boxed{}}{\boxed{}}, \textbf{ the reciprocal of 3.}$$

$$= \frac{\boxed{}}{\boxed{}} \text{ yd, or } \boxed{}\frac{\boxed{}}{\boxed{}} \text{ yd}$$

Check Understanding

1. Complete each statement.

a. 45 in. = ⬚ $= \boxed{}\dfrac{\boxed{}}{\boxed{}}$ ft

b. $56\frac{1}{3}$ in. = ⬚ $= \boxed{}\dfrac{\boxed{}}{\boxed{}}$ ft

c. How many yards of fabric are in $7\frac{1}{2}$ feet of fabric?

Examples

❷ Changing Units of Weight and Capacity Complete the statement.

19 cups = ☐ qt

19 cups = (19 ÷ 4) qt   ← **Divide to go from a smaller unit to a larger unit.**

$= \left(\dfrac{19}{1} \times \dfrac{☐}{☐} \right)$ qt   ← **Multiply by $\dfrac{☐}{☐}$, the reciprocal of 4.**

$= \dfrac{☐}{☐}$ qt, or $☐\dfrac{☐}{☐}$ qt

❸ Computing With Units A craftsperson is shipping a ceramic vase that weighs 3 lb 12 oz. The weight of the packing crate is 2 lb 6 oz. What is the total weight of the vase and the packing crate?

Add: 3 lb   12   oz
         + 2 lb   6   oz
         ☐ lb ☐   oz

Think: 5 lb   18   oz = 5 lb + ☐ lb + 2 oz ← **Rename 18 oz as 1 lb 2 oz.**

                = ☐ lb ☐ oz   ← **Combine 5 lb and 1 lb.**

The total weight is ☐ lb ☐ oz.

Check Understanding

2. Complete each statement.

a. 13 c = ☐ = $☐\dfrac{☐}{☐}$ qt

b. $2\dfrac{1}{4}$ t = ☐ = ☐ lb

3. Your baby cousin was 6 pounds 8 ounces at birth. She gained 1 pound 9 ounces. How much does she weigh now?

Lesson 6-1 *(pp. 269–272)*   Ratios

Lesson Objective	**NAEP 2005 Strand:** Number Properties and Operations
▼ Write ratios	**Topic:** Ratios and Proportional Reasoning
	Local Standards: _______________________________

Vocabulary

A ratio is ____

____

Two ratios are equal if ____

____

Example

❶ **Three Ways to Write a Ratio** During a school trip, there are 3 teachers and 25 students on each bus. Write each ratio in three ways.

    a. teachers to students

        There are ☐ teachers and ☐ students on each bus.

        teachers to students → 3 to ☐ or 3 : ☐ or $\dfrac{3}{\boxed{}}$

    b. students to teachers

        There are ☐ students and ☐ teachers on each bus.

        students to teachers → 25 to ☐ or 25 : ☐ or $\dfrac{25}{\boxed{}}$

Check Understanding

1. Use the recipe at the right to write each ratio in three ways.

    a. pretzels to cereal

    b. pretzels to party mix

Name_____________________________________ Class_________________________________ Date _______________

Examples

❷ **Writing Equal Ratios** Write two different ratios equal to 24 : 8.

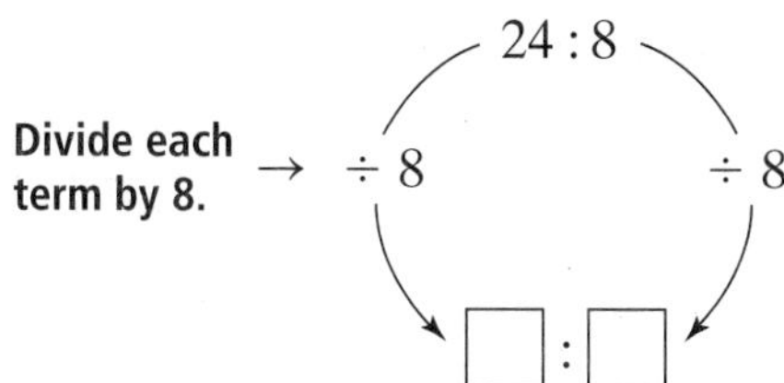

Two ratios equal to 24 : 8 are ☐ and ☐ .

❸ **Ratios in Simplest Form** Write each ratio in simplest form.

a. 121 to 11

b. 28 : 16

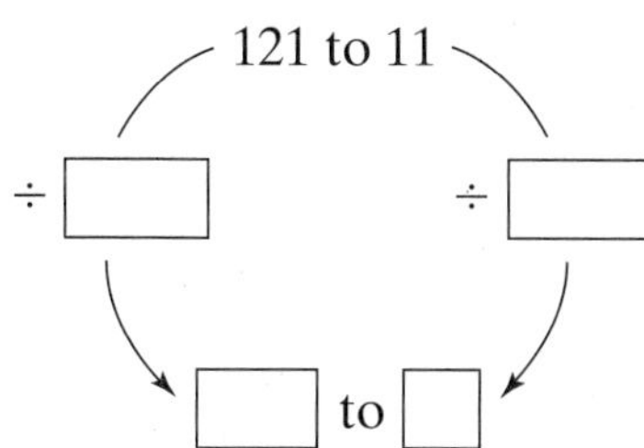

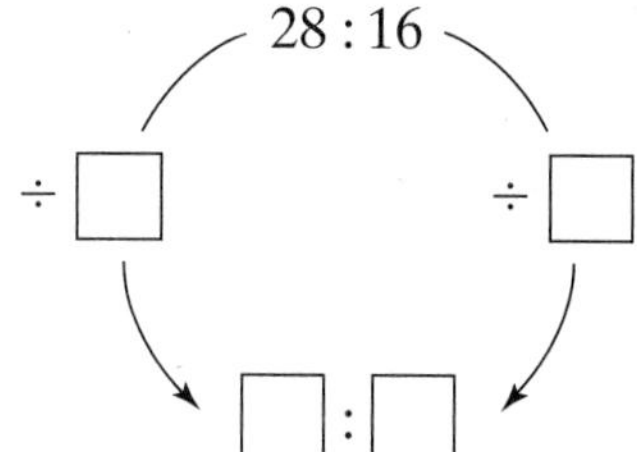

In simplest form, the ratio
121 to 11 is ☐ .

In simplest form, the ratio
28 : 16 is ☐ .

Check Understanding

2. Write two different ratios equal to each ratio.

a. $\frac{10}{35}$

b. 12 : 3

c. 8 to 22

d. Number Sense Use the definition of a ratio to explain why $\frac{9}{5}$ is a ratio but $1\frac{4}{5}$ is not a ratio.

3. Write each ratio in simplest form.

a. 4 : 20

b. 50 to 45

c. $\frac{39}{3}$

Lesson 6-2 *(pp. 273–276)* Unit Rates

Lesson Objectives	NAEP 2005 Strand: Number Properties and Operations
▼ Estimate products of mixed numbers ▼ Multiply mixed numbers	Topic: Ratios and Proportional Reasoning Local Standards: ________________________

Vocabulary

A rate is ____

____

A unit rate is _____________________________________

____

A unit price is ____________________________________

____

Example

1 **Finding a Unit Rate** Find the unit rate for typing 145 words in 5 minutes.

$$\begin{array}{l} \text{words} \rightarrow \\ \text{minutes} \rightarrow \end{array} \frac{145}{5} = \boxed{} \quad \leftarrow \begin{array}{l}\textbf{Divide the first quantity by}\\ \textbf{the second quantity.}\end{array}$$

The unit rate is $\boxed{}$ or $\boxed{}$ words per minute.

Check Understanding

1. Find the unit rate for each situation.

a. 66 pages read in 2 hours

b. $2.37 for 3 pounds of grapes

c. **Reasoning** Which of the following rates, $\frac{36 \text{ inches}}{3 \text{ feet}}$ or $\frac{12 \text{ inches}}{1 \text{ foot}}$, is a unit rate?

Name_______________________________ Class_______________________________ Date _______________

Examples

❷ Using a Unit Rate Apples cost $1.49 for 1 pound. How much do 5 pounds of apples cost?

Write the unit ratio. Then find an equal ratio.

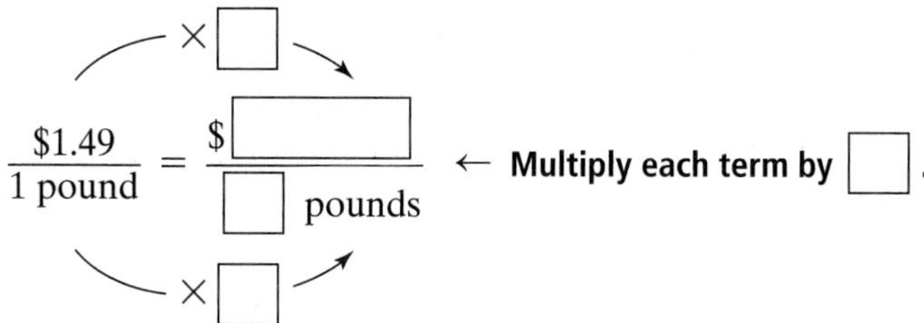

Five pounds of apples cost ⬚ .

❸ Comparing Unit Prices The same brand of pretzels comes in two sizes: a 10-ounce bag for $.99, and an 18-ounce bag for $1.49. Which size is a better buy? Round each unit price to the nearest cent.

Divide to find the unit price of each size.

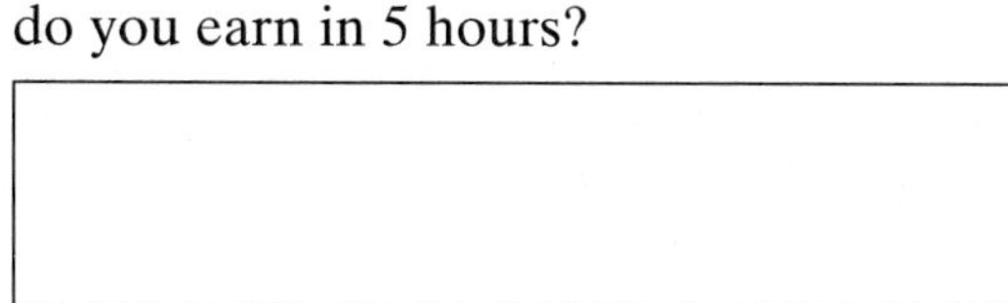

The better buy costs less per ounce. Since ⬚ is less than ⬚ , the ⬚ -ounce bag is the better buy.

Check Understanding

2. Write each unit rate as a ratio. Then find an equal ratio.

a. You can earn $5.25 in 1 hour. How much do you earn in 5 hours?

b. You type 25 words in 1 minute. How many words can you type in 10 minutes?

3. Find each unit price. Round to the nearest cent. Then determine the better buy.

a. yogurt: 6 ounces for $.68
      32 ounces for $2.89

b. phone call: 3 minutes for $.42
      15 minutes for $1.35

c. Reasoning Explain how unit pricing helps you compare costs in a grocery store.

Lesson 6-3 *(pp. 278–282)*   **Understanding Proportions**

Lesson Objectives	**NAEP 2005 Strand:** Number Properties and Operations
▼ Testing ratios ▼ Completing proportions	**Topic:** Ratios and Proportional Reasoning **Local Standards:** _______________________

Vocabulary and Key Concepts

Proportions

A proportion is ____

____

Examples $\frac{1}{2}=$ ☐ $\frac{27}{18}=$ ☐

Example

❶ **Recognizing Proportions** Do the ratios in each pair form a proportion?

a. $\frac{6}{14}, \frac{42}{77}$

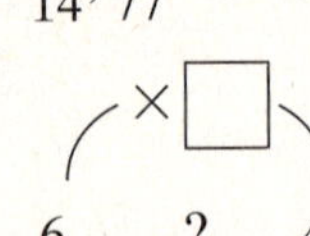

$\frac{6}{14} \overset{?}{=} \frac{42}{77}$ ← $14 \times$ ☐ $= 98$, not ☐

$\frac{6}{14}$ ☐ $\frac{42}{77}$ ← Compare ratios.

$\frac{6}{14}$ and $\frac{42}{77}$ do *not* form a proportion.

b. $\frac{3}{13}, \frac{9}{39}$

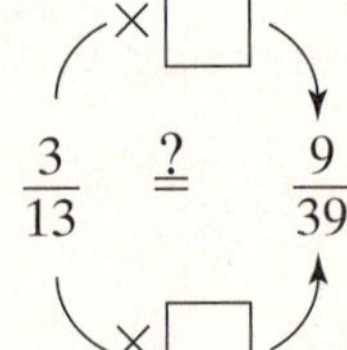

$\frac{3}{13} \overset{?}{=} \frac{9}{39}$

$\frac{3}{13}$ ☐ $\frac{9}{39}$ ← Compare ratios.

$\frac{3}{13}$ and $\frac{9}{39}$ form a proportion.

Check Understanding

1. Do the ratios in each pair form a proportion?

a. $\frac{2}{5}, \frac{8}{20}$

b. $\frac{8}{5}, \frac{36}{20}$

c. $\frac{12}{52}, \frac{4}{14}$

Example

❷ **Completing a Proportion** Leslie biked 45 mi in 5 h. How far could she bike in 3 hours?

Write a proportion that compares miles biked to hours.

miles → $\dfrac{45}{\square}$ = $\dfrac{\blacksquare}{\square}$ ← miles
hours → ← hours

The denominators $\square$ and $\square$ are not easy to relate by multiplication, so find a unit rate for 45 miles and 5 hours.

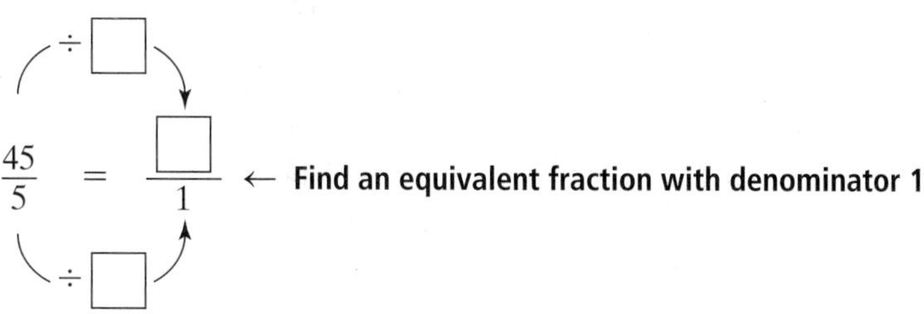

$\dfrac{45}{5}$ = $\dfrac{\square}{1}$ ← **Find an equivalent fraction with denominator 1.**

9 miles per hour $\times$ 3 hours = $\boxed{}$ miles

Leslie can bike $\boxed{}$ miles in 3 hours.

Check Understanding

2. Find the value that completes each proportion.

a. $\dfrac{12}{4} = \dfrac{\blacksquare}{5}$

b. $\dfrac{3}{9} = \dfrac{2}{\blacksquare}$

Lesson 6-4 *(pp. 283–287)*   **Using Cross Products**

Lesson Objective	**NAEP 2005 Strand:** Number Properties and Operations
▼ Use cross products to identify proportions	**Topic:** Ratios and Proportional Reasoning
	Local Standards: _________________________

Vocabulary

The cross products of two ratios are found by _______________________________________

____

Examples

① Using Cross Products Does each pair of ratios form a proportion?

a. $\dfrac{9}{10}, \dfrac{18}{30}$ **b.** $\dfrac{9}{27}, \dfrac{7}{21}$

$\dfrac{9}{\boxed{}} \overset{?}{=} \dfrac{18}{\boxed{}}$ ← Write a possible proportion. → $\dfrac{9}{\boxed{}} \overset{?}{=} \dfrac{7}{\boxed{}}$

$9 \times \boxed{} \overset{?}{=} \boxed{} \times 18$ ← Write the cross products. → $9 \times \boxed{} \overset{?}{=} \boxed{} \times 7$

$270 \ \boxed{} \ 180$ ← Multiply. → $189 \ \boxed{} \ 189$

The ratios $\dfrac{9}{10}$ and $\dfrac{18}{30}$ The ratios $\dfrac{9}{27}$ and $\dfrac{7}{21}$

$\boxed{}$ form a proportion. $\boxed{}$ form a proportion.

② Solving Proportions Using Cross Products Solve $\dfrac{14}{26} = \dfrac{21}{n}$.

$\dfrac{14}{26} = \dfrac{21}{n}$ ← Start with the proportion.

$14 \cdot \boxed{} = \boxed{} \cdot 21$ ← Write the cross products.

$14n = 546$ ← Multiply.

$\dfrac{14n}{\boxed{}} = \dfrac{546}{\boxed{}}$ ← Divide each side by $\boxed{}$.

$n = \boxed{}$ ← Simplify.

Name_________________________________ Class_________________________________ Date _____________

❸ Jobs Janet earned \$31.50 for 5 hours of work. How much does she earn for 7 hours of work at the same rate of pay?

Write a proportion that compares hours of work to pay.

Let p = the amount of pay.

hours → $\dfrac{5}{\boxed{}}$ = $\dfrac{7}{\boxed{}}$ ← hours ← **Write a proportion.**
pay (\$) →   ← pay (\$)

$5 \cdot \boxed{} = \boxed{} \cdot 7$ ← **Write the cross products.**

$5p = \boxed{}$ ← **Multiply.**

$\dfrac{5p}{\boxed{}} = \dfrac{\boxed{}}{\boxed{}}$ ← **Divide each side by** $\boxed{}$.

$p = \boxed{}$ ← **Simplify.**

Janet will earn \$$\boxed{}$ for 7 hours of work.

Check Understanding

1. Do the ratios $\frac{2}{4}$ and $\frac{8}{16}$ form a proportion? Explain.

2. Solve each proportion.

a. $\dfrac{6}{8} = \dfrac{n}{20}$

b. $\dfrac{9}{12} = \dfrac{3}{x}$

c. $\dfrac{2}{8} = \dfrac{t}{20}$

3. a. If 5 notebooks cost \$7.50, how much do 3 notebooks cost?

b. Estimation If 7 pens cost \$5.53, about how much will 4 pens cost?

Lesson 6-5 *(pp. 288–292)*   Scale Drawings

Lesson Objectives	NAEP 2005 Strands: Number Properties and Operations; Measurement
V1 Find the scale **V2** Find actual dimensions	**Topics:** Ratios and Proportional Reasoning; Measuring Physical Attributes; Systems of Measurement **Local Standards:** _______________________________

Vocabulary

A scale is ____

____

Examples

1 **Finding the Scale of a Drawing** The length of a drawing of a kitten is 3 cm. The actual length of the kitten is 27 cm. What is the scale of the drawing?

$$\text{drawing length} \rightarrow \quad \frac{3 \text{ cm}}{\boxed{} \text{ cm}} = \frac{1}{\boxed{}} \leftarrow \begin{array}{l}\textbf{Divide each measure by}\\ \textbf{the GCF } \boxed{}\,.\end{array}$$

The scale is $\boxed{}$ cm to $\boxed{}$ cm, or $\boxed{}$.

2 **Finding Distances on a Map** Use a map scale of 1 in. : 20 mi to find the actual distance represented on the map by 3.4 in.

Step 1 Write the scale ratio: $\dfrac{\boxed{}}{\boxed{}}$.

Step 2 Find the number of miles represented by 3.4 in.

Let y = the actual distance represented by 3.4 in.

$$\frac{1 \text{ in.}}{\boxed{} \text{ mi.}} = \frac{3.4 \text{ in.}}{\boxed{} \text{ mi.}} \quad \leftarrow \textbf{ map distances}$$
$$ \leftarrow \textbf{ actual distances}$$

$$1\boxed{} = \boxed{} \cdot 3.4 \quad \leftarrow \textbf{ Write the cross products.}$$

$$y = \boxed{} \quad \leftarrow \textbf{ Multiply.}$$

The actual distance is $\boxed{}$ miles.

❸ Models Suppose you are making a model of an 18-meter boat. Use a scale of 1 cm : 2.5 m to find the length of your model boat.

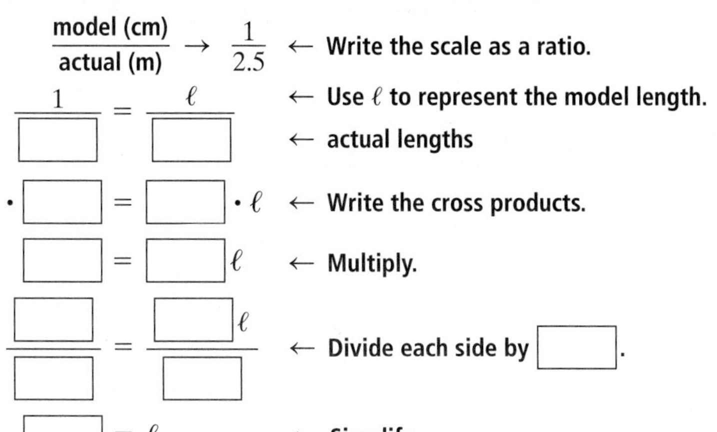

The model will be ⬚ cm long.

Check Understanding

1. The length of a drawing of an object is 6 inches. The length of the actual object is 84 inches. What is the scale of the drawing?

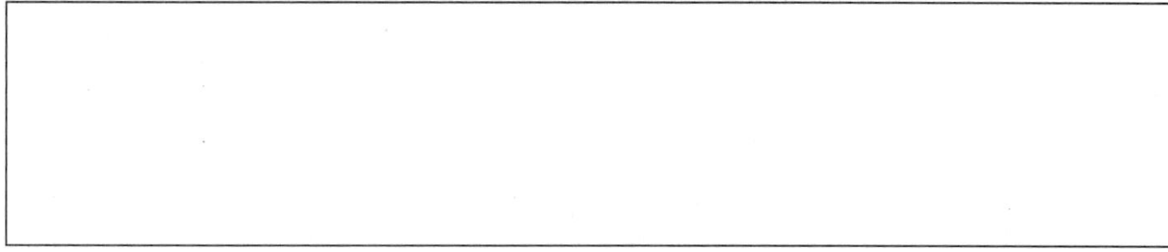

2. Use the map and scale to find the approximate distance from Winfield to Montgomery.

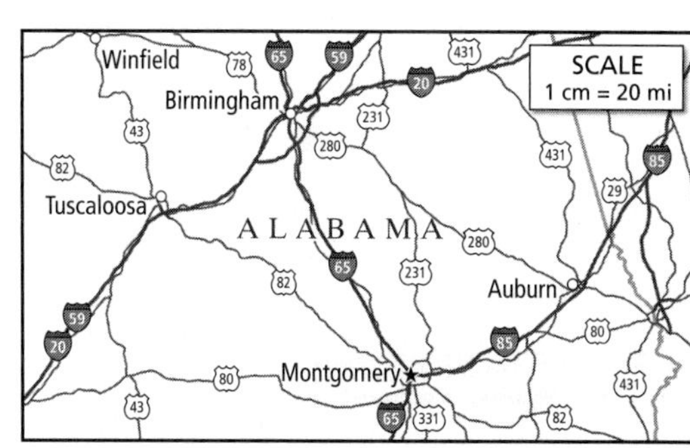

3. Suppose the boat in Example 3 is 1.5 meters tall. How tall will the model be?

Lesson 6-6 *(pp. 294–298)*

Percents, Fractions, and Decimals

Lesson Objectives	**NAEP 2005 Strand:** Number Properties and Operations
▼ Write percents as decimals and fractions ▼ Write decimals and fractions as percents	**Topic:** Number Sense **Local Standards:** _______________________________

Vocabulary

A percent is ____

____

Examples

❶ **Writing Percents as Decimals** Write each percent as a decimal.

a. 87%　　　　　　　　　　　　　　　　**b.** 9%

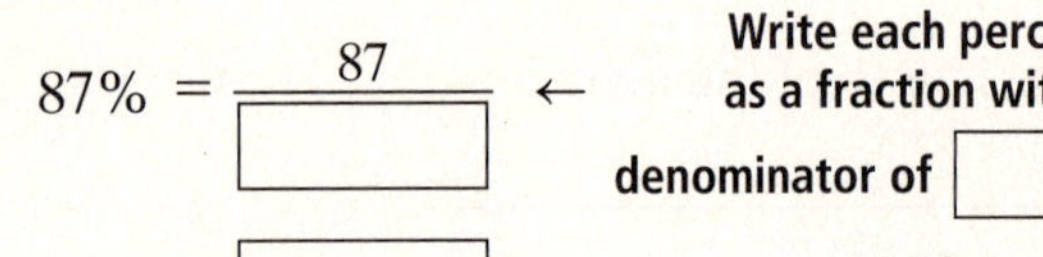
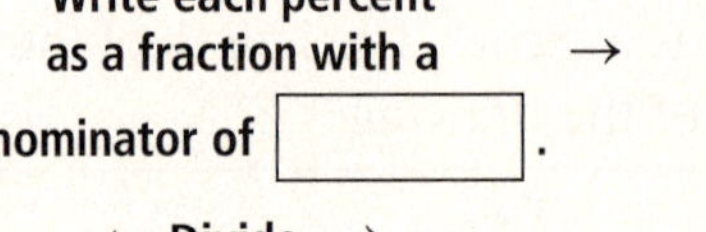

❷ **Writing Percents as Fractions** Write 4% as a fraction in simplest form.

$$4\% = \frac{4}{\boxed{}} \quad \leftarrow \quad \text{Write the percent as a fraction with a denominator of } \boxed{}.$$

$$= \frac{\boxed{}}{\boxed{}} \quad \leftarrow \quad \text{Write the fraction in simplest form.}$$

Check Understanding

1. Write 18% as a decimal.

2. **a.** Write 12% as a fraction in simplest form.

   b. **Mental Math** Write 20% as a fraction in simplest form.

Examples

❸ Writing Decimals as Percents Write each decimal as a percent.

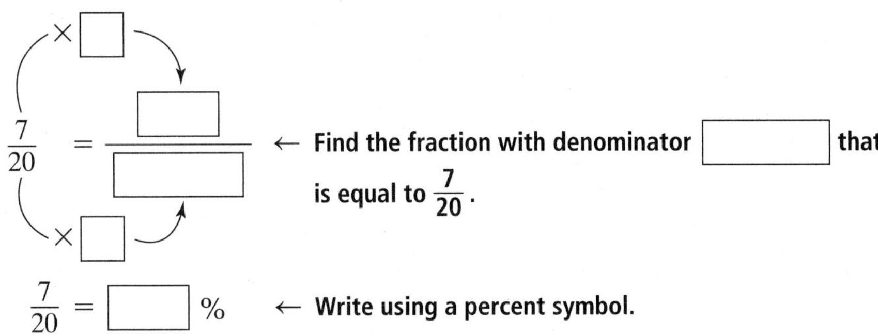

a. 0.16   0.16 → ☐ %   Move each decimal point

b. 0.03   0.03 → ☐ %   ← ☐ places to the right.

❹ Writing Fractions as Percents Write $\frac{7}{20}$ as a percent.

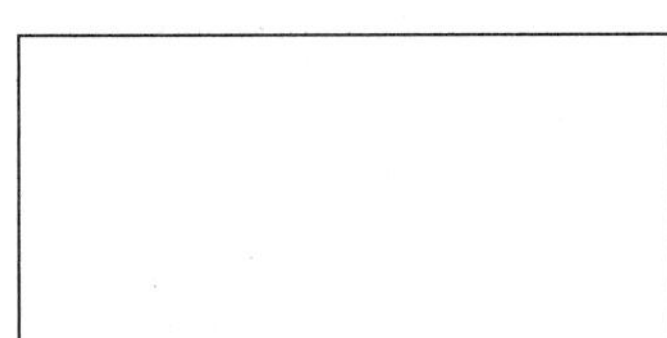

$\frac{7}{20} = \dfrac{\boxed{}}{\boxed{}}$ ← Find the fraction with denominator ☐ that is equal to $\frac{7}{20}$.

$\frac{7}{20} = \boxed{}$ %   ← Write using a percent symbol.

Check Understanding

3. Write each decimal as a percent.

a. 0.52   **b.** 0.05   **c.** 0.5

d. Reasoning Explain how you could write 72% as a decimal by moving a decimal point.

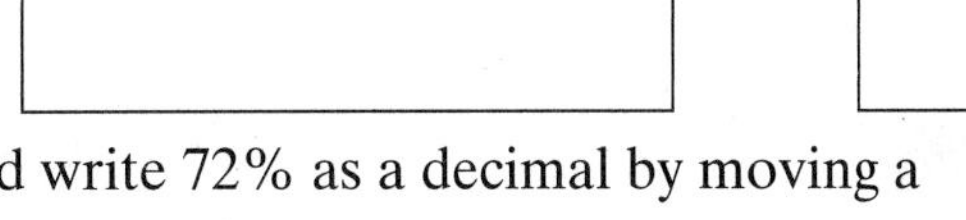

4. a. According to a news article, 1 out of every 20 neurosurgeons in the United States is a woman. Write the fraction $\frac{1}{20}$ as a percent.

b. Number Sense List all possible denominators that are factors of 100.

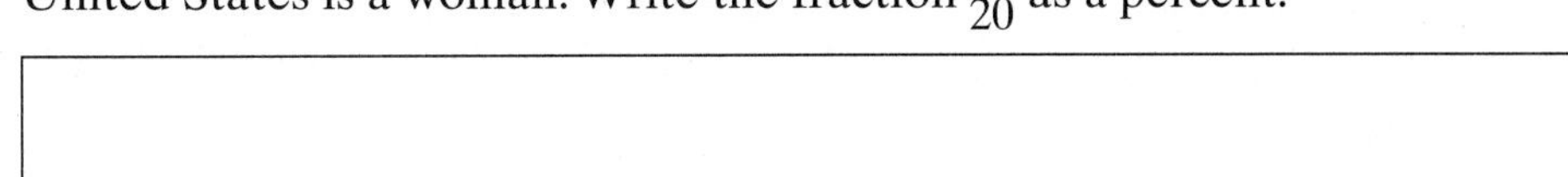

Lesson 6-7 *(pp. 289–302)*

Finding Percent of a Number

Lesson Objectives	NAEP 2005 Strand: Number Properties and Operations
1 Use proportions with percents **2** Use decimals with percents	**Topic:** Ratios and Proportional Reasoning **Local Standards:** ________________________

Examples

1 **Using a Proportion** Use a proportion to find 60% of 45.

Let n represent the number you want to find.

$$\dfrac{n}{\boxed{}} = \dfrac{60}{\boxed{}} \quad \leftarrow \textbf{ part}$$
$$\leftarrow \textbf{ whole}$$

$\boxed{} \times n = 60 \times \boxed{} \quad \leftarrow$ **Write the cross products.**

$100n = 2{,}700 \quad \leftarrow$ **Multiply.**

$n = \boxed{} \quad \leftarrow$ **Divide each side by** $\boxed{}$.

60% of 45 is $\boxed{}$.

2 **Using a Decimal** Find 88% of 250.

$88\% = \boxed{} \quad \leftarrow$ **Write 88% as a decimal.**

$\boxed{} \times 250 = \boxed{} \quad \leftarrow$ **Multiply.**

So, 88% of 250 is $\boxed{}$.

Check Understanding

1. Brendan has read 60% of a novel that has 80 pages. Use a proportion to find the number of pages Brendan has read.

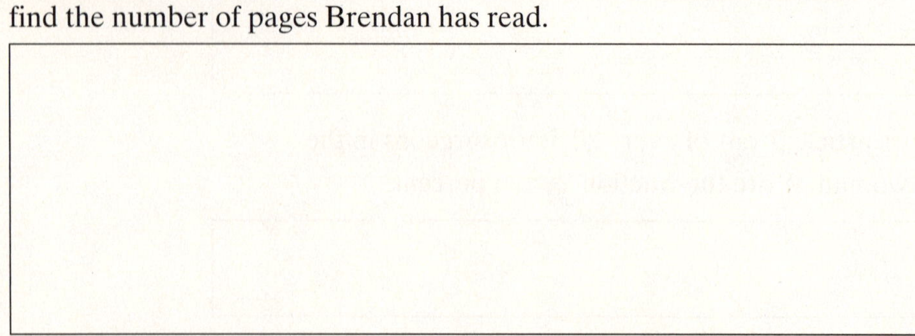

Name_____________________________ Class_____________________________ Date _____________

Example

❸ **Using Mental Math** Use mental math to find 75% of 84.

What you think

75% is equivalent to $\frac{3}{4}$. $\frac{3}{4} \times 84 = \boxed{}$.   75% of 84 is $\boxed{}$.

Why it works

$$75\% = \frac{75}{\boxed{}}$$

$$= \frac{\boxed{}}{\boxed{}} \quad \leftarrow \textbf{Write 75\% as a fraction in simplest form.}$$

$$\frac{3}{4} \times 84 = \frac{3}{4} \times \frac{\boxed{}}{\boxed{}} \quad \leftarrow \textbf{Multiply 84 by } \tfrac{3}{4}. \textbf{ Rewrite 84 as } \frac{\boxed{}}{\boxed{}}.$$

$$= \frac{\boxed{}}{\boxed{}} \quad \leftarrow \textbf{Simplify.}$$

$$= \boxed{} \quad \leftarrow \textbf{Divide.}$$

Check Understanding

2. Find each answer.

   a. 12% of 91

   b. 18% of 121

3. Use mental math to find each of the following.

   a. 10% of 56

   b. 75% of 12

   c. 50% of 36

Lesson 6-8 *(pp. 303–306)*   **Estimating With Percents**

Lesson Objective ▼ Estimate with percents	**NAEP 2005 Strand:** Number Properties and Operations **Topic:** Ratios and Proportional Reasoning **Local Standards:** ____________________

Examples

❶ Estimating Sales Tax Using a 5% sales tax, estimate the sales tax and the total cost for a pair of sneakers that costs $34.99.

Method 1 The sneakers cost about $35.

$$5\% \text{ of } 35 = \boxed{} \times 35 \quad \leftarrow \text{ Write 5\% as a decimal.}$$

$$= \boxed{} \quad \leftarrow \text{ Multiply to find the tax.}$$

$$35 + \boxed{} = \boxed{} \quad \leftarrow \text{ Find the sum of the price and the tax.}$$

The cost of the sneakers, including tax, is about $\boxed{}$.

Method 2 The sneakers cost about $35. The sales tax rate is 5%, or $\boxed{}$ cents for every dollar.

$$\$35 \times \boxed{} \text{cents/dollar} = \boxed{} \text{¢, or } \$\boxed{}$$

$$\$35 + \boxed{} = \boxed{}$$

The cost of the sneakers, including tax, is about $\boxed{}$.

❷ Estimating a Tip Estimate a 15% tip for a bill of $29.34.

What you think

The bill is about $29. I can break apart 15% into 10% and $\boxed{}$%.

Since 10% of $29 is $\boxed{}$, 5% is half of $2.90, or $\boxed{}$.

A 15% tip is about $\boxed{}$ + $\boxed{}$, or $\boxed{}$.

Why it works

$$15\% \times \$29 = (10\% + \boxed{}\%) \times \$29 \quad \leftarrow \text{ Replace 15\% with 10\% + } \boxed{}\%.$$

$$= \left(10\% \times \boxed{}\right) + \left(5\% \times \boxed{}\right) \quad \leftarrow \boxed{} \text{ property.}$$

$$= \$2.90 + \left(\tfrac{1}{2} \times 10\% \times \$29\right) \quad \leftarrow \text{ Replace 5\% with } \tfrac{1}{2} \times 10\%.$$

$$= \$2.90 + \boxed{} \quad \leftarrow \text{ Simplify inside the parentheses.}$$

$$= \boxed{} \quad \leftarrow \text{ Add.}$$

Name_______________________________ Class_______________________________ Date _______________

❸ Estimating a Sale Price A jacket is on sale for 20% off the regular price of $49.95. Estimate the sale price of the jacket.

What you think

The regular price of the jacket is about $50.

If the price is 20% off, you pay 100% − 20%, or ☐ of the regular price.

80% of $50 = ☐ .

The sale price is ☐ .

Why it works

The sale price is 20% off the regular cost.

20% × $50 = ☐ × $50   ← **Write 20% as a decimal.**

$\quad\quad\quad$ = ☐   ← **Simplify.**

Subtract the amount off the regular price to find the sale price.

$50 − ☐ = ☐

Check Understanding

1. **a.** Using a 5% sales tax rate, estimate the sales tax and total cost for a hat that costs $9.99.

   b. Reasoning When estimating tax, would it be better to round a price like $34.48 up to $35, or down to $34? Explain.

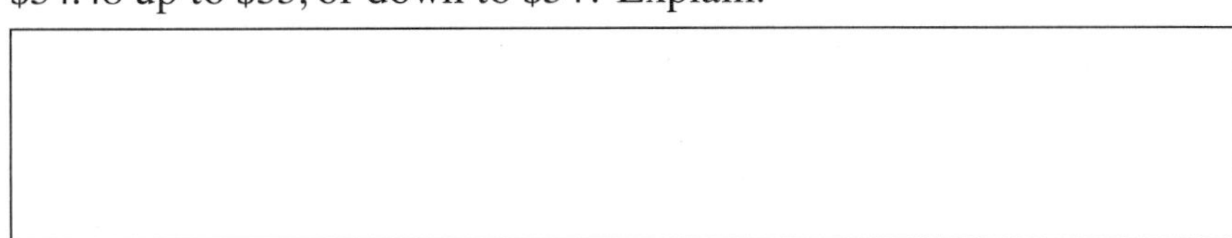

2. Estimate a 15% tip for a bill of $41.63.

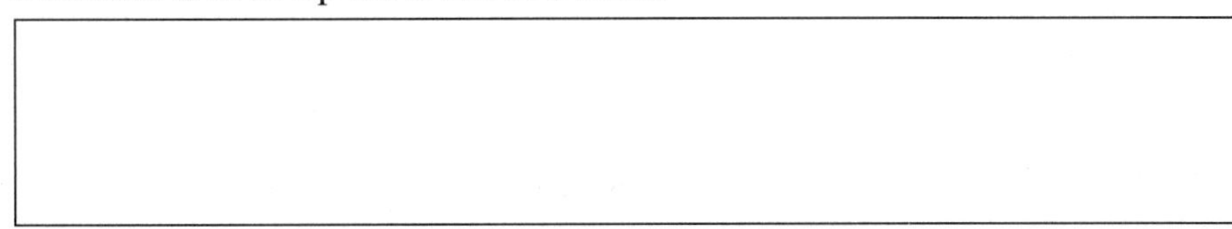

3. A baseball glove is on sale for 40% off the original price of $40.19. Estimate the sale price of the glove.

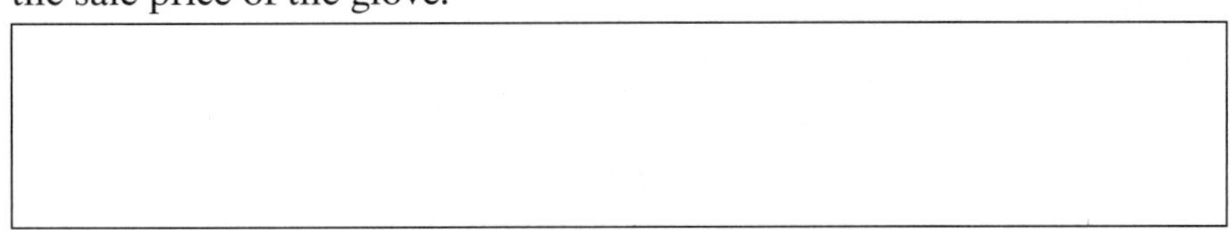

Lesson 6-9 *(pp. 307–309)*   **Write an Equation**

Lesson Objective	**NAEP 2005 Strand:** Algebra
▼ Solve problems by writing an equation	**Topic:** Equations and Inequalities
	Local Standards: ________________________

Example

1 **Sports** Solve by writing an equation. Soccer shoes are on sale for $67.97. The sale price is 15% off the regular price. What is the regular price of the shoes?

Read and Understand

The sale price of the soccer shoes, ⬚ , is 15% off the regular price. You need to find the regular price.

Plan and Solve

You will pay 100% − ⬚ , or ⬚ , of the regular price.

Words | percent you pay | times | regular price | equals | sale price |

Let | r | = the regular price.

Equation   ⬚   ×   ⬚   =   ⬚

⬚ $r = 67.97$ ← **Write 85% as a decimal.**

$$\frac{0.85r}{\boxed{}} = \frac{67.97}{\boxed{}}$$ ← **Divide each side by** ⬚ **to find r.**

$r \approx \$$ ⬚   ← **Simplify. Round to the nearest cent.**

The regular price of the shoes is ⬚ .

Look Back and Check

The regular price is about $80. The sale price is about ⬚ of $80, or ⬚ . This is close to the sale price, ⬚ .

Check Understanding

1. A sleeping bag is on sale for $29.97. This is 25% off the original price. What is the regular price of the sleeping bag?

Lesson 7-1 *(pp. 322–325)*

Mean, Median, and Mode

Lesson Objectives	**NAEP 2005 Strand:** Data Analysis and Probability
▼ Find the mean	**Topic:** Characteristics of Data Sets
▼ Find the mean and the mode	**Local Standards:** ______________________

Vocabulary

The mean is ____

An outlier is ____

The median is ____

The mode is ____

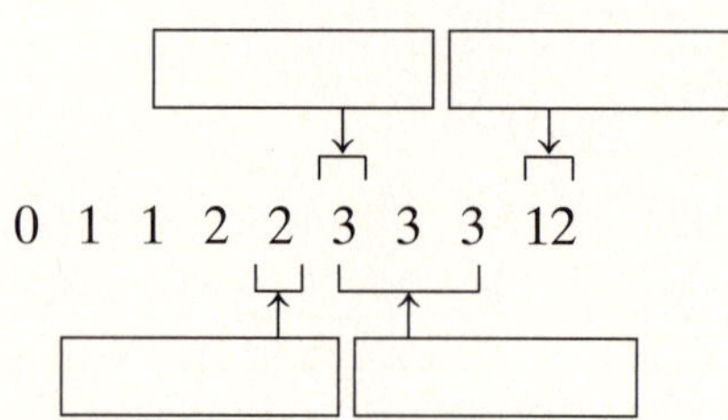

0 1 1 2 2 3 3 3 12

Example

❶ **Finding the Mean** Find the mean test score of 78, 85, 94, 88, and 91.

$78 + 85 + 94 + 88 + 91 = $ ☐ ← **Add the test scores.**

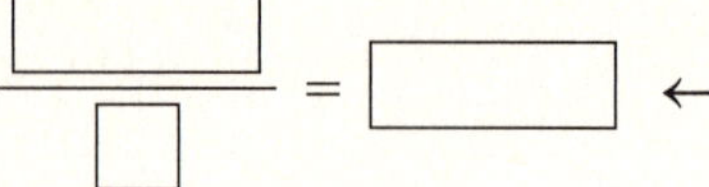 ← **Divide by the number of test scores.**

The mean test score is ☐ .

Check Understanding

1. Find the mean of each data set.
   a. 3, 2, 8, 4, 2, 3, 1, 5   **b.** 12, 23, 19, 32, 26   **c.** 4, 16, 20, 40   **d.** 5, 15, 75, 105, 85

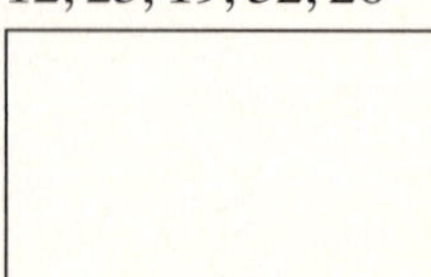

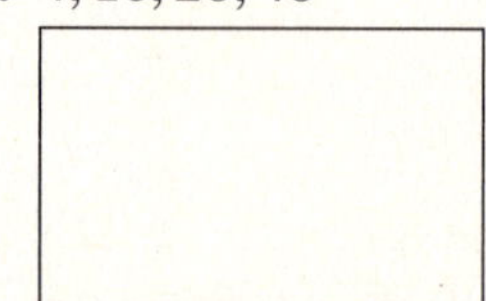

   e. Reasoning Using the set of data from part (d), find the mean of the numbers without the value 105. What do you notice?

Examples

❷ Finding the Median Find the median of 23, 35, 27, 55, 41, 23, 45, and 69.

$$23, 23, 27, 35, 41, 45, 55, 69 \quad \leftarrow \text{Order the data.}$$

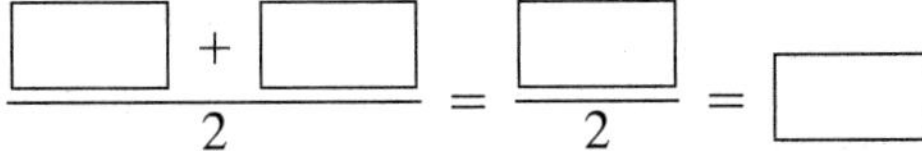

$$23, 23, 27, 35, 41, 45, 55, 69 \quad \leftarrow$$ Since there are 8 items (an even number), use the [______] values.

$$\frac{[\quad] + [\quad]}{2} = \frac{[\quad]}{2} = [\quad] \quad \leftarrow \text{Find the mean of } [\quad] \text{ and } [\quad].$$

The median is [______].

❸ Finding the Mode Find the mode of the following data:

blue, red, blue, yellow, yellow, blue, red, blue, yellow, blue, red, yellow

Group the data.

   blue, blue, blue, blue, blue

   red, red, red

   yellow, yellow, yellow, yellow

[______] occurs most often. It is the [______].

Check Understanding

2. Find the median of each data set.

a. 86, 90, 88, 84, 102, 95, 7

b. 8, 42, 13, 7, 50, 91

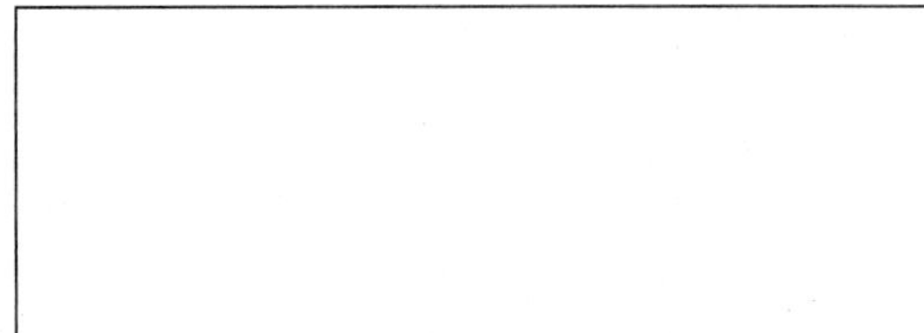

3. Find the mode of the following data.

orange, banana, apple, orange, apple, apple, orange, apple

Lesson 7-2 *(pp. 326–330)*

Organizing and Displaying Data

Lesson Objectives	NAEP 2005 Strand: Data Analysis and Probability
▼ Make a frequency table	Topic: Data Representation
▼ Make a plot and find the range	Local Standards: _________________

Vocabulary

A frequency table is ____

____

A line plot ____

____

The range is ____

____

Examples

❶ **Making a Frequency Table** The favorite lunch for ten students is: pizza, pizza, chicken, hamburger, chicken, pizza, chicken, pizza, pizza, pizza. Organize the data by making a frequency table. What is the mode?

Favorite Lunch

Lunch	Tally	Freq.

Make a tally mark for each lunch item chosen.

The number of tally marks in each row is the ______________.

Since most of the students selected ____________ as their favorite lunch item, the mode is ____________.

❷ **Making a Line Plot** Make a line plot to display the dinner hour for seven families:

5:00 7:00 6:00 6:00 8:00 7:00 6:00

Dinner Hours

← Each **X** represents one hour.

← The data range from ☐ to ☐.

Name_______________________________ Class_______________________________ Date _______________

❸ Finding the Range Find the range of the data in Example 2.

☐ − ☐ = ☐ ← **Subtract the least value from the greatest value.**

The range is ☐ hours.

Check Understanding

1. The first initial of the names of fifteen students are listed below.

A J B K L C K D L S T D V P L

a. Organize the data by making a frequency table. What is the mode?

Initial	A	B	C	D	J	K	L	P	S	T	V
Tally											
Frequency											

The mode is ☐.

b. Reasoning Explain why you cannot find the mean of the data in part (a).

☐

2. Make a line plot of the number of phone calls made by employees in one day: 2, 3, 0, 7, 1, 1, 9, 8, 2, 8, 1, 2, 8, 7, 1, 8, 6, 1.

Number of Phone Calls

0   1   2   3   4   5   6   7   8   9
Phone Calls

3. Find the range of each data set.

a. 36, 21, 9, 34, 36, 10, 4, 35, 5, 30, 28, 27, 5, 10 ☐

b. 0.12, 0.11, 0.16, 0.15, 0.20, 0.18, 0.24, 0.7 ☐

c. Reasoning If two sets of data have the same range, do they also have the same median? Explain your reasoning.

☐

Lesson 7-3 *(pp. 331–334)*

Make an Organized List

Lesson Objective	Local Standards: _______________________________
▼ Solve problems by making an organized list	

Example

❶ **Using an Organized List** How many ways can you make 18¢? Solve by making an organized list.

(Read and Understand) You need to find all the different combinations of pennies, nickels, and dimes that make 18¢.

(Plan and Solve) Make an organized list that shows each coin and the number of each needed to make 18¢. Let each column be one set of pennies, nickels, and dimes. For example, one combination is one dime and eight pennies.

Dimes					
Nickels					
Pennies					

There are [   ] ways to make 18¢.

(Look Back and Check) You know that you cannot have more than [ ] dime in any one combination, nor can you have more than [ ] nickels.

You can use this information to see if you have considered all possibilities.

❷ Running Tara wants to walk in a charity event. In her first week of training, she walks three miles each day. Each week after that, she adds $\frac{3}{4}$ mile to her daily distance. In which week of training does Tara walk six miles per day?

Read and Understand During the first week of training, Tara walks

[   ] miles each day. Each week, she walks an additional

[ ] mile every day. You need to find

[   ]

Plan and Solve Make an organized list that shows week and distance. Stop when the distance reaches [   ] miles.

Week	Distance (miles/day)
1	3
2	$3 + \dfrac{\square}{\square} = \square\dfrac{\square}{\square}$
3	$\square\dfrac{\square}{\square} + \dfrac{3}{4} = \square\dfrac{\square}{\square}$
4	$\square\dfrac{\square}{\square} + \dfrac{3}{4} = \square\dfrac{\square}{\square}$
5	$\square\dfrac{\square}{\square} + \dfrac{3}{4} = \square$

Tara walks six miles per day during the [   ] week of training.

Look Back and Check You can check by **working backward.** In five weeks, there were [ ] increases of $\frac{3}{4}$ mile. $4 \times \frac{3}{4} = \boxed{}$. So the total increase was [ ] miles. The [ ]-mile increase plus the original 3 miles per day = [ ] miles.

Check Understanding

1. Suppose you plan to read a novel. Every day, you want to read two more pages than you did the day before. If you read just one page on the first day, on what day will you reach page 64?

[   ]

Lesson 7-4 *(pp. 335–339)*

Bar Graphs and Line Graphs

Lesson Objectives	NAEP 2005 Strand: Data Analysis and Probability
▼ Make bar graphs	Topic: Data Representation
▼ Make line graphs	Local Standards: ____________________

Vocabulary

A bar graph is ____

A histogram is ____

A line graph is ____

Example

❶ **Making a Bar Graph** Make a bar graph of the data.

Students With Employer Jobs

Age	Percent
14	33%
15	60%
16	74%

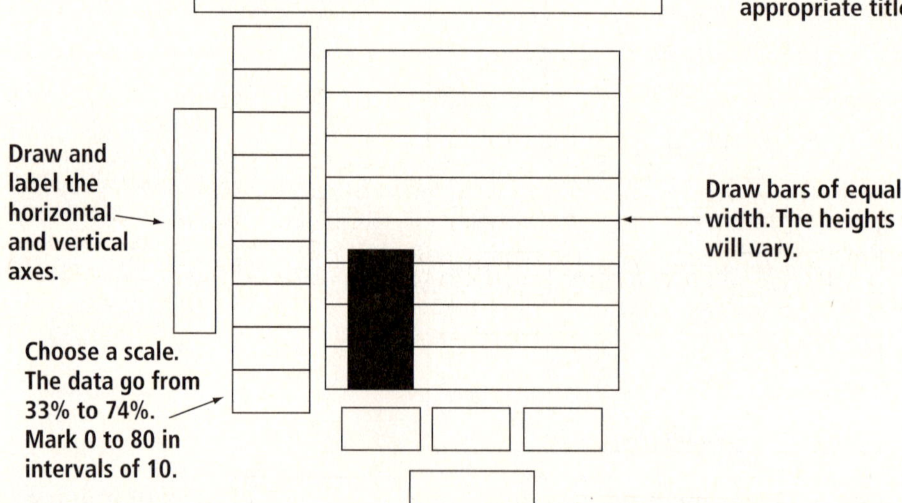

Check Understanding

1. Make a bar graph to display the data below.

Allowance Each Week					
Amount of Money ($)	3	4	5	6	7
Number of Students	10	21	34	12	6

Course 1 Daily Notetaking Guide

Examples

❷ Making a Histogram Make a histogram to display the speeds of the ticketed drivers.

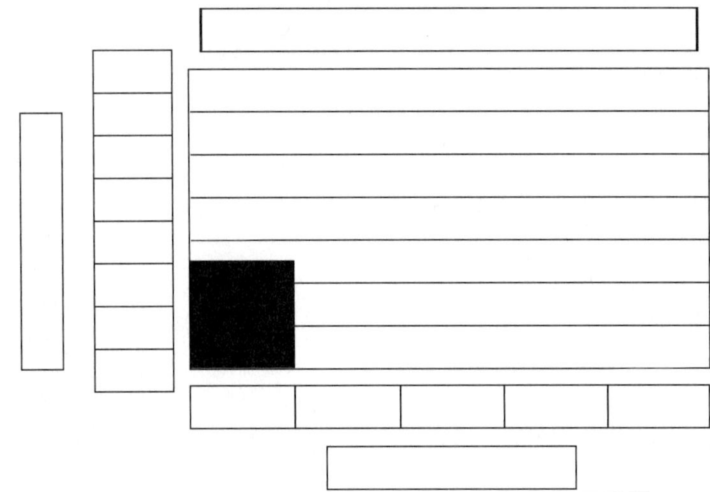

Speed	Frequency
36–40	5
41–45	8
46–50	12
51–55	6
56–60	3

❸ Making a Line Graph Make a line graph of the data.

Choose a scale. The data range from 45 to 121. Mark 0 to 140 in units of 20.

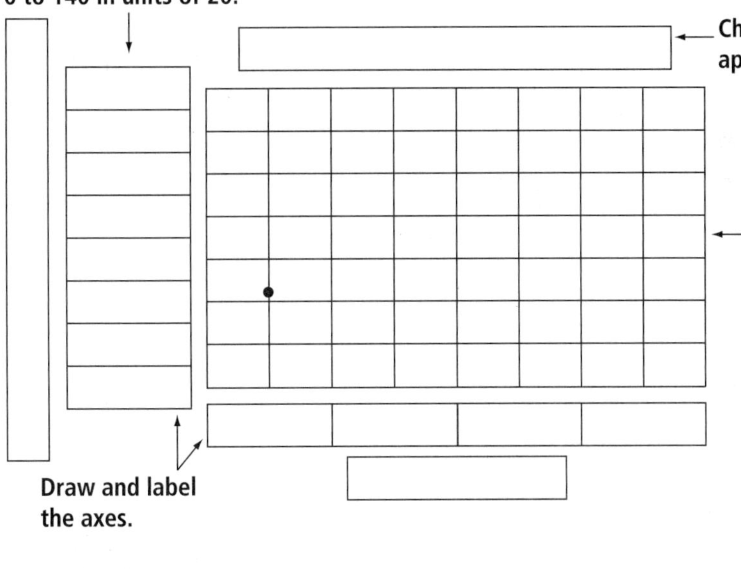

Running Shoes Sold

Month	Pairs Sold
February	45
March	86
April	121
May	115

Check Understanding

2. In Example 2, which interval contains the median?

3. Use the table to make a line graph.

Ticket Sales				
Week	1	2	3	4
Tickets Sold	22	35	33	46

Ticket Sales

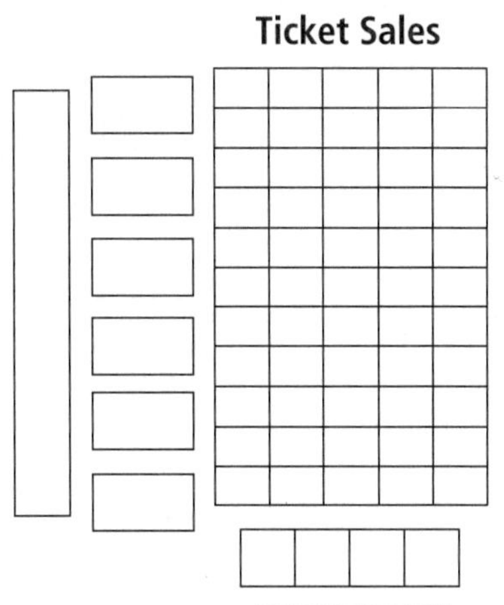

Lesson 7-5 *(pp. 341–345)*   Circle Graphs

Lesson Objective	NAEP 2005 Strand: Data Analysis and Probability
▼ Read and make circle graphs	Topic: Data Representation
	Local Standards: _____________________

Example

Brands of Jackets Sold

❶ **Reading a Circle Graph** Use the circle graph.

  a. What brand of jacket sold 43%?

  Brand ☐ sold 43%.

  b. What percent of Brand C were sold?

  ☐ % of Brand C were sold.

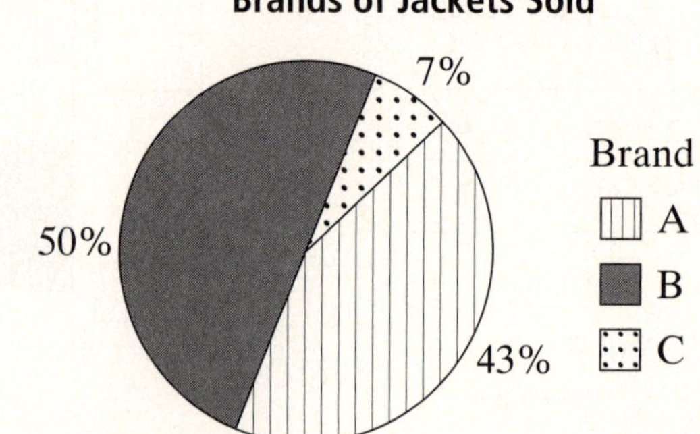

❷ **Making a Circle Graph** Make a circle graph of the data in the table.

First, use a calculator to change the data to percents of the total.

$56 + $33 + $18 + $24 = $ ☐

Round to the nearest percent.

Weekly Budget	
Savings	$56
Hobbies	$33
Food	$18
Other	$24

$\frac{56}{131} \approx$ ☐ % $\frac{33}{131} \approx$ ☐ %

$\frac{18}{131} \approx$ ☐ % $\frac{24}{131} \approx$ ☐ %

Use number sense to divide the circle.

43% is slightly less than ☐ the circle.

$25\% = \dfrac{☐}{☐}$

18% is slightly less than $\dfrac{☐}{☐}$ of the circle.

☐ % is what is left over.

Weekly Budget

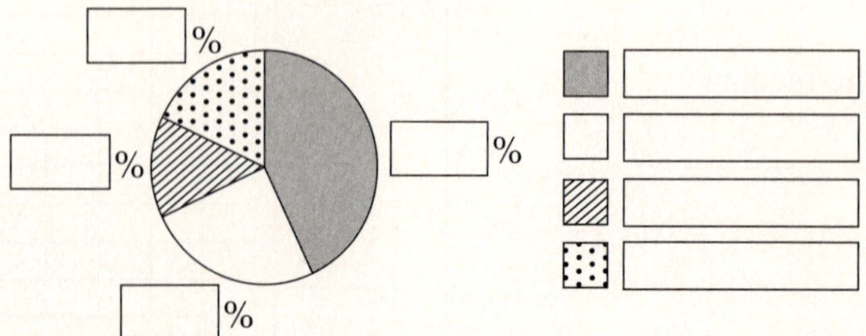

❸ More Than One Way Four NASA space shuttles flew 14 missions from 2000 through 2002. Draw a graph for the following data: *Atlantis*, 5 missions; *Columbia*, 1 mission; *Discovery*, 3 missions; *Endeavour*, 5 missions.

Method 1

Make a bar graph to display the data.

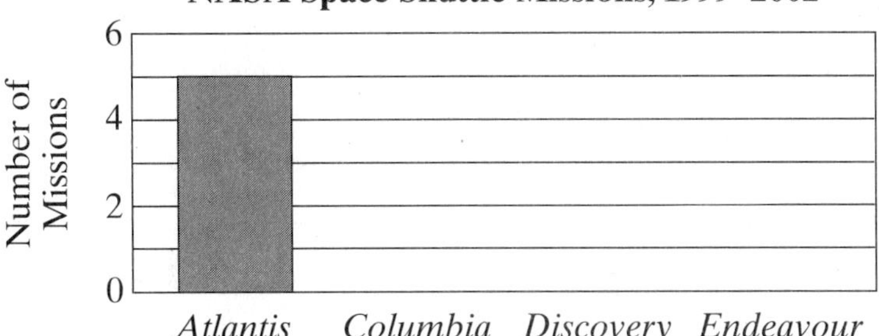

Method 2

Make a circle graph to display the data.

Space Shuttle Missions, 1999–2002

Check Understanding

1. a. According to the graph in Example 1, what brand of jacket sold 50%?

b. Which brands account for 93% of the jackets sold?

2. Of 50 students surveyed, 13 preferred hot lunch, 9 packed lunch, 6 ate at the salad bar, and 22 bought sandwiches. Make a circle graph of the data.

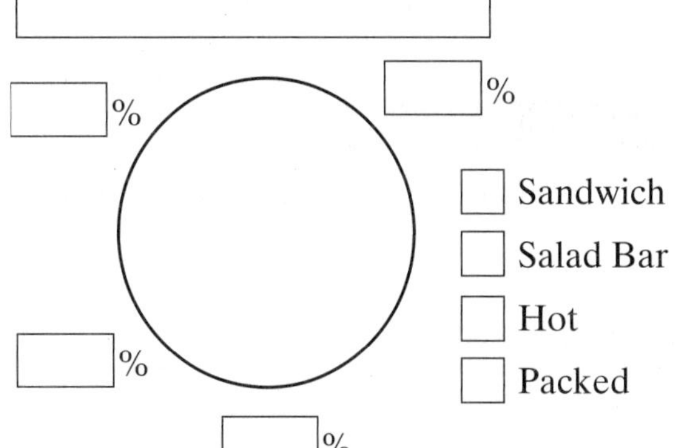

Lesson 7-6 *(pp. 347–350)*

**Using Spreadsheets
to Organize Data**

Lesson Objectives	**NAEP 2005 Strand:** Data Analysis and Probability
▼ Read data in a spreadsheet	**Topic:** Data Representation
▼ Write formulas for a spreadsheet	**Local Standards:** _______________________

Vocabulary

A spreadsheet is ____

____

A cell is ____

____

Example

❶ **Using a Spreadsheet** Use the spreadsheet below.

Column ☐

	A	**B**	**C**	**D**
1	Date	Phone	Utilities	Total
2	10/15	$68	$118	
3	11/15	$55	$143	
4	12/15	$72	$159	

Row ☐

Cell ☐

a. What is the value in cell C3?

$ ☐

b. Identify the cells that indicate the category *Phone*.

☐ , ☐ , ☐ , ☐

Check Understanding

1. a. What is the value in cell C4? What does this number represent?

☐

b. What cells are in row 2? What do the numbers in these cells represent?

☐

Example

❷ Formulas in a Spreadsheet Use the same spreadsheet as in Example 1.
Write a formula for cell D3 that will calculate the total for 11/15.

	A	B	C	D
1	Date	Phone	Utilities	Total
2	10/15	$68	$118	
3	11/15	$55	$143	
4	12/15	$72	$159	

← Add the entries in cells ⬚ and ⬚ .

The formula that should go in cell D3 is ⬚ .

Check Understanding

2. a. Write formula for cell B5 that will calculate the total amount for the
phone bills from 10/15, 11/15, and 12/15.

b. Write a formula for cell D4 that will calculate the total amount for 12/15.

Name_______________________________ Class_______________________________ Date_______________

Lesson 7-7 *(pp. 352–355)*   **Stem-and-Leaf Plots**

Lesson Objective	**NAEP 2005 Strand:** Data Analysis and Probability
▼ Use a stem-and-leaf plot	**Topic:** Data Representation
	Local Standards: _______________________

Vocabulary

A stem-and-leaf plot is ____

____

Example

1 Reading a Stem-and-Leaf Plot Use the stem-and-leaf plot.

Wait Times for Haircuts

```
0 | 1 1 3 4 5 6 9
1 | 0 0 1 3 4 4 9
2 | 1 2 4 6
3 | 0 2
```
Key: 0 | 5 means 5 min

[____] customers waited more than 10 minutes.

Their times were 11, [____], 14, 14, [____], 21,

22, [____], 26, [____], and 32.

The longest wait was [____] minutes.

a. How many customers waited more than 10 minutes?

[________________] customers waited more than 10 minutes.

b. How long was the longest wait?

The longest wait was [____] minutes.

Check Understanding

1. a. How many customers waited 10 minutes? [________________]

b. What is the range of the data?

[____]

c. **Reasoning** What advantage does a stem-and-leaf plot have compared to an ordered list of values?

[____]

   Course 1 Daily Notetaking Guide

Example

❷ Using a Stem-and-Leaf Plot Make a stem-and-leaf plot of the following bowling scores.

130	90	141	128	133	142
123	148	105	93	108	130
133	100	124	146	97	108

Step 1 Write the stems in order. Use the numbers in the tens and hundreds places. Draw a vertical line to the right of the stems.

Step 2 Write the leaves in order. Use the values in the ones place.

Step 3 Choose a title and include a key to explain what your stems and leaves represent.

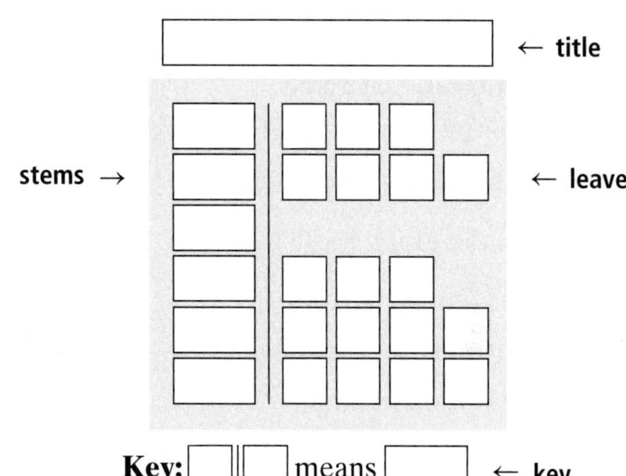

Check Understanding

2. Make a stem-and-leaf plot of the data: 137, 125, 145, 123, 181, 132, 155, 141, 140, 133, 138, 127, 150, 126, 124, 130, 125, 138, 144, 121, and 136.

(*Hint:* Use the ones digits for the leaves.)

Key: [ ] | [ ] means [ ]

Lesson 7-8 *(pp. 358–362)*
Misleading Graphs and Statistics

Lesson Objectives	NAEP 2005 Strand: Data Analysis and Probability
▼ Identify and fix misleading graphs ▼ Identify misleading statistics	Topic: Data Representation Local Standards: _____________________________

Examples

❶ Misleading Line Graphs

a. What impression is given by the graph?

The admission price is gradually [____________].

b. Why is the graph misleading?

The vertical scale uses [____________] intervals.

So, the increase from 1995 to [____________]

does not look so large.

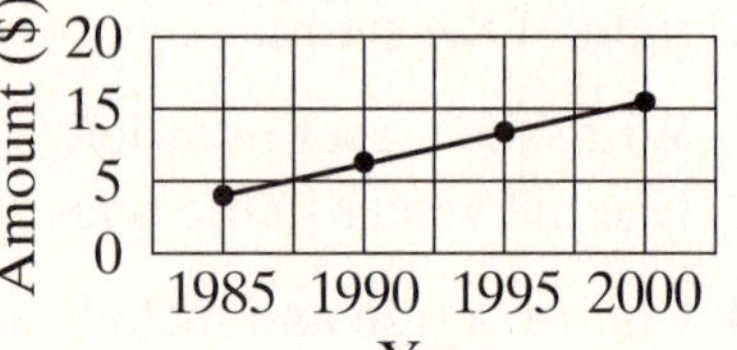

❷ Misleading Bar Graphs

a. What impression is given by the graph?

The number of females enrolled is more than

[____________] the number of males enrolled.

b. Why is the graph misleading?

The [____________] scale does not start at 0. So, you are

looking just at the [____________] of the graph.

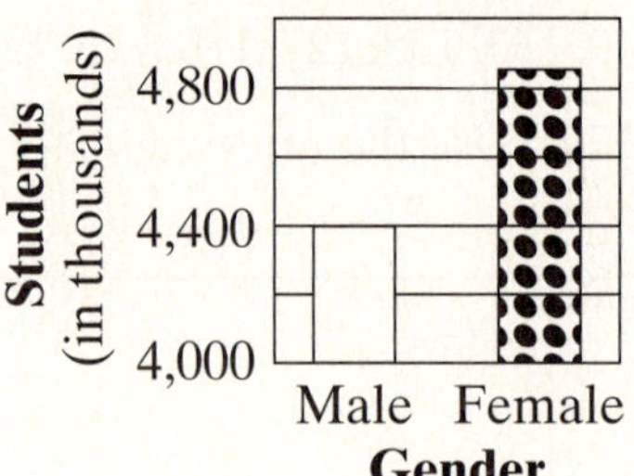

❸ Misleading Statistics Five hourly wages are $5, $8, $7.50, $35, and $7. Why might the mean wage be misleading?

Only one person makes more than the mean of $[____________]. The

$[____________] hourly wage is an [____________] and greatly increases

the mean.

Name_____________________________ Class_____________________________ Date _____________

Check Understanding

1. Redraw the graph in Example 1 so that it is not misleading.

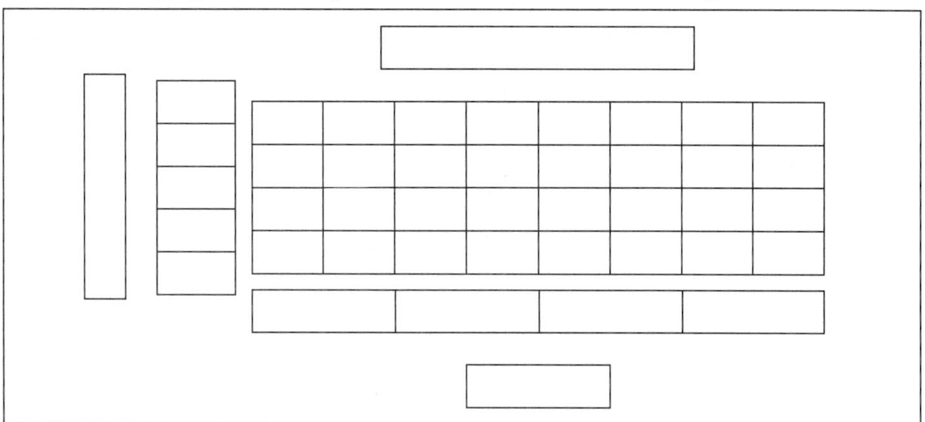

2. a. In Example 2, how many times as tall is the bar for Females as the bar for Males?

b. How many more females were enrolled?

c. Redraw the graph so that it is not misleading.

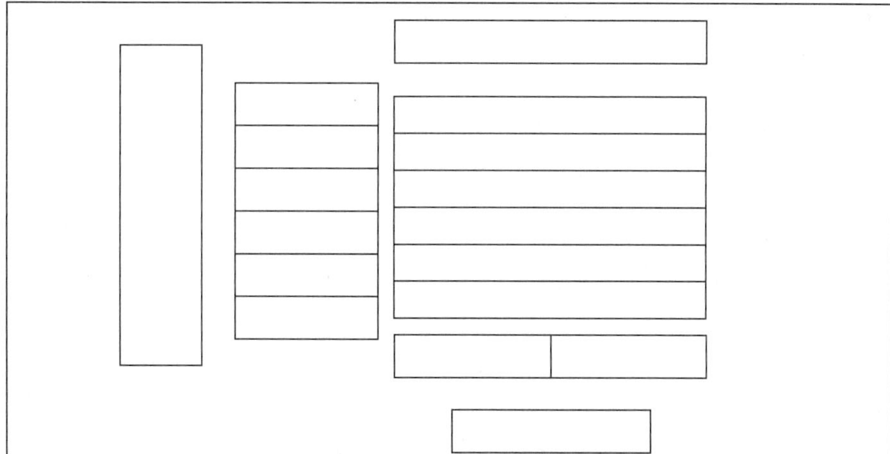

3. a. Find the mean hourly wage in Example 3 without the outlier.

b. Reasoning In Example 3, which would better describe the hourly wages, the median or the mode? Explain.

Lesson 8-1 *(pp. 373–377)*

Points, Lines, Segments, and Rays

Lesson Objectives	NAEP 2005 Strand: Geometry
▼ Points, lines, segments, and rays ▼ Parallel and skew lines	**Topic:** Relationships Among Geometric Figures **Local Standards:** _______________________________

Vocabulary

Points *A*, *B*, and *C*

A point is ________________________________

____

$\overleftrightarrow{DE}$ or $\overleftrightarrow{ED}$

A line is ________________________________

____

$\overline{DE}$ or $\overline{ED}$

A segment is ____________________________

____

____

$\overrightarrow{DE}$

A ray is _________________________________

____

____

A collection of points is collinear if ________________________

____

A plane is _______________________________________

____

Intersecting lines have ____________________________

Parallel lines ___________________________________

Skew lines are __________________________________

____

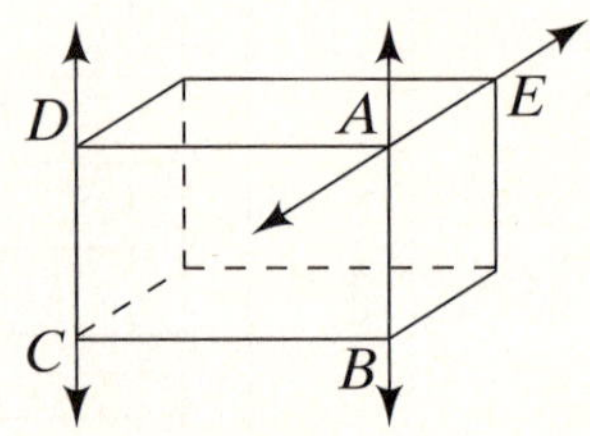

Plane *ABCD*

$\overleftrightarrow{AB}$ is [ ] to $\overleftrightarrow{DC}$.

$\overleftrightarrow{AE}$ [ ] $\overleftrightarrow{AB}$.

$\overleftrightarrow{AE}$ and $\overleftrightarrow{DC}$ are [ ].

Examples

❶ **Naming Lines, Segments, and Rays** Name each line, segment, or ray.

a.

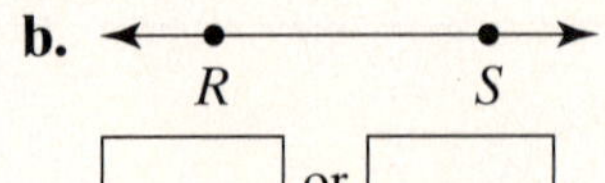

[ ] or [ ]

b.

[ ] or [ ]

c.

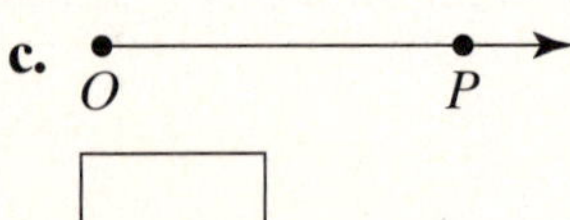

[ ]

❷ Collinear and Noncollinear Points

   a. Name three collinear points.

      Points ☐, ☐, and ☐ are collinear.

   b. Name three noncollinear points.

      Points A, B, and ☐ are noncollinear. Points A, C, and ☐ are

      noncollinear. Points B, C, and ☐ are noncollinear.

❸ Identifying Line Relationships Name each of the following.

   a. two parallel lines

      $\overleftrightarrow{XY}$ and ☐ are parallel. $\overleftrightarrow{XW}$ and ☐ are also parallel.

   b. two skew lines

      $\overleftrightarrow{WX}$ and ☐ are skew. $\overleftrightarrow{WX}$ and ☐ , $\overleftrightarrow{YZ}$ and ☐ , or

      $\overleftrightarrow{ZU}$ and ☐ are also pairs of skew lines.

Check Understanding

1. Use the figure at the right.

   a. Give two names for the line. ☐

   b. Name three segments. ☐

   c. **Reasoning** How is $\overrightarrow{VM}$ different from $\overrightarrow{MV}$?

      ☐

2. a. Points *L*, *Q*, and *T* are collinear. Name a different set of three collinear points.

      ☐

   b. Name three points that are noncollinear.

      ☐

3. a. $\overleftrightarrow{AB}$ and $\overleftrightarrow{TW}$ are parallel. Name two other streets on the map that are parallel.

      ☐

   b. **Reasoning** Can streets on this map represent skew lines? Explain.

      ☐

Name_______________________________ Class_______________________________ Date_______________

Lesson 8-2 *(pp. 379–383)*   **Angles**

Lesson Objective	**NAEP 2005 Strand:** Geometry
▼ Measuring and classifying angles	**Topic:** Dimension and Shape
	Local Standards: _________________________

Vocabulary

An angle has ____

____

The vertex of an angle is ____

____

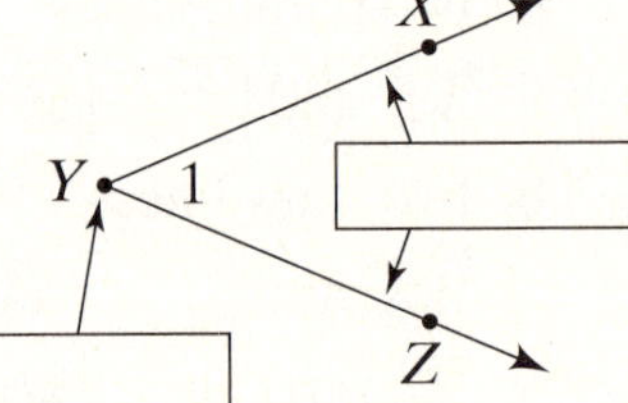

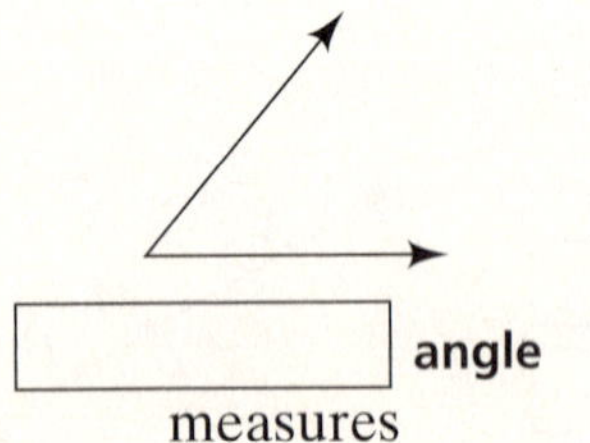

[____] **angle**
measures
[________]

[____] **angle**
measures
[__]

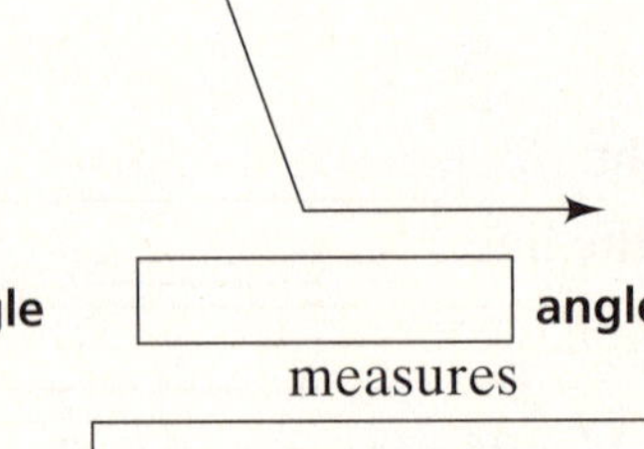

[____] **angle**
measures
[________]

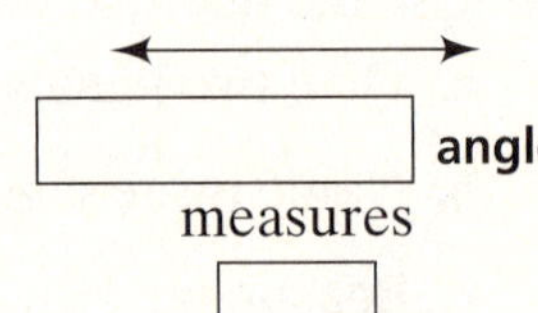

[____] **angle**
measures
[__]

Perpendicular lines are ____

____

Example

❶ Use a protractor to measure the angle.

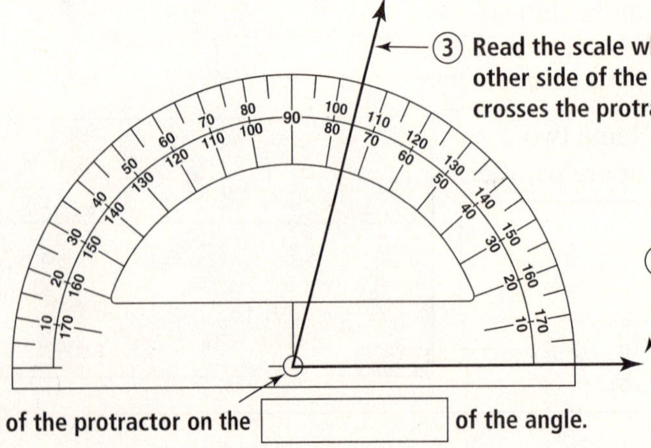

The angle measure is [________].

Example

❷ **Classifying Angles** Classify each angle as *acute*, *right*, *obtuse*, or *straight*.

a. 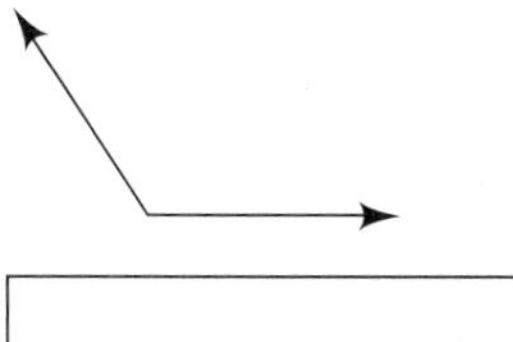

b. 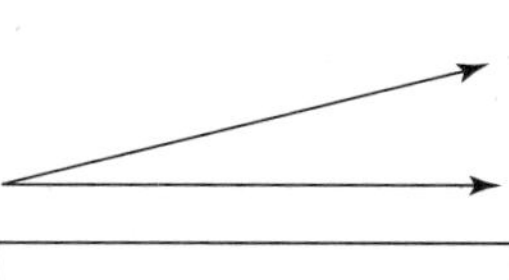

c. 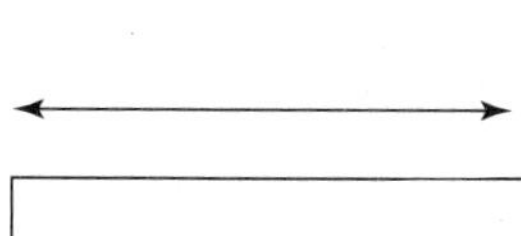

Check Understanding

1. a. Use a protractor to measure the angles.

i.

ii. 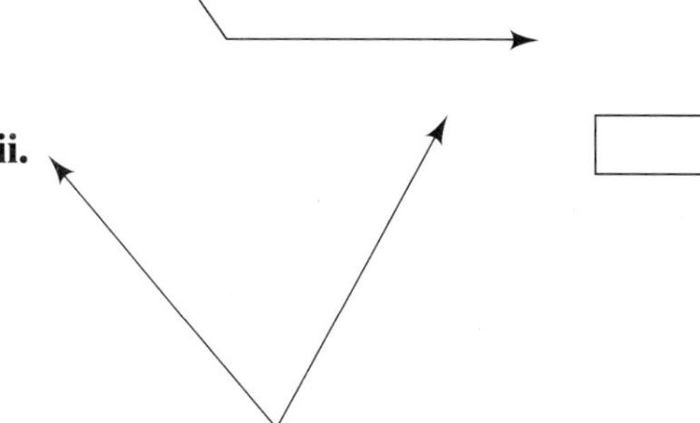

b. Reasoning Will an angle that measures 100° be greater than or less than the angle formed by a corner of a piece of paper?

2. a. Estimation Estimate the measure of the angle.

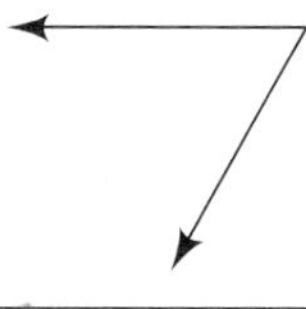

b. Classify the angle as *acute*, *right*, *obtuse*, or *straight*.

Lesson 8-3 *(pp. 386–390)*   Special Pairs of Angles

Lesson Objectives	**NAEP 2005 Strand:** Geometry
▼ Complement and supplement of an angle	**Topics:** Dimension and Shape; Relationships Among Geometric Figures
▼ Special pairs of angles	**Local Standards:** _________________________

Vocabulary

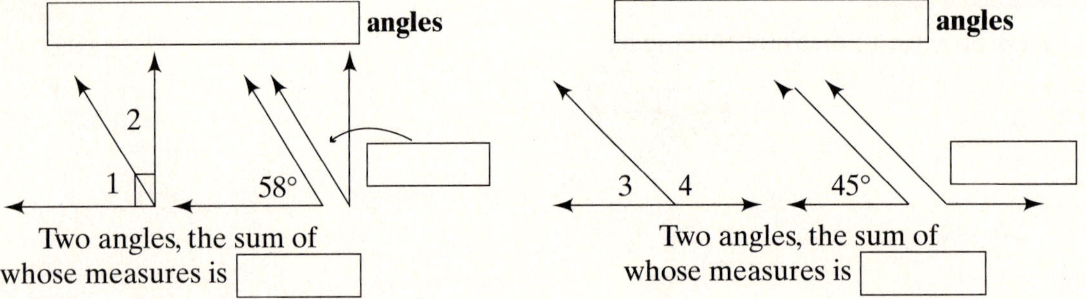

Vertical angles are ____

Congruent angles have ____

A transversal is a line that _______________________________________

Interior angles are ____

____

Exterior angles are ____

Example

❶ **Finding the Complement and Supplement of an Angle** Find the
complement and supplement of a 66° angle.

Let x = the measure of the angle's complement.

$$x + 66° = \boxed{}$$ ← **The angles are** $\boxed{}$.

$$x + 66° - \boxed{} = 90° - \boxed{}$$ ← **Subtract** $\boxed{}$ **from each side.**

$$x = \boxed{}$$ ← **Simplify.**

Let y = the measure of the angle's supplement.

$$y + 66° = \boxed{}$$ ← **The angles are** $\boxed{}$.

$$y + 66° - \boxed{} = 180° - \boxed{}$$ ← **Subtract** $\boxed{}$ **from each side.**

$$y = \boxed{}$$ ← **Simplify.**

The complement of a 66° angle measures 24°. Its supplement measures 114°.

Name_________________________________ Class_____________________________ Date ______________

Examples

❷ Using Diagrams Find the value of x.

a.

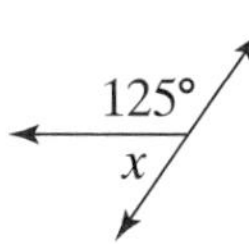

$$x + 125° = \boxed{} \qquad \leftarrow \text{The angles are } \boxed{}.$$

$$x + 125° - \boxed{} = 90° - \boxed{} \qquad \leftarrow \text{Subtract } \boxed{} \text{ from each side.}$$

$$x = \boxed{} \qquad \leftarrow \text{Simplify.}$$

b.

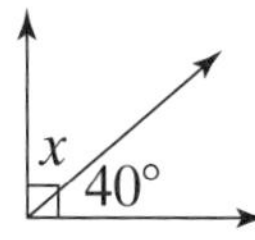

$$y + 40° = \boxed{} \qquad \leftarrow \text{The angles are } \boxed{}.$$

$$y + 40° - \boxed{} = 180° - \boxed{} \qquad \leftarrow \text{Subtract } \boxed{} \text{ from each side.}$$

$$y = \boxed{} \qquad \leftarrow \text{Simplify.}$$

❸ Identifying Special Pairs of Angles Use the diagram to identify each of the following.

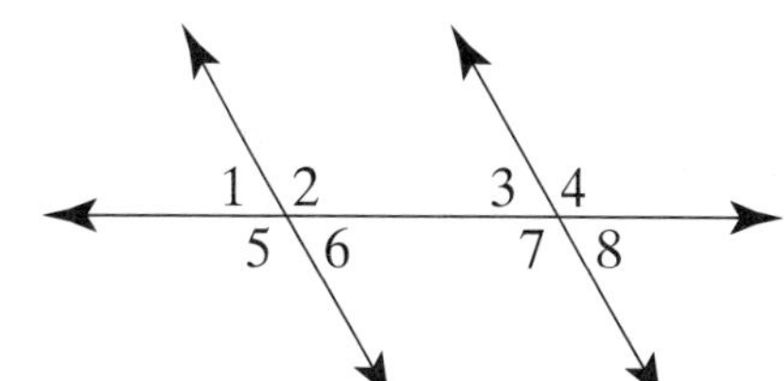

a. a pair of obtuse vertical angles

∠2 and $\boxed{}$, ∠4 and $\boxed{}$

b. two supplementary exterior angles

∠1 and $\boxed{}$, ∠4 and $\boxed{}$

Check Understanding

1. a. Find the value of x.

$\boxed{}$

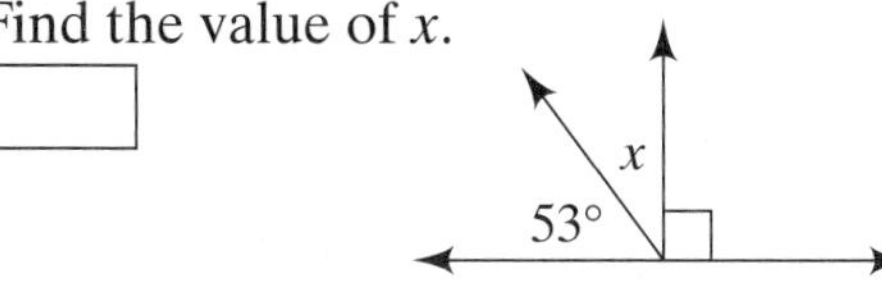

b. Find the value of x.

$\boxed{}$

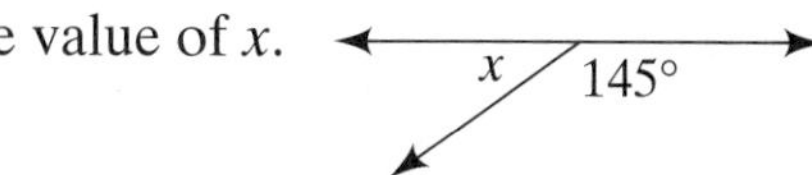

2. Use the diagram to identify each of the following.

a. a pair of obtuse vertical angles

$\boxed{}$

b. a pair of supplementary angles

$\boxed{}$

Lesson 8-4 *(pp. 392–396)*

Classifying Triangles

Lesson Objectives	NAEP 2005 Strand: Geometry
▼1 Classifying triangles by angles ▼2 Classifying triangles by sides	**Topics:** Dimension and Shape; Relationships Between Geometric Figures **Local Standards:** _______________________

Vocabulary

Classifying by Angles

acute triangle	**obtuse triangle**	**right triangle**
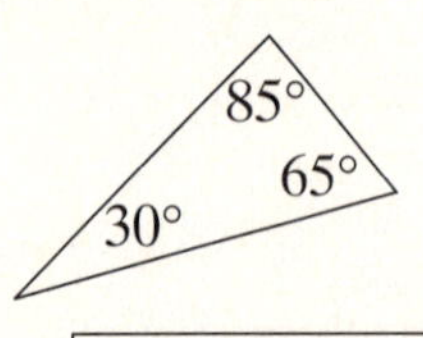	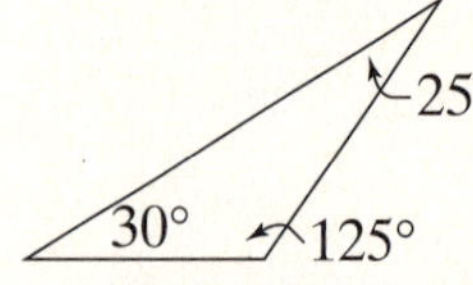	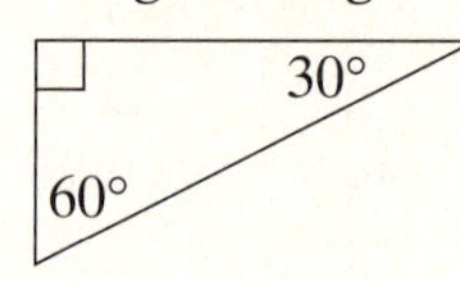
Three [____] angles	One [____] angle	One [____] angle

Classifying by Sides

equilateral triangle	**isosceles triangle**	**scalene triangle**
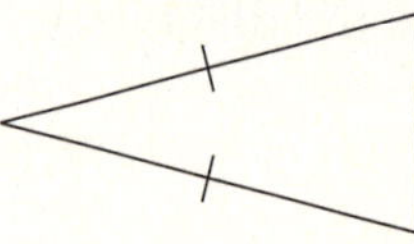	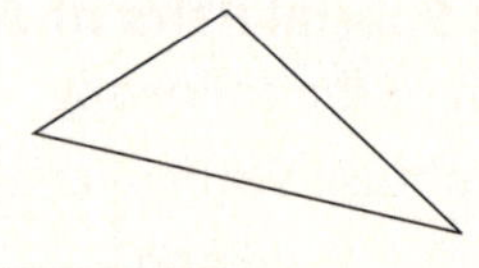	
[____] congruent sides	At least [____] congruent sides	[____] congruent sides

Congruent segments are _______________________

Example

1 **Classifying Triangles by Angles** Classify each triangle by its angles.

a.
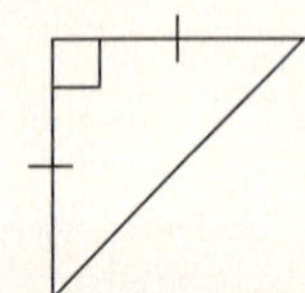
[____] triangle

b.
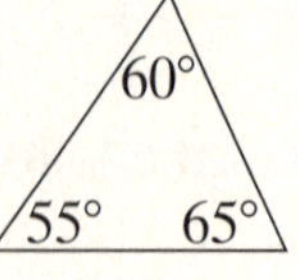
[____] triangle

Check Understanding

1. a. Classify the triangle at the right by its angles. [____]

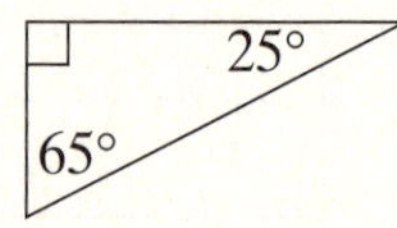

   b. A triangle has three equal angles. Classify the triangle by its angles.

[__________]

Name_________________________________ Class_________________________________ Date _____________

Examples

❷ Finding an Angle's Measure Two angles of a triangle measure 48° and 90°. What is the measure of the third angle?

$$x + 48° + 90° = \boxed{}$$

$$x + \boxed{} = 180° \qquad \leftarrow \textbf{ Add 48° and 90°.}$$

$$x + 138° - \boxed{} = 180° - \boxed{} \qquad \leftarrow \textbf{ Subtract } \boxed{} \textbf{ from each side.}$$

$$x = \boxed{} \qquad \leftarrow \textbf{ Simplify.}$$

The third angle measures $\boxed{}$.

❸ Classifying Triangles by Sides Classify each triangle by its sides.

a.

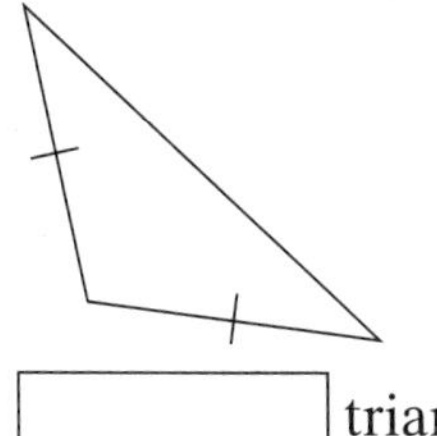

$\boxed{}$ triangle

b.

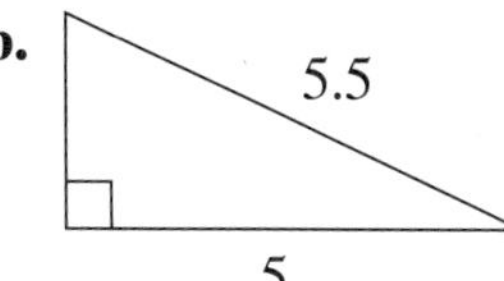

$\boxed{}$ triangle

❹ Name the triangle by its angles and its sides.

The triangle has three $\boxed{}$ angles.
It is $\boxed{}$.

The triangle has $\boxed{}$ congruent sides.
It is $\boxed{}$.

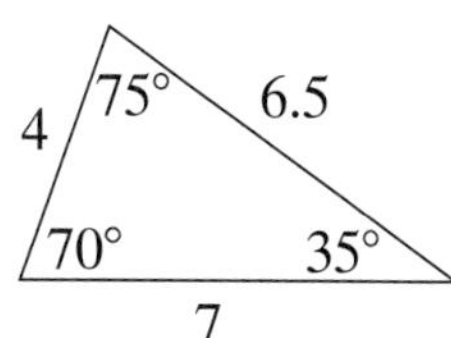

Check Understanding

2. Two angles of a triangle measure 58° and 72°. What is the measure of the third angle?

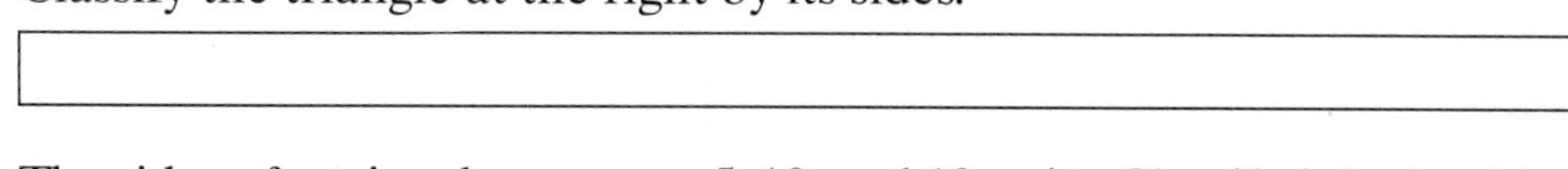

3. a. Classify the triangle at the right by its sides.

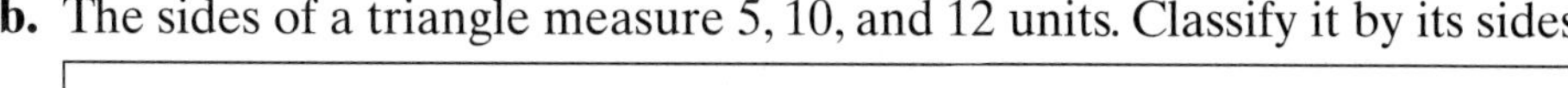

b. The sides of a triangle measure 5, 10, and 12 units. Classify it by its sides.

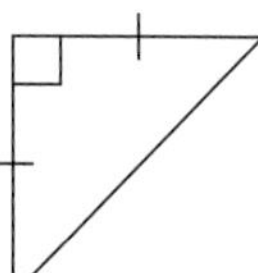

4. Name the triangle shown at the right by its angles and its sides.

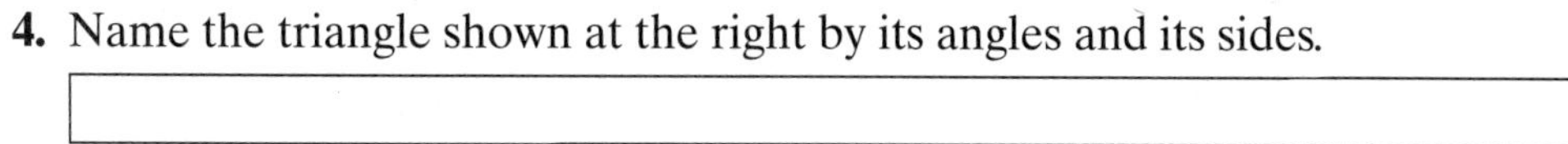

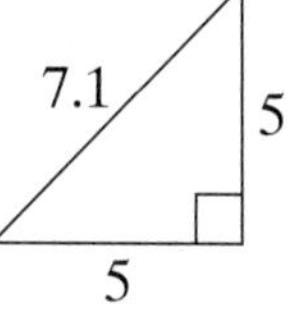

Lesson 8-5 *(pp. 397–400)*   **Exploring and Classifying Polygons**

Lesson Objectives	NAEP 2005 Strand: Geometry
▼ Identify polygons ▼ Classify quadrilaterals	**Topics:** Dimension and Shape; Relationships Among Geometric Figures **Local Standards:** ________________________

Vocabulary

A polygon is ___________________________________

____

____

A quadrilateral is ___________________________________

____

____

Polygon	Number of Sides
Triangle	
Quadrilateral	
Pentagon	
Hexagon	
Octagon	
Decagon	

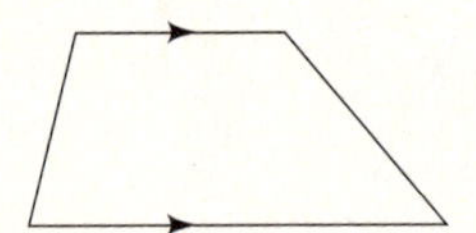

A trapezoid has ______________________

____

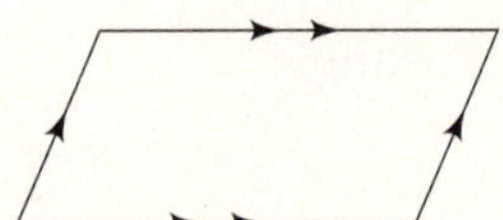

A parallelogram has ______________________

____

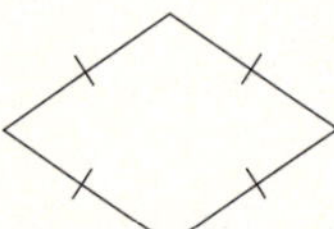

A rectangle has ________

____

____

A rhombus has ________

____

____

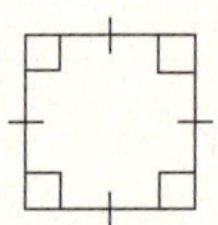

A square has ________

____

____

Examples

① Identifying Polygons Identify each polygon according to the number of sides.

a. 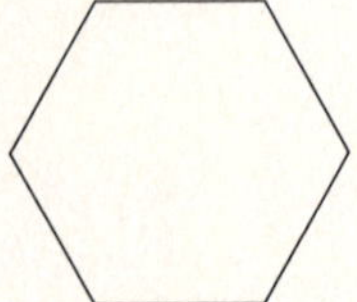

b. 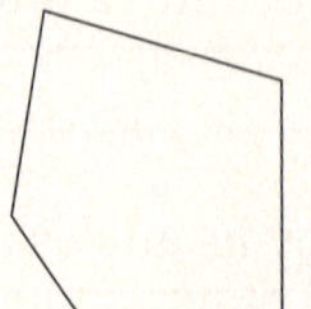

Name_________________________________ Class_________________________________ Date _______________

❷ Write all the possible names for the quadrilateral. Then give the best name.
Exactly one pair of opposite sides is [   ].

Its only possible name is [   ].

Check Understanding

1. Name each polygon according to the number of sides.

   a.   **b.**   **c.**

2. a. Write all possible names for the quadrilateral at the right.

   b. Which is the best name? Explain.

   c. Reasoning Draw a rhombus and a square. Is every square a rhombus? Explain.

                rhombus   square

Lesson 8-6 *(pp. 401–404)*

Use Logical Reasoning

Lesson Objective	Local Standards: _______________________
▼ Solve problems using logical reasoning	

Example

1 **Puzzles** A word square shows words that read the same across and down. Use these clues to make a 4-by-4 word square.

a. metric standard unit for mass

b. seldom occurring or found

c. square units inside a figure

d. average for a set of data

Read and Understand The goal is to complete a word square using the given clues.

Plan and Solve Fill in the words using the clues. The word "gram" goes in row [   ] and column [   ]. Complete the word square.

Look Back and Check Check that the words match the clues and that they all read the same across and down.

Check Understanding

1. Use these clues to complete a 4-by-4 word square.

a. This and _____?_____

b. Prefix meaning "six"

c. Plural of "axis"

d. Chore

Name_________________________________ Class_________________________________ Date _______________

Example

❷ Sports Jude, Cecily, and Gloria each play one of the three bases in softball. Jude does not play 1st base. Gloria lives next door to the 1st base player. Gloria does not play 2nd base. Which girl plays each base?

(Read and Understand) The problem gives clues about the playing positions of Jude, Cecily, and Gloria. The goal is to match each girl with her position.

(Plan and Solve) Use the table. Use the clues and record your conclusions.

Jude does not play 1st base. →

Gloria lives next door to the 1st base player. Cecily must → be the 1st base player.

	1st	2nd	3nd
Jude	No		
Cecily	Yes		
Gloria	No		

- Gloria does not play 2nd base. She must play ____________.

- Complete the table. Jude must play ____________.

	1st	2nd	3rd
Jude	No		
Cecily	Yes		
Gloria	No		

(Look Back and Check) Reread the problem. Make sure your solution matches all the facts given.

Check Understanding

2. Janna, Georgine, and Tanika were born in Jamaica, Peru, and France. Janna has never been to France. Tanika plays softball with the girl from Jamaica, but not with the one who came from France. Where was each girl born?

	Jamaica	Peru	France
Janna			
Georgine			
Tanika			

Lesson 8-7 *(pp. 405–409)*   **Congruent and Similar Figures**

Lesson Objective	**NAEP 2005 Strand:** Geometry
▼ Identify congruent figures	**Topic:** Transformation of Shapes and Preservation of Properties
	Local Standards: ____________________________

Vocabulary

Congruent figures have ____

____

Corresponding sides of congruent figures are [   ], and

corresponding angles of congruent figures are [   ].

Similar figures have ____

____

Corresponding angles of similar figures are [   ], and

corresponding sides of similar figures are [   ].

Example

❶ Identifying Congruent Figures Are the pentagons congruent?
The corresponding sides and angles are [   ], so the
pentagons are [   ].

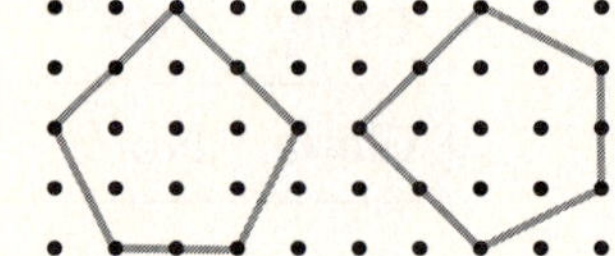

Check Understanding

2. Is each trapezoid congruent to the given trapezoid?

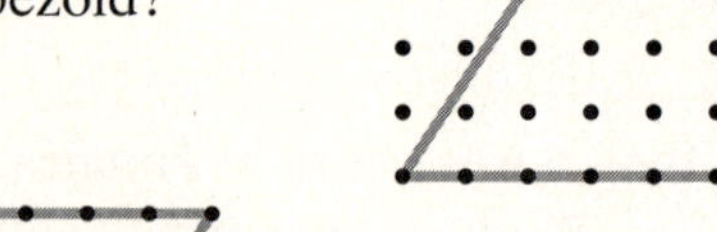

a. 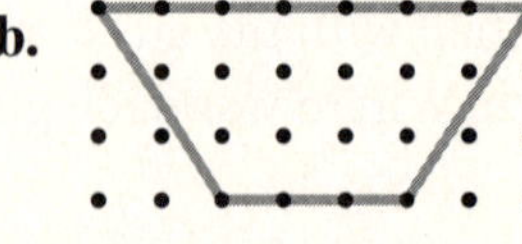

[   ]

b.

[   ]

                    Course 1 Daily Notetaking Guide

Name_______________________ Class_______________________ Date _______________

❷ **Identifying Similar Figures** Which triangle appears to be similar to $\triangle HJK$? Confirm your answer by finding whether the corresponding sides are proportional.

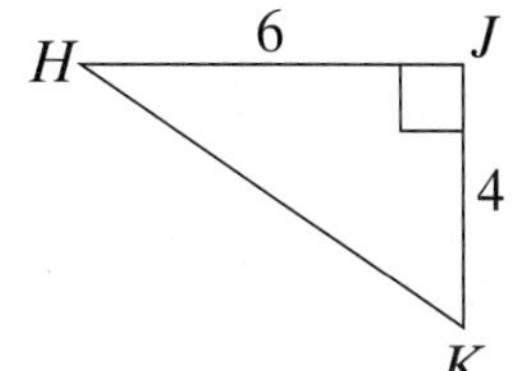

a.

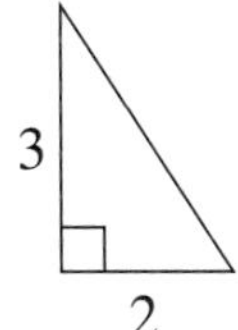

$$\frac{4}{\square} = \frac{6}{\square}$$

This triangle is [ ] to $\triangle HJK$.

b.

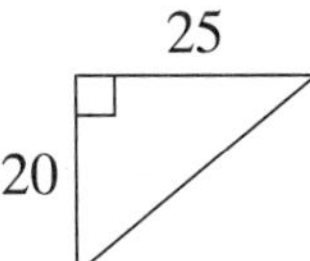

$$\frac{4}{\square} \neq \frac{6}{\square}$$

This triangle is [ ] to $\triangle HJK$.

❸ Are the figures *congruent* or *similar*? Explain.

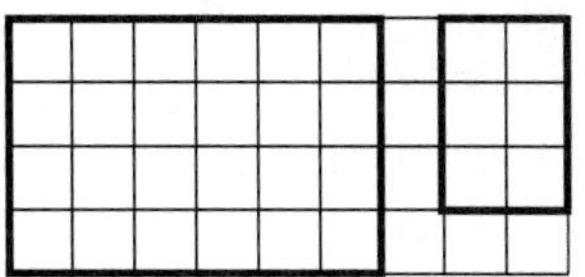

The two rectangles are not congruent, because their corresponding sides are [ ].

The two rectangles are similar, because their corresponding sides are [ ] and their corresponding angles are [ ].

Check Understanding

2. Is the given triangle similar to $\triangle KJH$ in Example 2?

a.

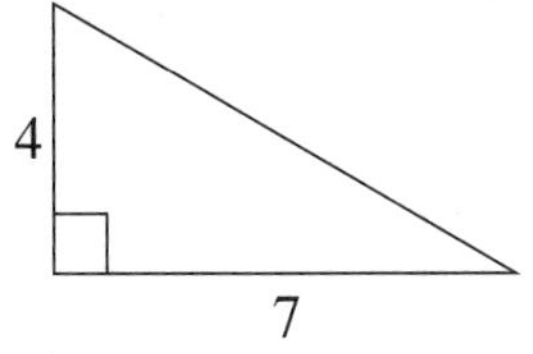

b.

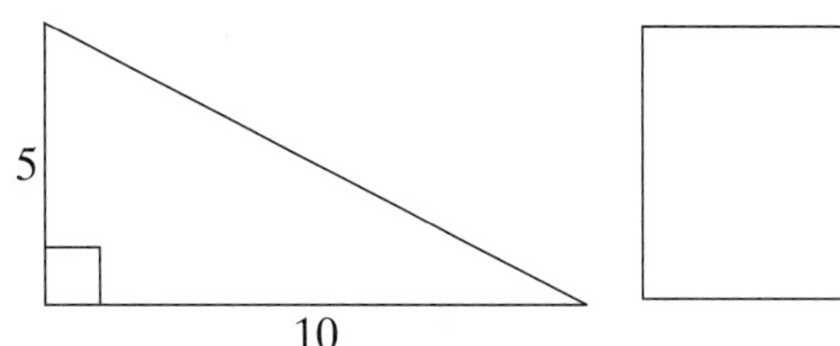

3. Are the figures congruent or similar? Explain.

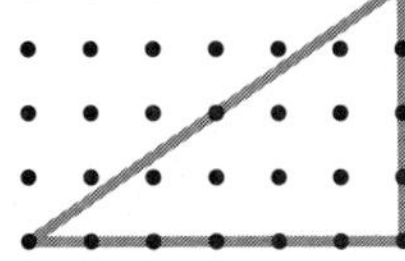 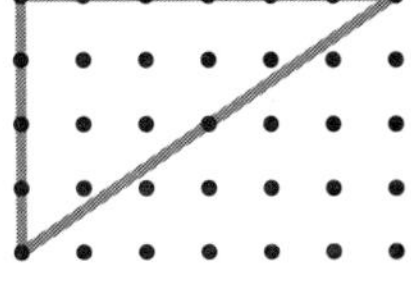

Lesson 8-8 *(pp. 410–414)*   **Line Symmetry**

Lesson Objective	**NAEP 2005 Strand:** Geometry
▼ Find the line of symmetry	**Topic:** Transformation of Shapes and Preservation of Properties
	Local Standards: ______________________

Vocabulary

A figure has line symmetry if ____

____

The line is called the [   ].

Example

① Testing for Line Symmetry Is the dashed line shown in each figure a line
of symmetry? Explain.

a. 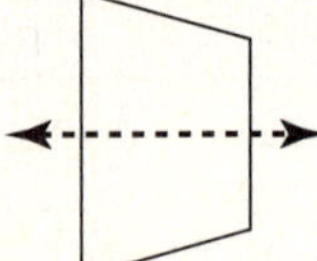   [   ] : if you fold the figure along the line, the two parts match.

b. 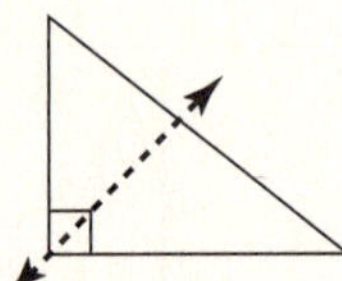   [   ] : if you fold the figure along the line, the two parts do not match.

Check Understanding

1. Is the dashed line in the figure a line of symmetry? Explain.

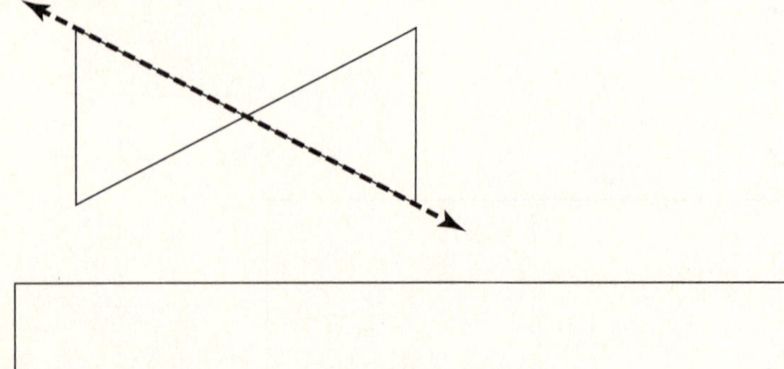

[   ]

                              Course 1 Daily Notetaking Guide

Example

❷ How many lines of symmetry does each figure have? Draw the lines of symmetry.

a. The rectangle has ⬚ lines of symmetry.

b. The hexagon has ⬚ lines of symmetry.

Check Understanding

2. How many lines of symmetry does each figure have? Draw the lines of symmetry.

a. 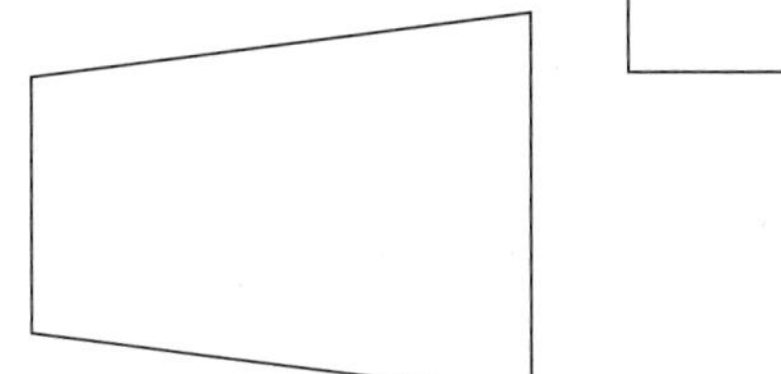

b. 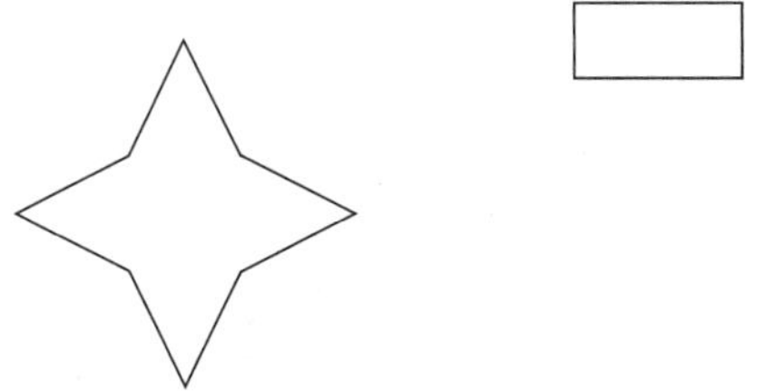

c. **Reasoning** How many lines of symmetry does a circle have? Explain your reasoning.

Lesson 8-9 *(pp. 415–419)*

Transformations

<table>
<tr><td>

Lesson Objectives

▼ Translations and reflections
▼ Rotations

</td><td>

NAEP 2005 Strand: Geometry

Topic: Transformation of Shapes and Preservation of Properties

Local Standards: _________________________

</td></tr>
</table>

Vocabulary

A transformation of a figure is ____

____

The new figure is the [   ] of the original.

A translation, or [   ], is ____

____

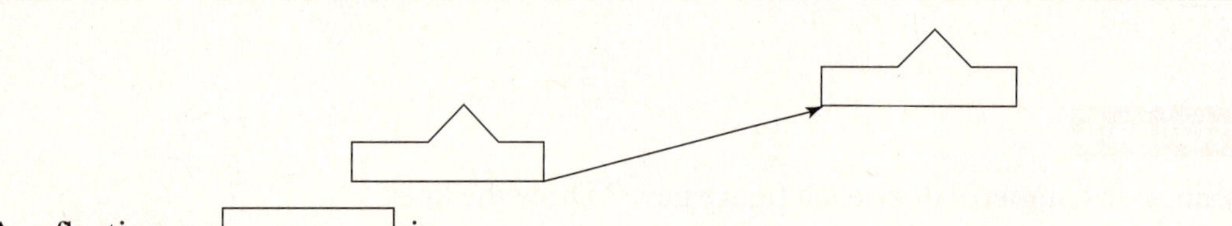

A reflection, or [   ], is ____

____

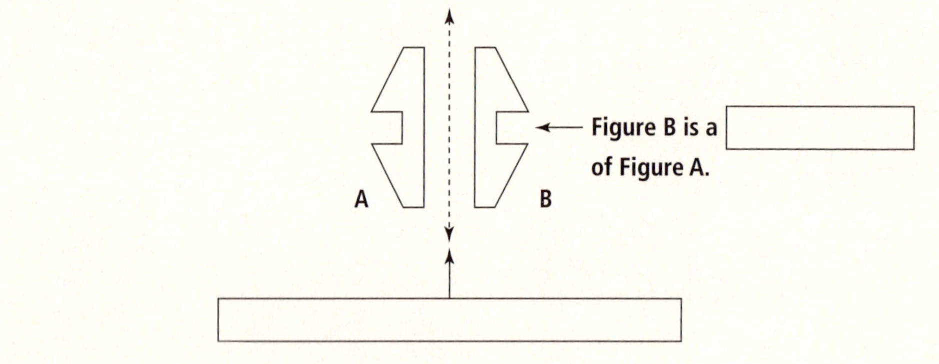

A rotation, or [   ], is ____

____

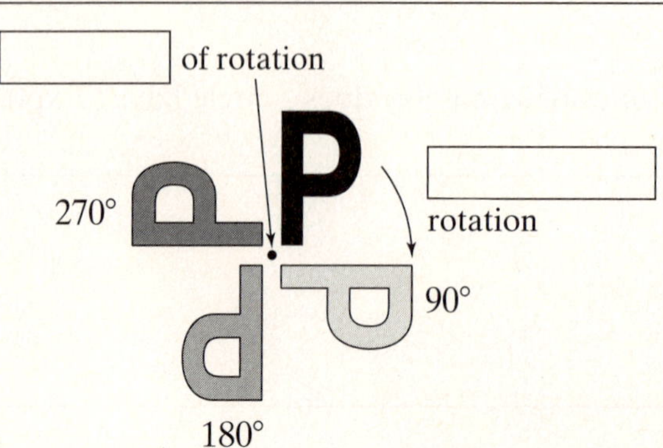

Course 1 Daily Notetaking Guide

Name________________________________ Class________________________________ Date ______________

Examples

❶ Identifying Translations Is the second figure
a translation of the first figure?

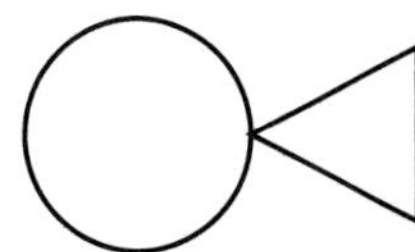 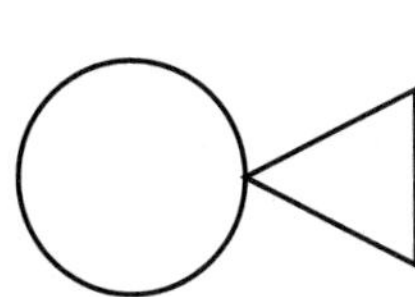

❷ Drawing Reflections Draw the reflection over the given line of reflection.

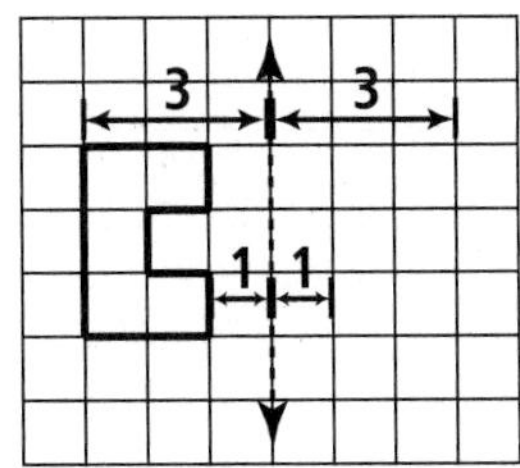

← **Use the grid to locate vertices the same
distance from the line of reflection.
Then connect the vertices.**

❸ Tell whether each figure is a rotation of the shape at right.
If so, give the angle of rotation.

a. 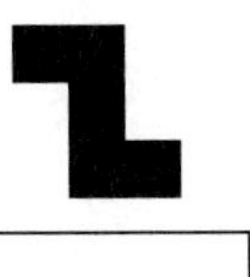

b. 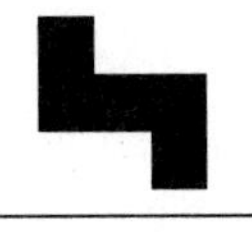

c. 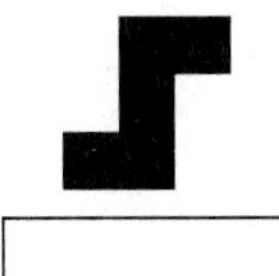

Check Understanding

1. Is the second figure a translation of the first figure?

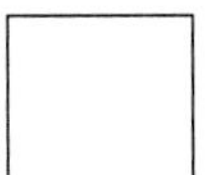 

2. Draw the reflection of each figure over the given line of reflection.

a. 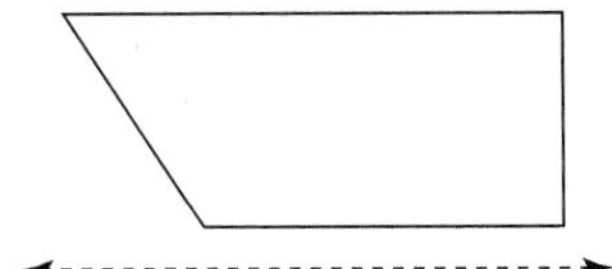

b. 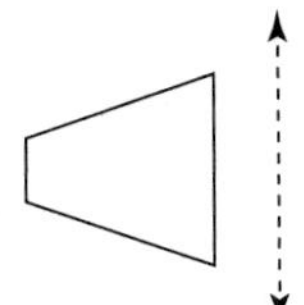

3. Tell whether each figure is a rotation of the shape at right.
If so, give the angle of rotation.

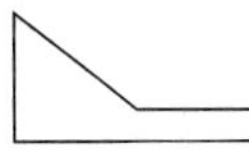

a. 

b. 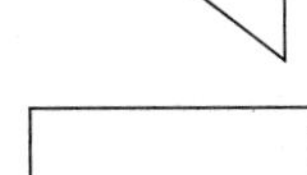

c. 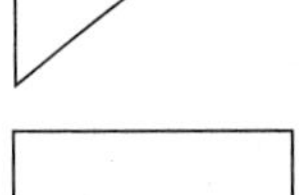

Lesson 9-1 *(pp. 431–435)*

Metric Units of Length, Mass, and Capacity

Lesson Objectives	**NAEP 2005 Strand:** Measurement
▼ Use metric units of length ▼ Choose units for mass and capacity	**Topic:** Systems of Measurement **Local Standards:** _________________________

Vocabulary

The metric system is ____

____

A meter (m) is ____

____

Mass is ____

____

A gram (g) is ____

____

Capacity is ____

____

A liter (L) is ____

____

Examples

❶ Choosing a Unit of Length Choose an appropriate metric unit of length for a classroom.

A classroom is much shorter than a [   ] but longer than a [   ]. The most appropriate unit of measure is [   ].

❷ Using a Metric Ruler Find the length of the segment at the right.

The length of the segment is [   ] millimeters, or [   ] centimeters.

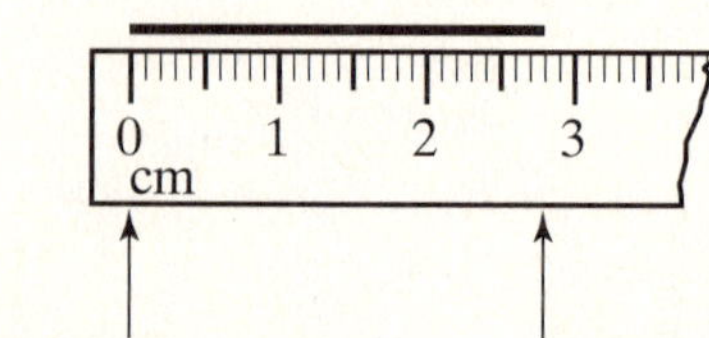

Align the zero mark on the ruler with one end of the segment.

Read the length at the other end of the segment.

Name_________________________________ Class_____________________________ Date _______________

❸ Choosing a Unit of Mass Choose an appropriate metric unit of mass.

a. a sewing needle

The mass of a sewing needle is much less than the mass of a paperclip. An appropriate unit of measure

is [ ].

b. a compact disc

The mass of a compact disc is much greater than the mass of an eyelash. An appropriate unit of measure

is [ ].

❹ Choosing a Unit of Capacity Choose an appropriate metric unit of capacity.

a. a kitchen sink

The capacity of a kitchen sink is much less than the capacity of 2 or 3 bathtubs. An appropriate unit of measure is

[ ].

b. a shampoo bottle

The capacity of a shampoo bottle is less than the capacity of a bottle of juice. An appropriate unit of measure is

[ ].

Check Understanding

1. Choose an appropriate metric unit of length for a city block. [ ]

2. Use a metric ruler to find each length in millimeters and in centimeters.

a.

[ ]

b.

[ ]

c.

[ ]

3. Choose an appropriate metric unit of mass.

a. a car

[ ]

b. a desk

[ ]

c. a robin's feather

[ ]

d. a pencil

[ ]

4. Choose an appropriate metric unit of capacity.

a. a car's fuel tank [ ]

b. a pond [ ]

c. a test tube [ ]

Lesson 9-2 *(pp. 436–439)*

Converting Units
in the Metric System

Lesson Objective	NAEP 2005 Strand: Measurement
▼ Convert units to the metric system	Topic: Systems of Measurement
	Local Standards: _______________________

Examples

❶ Converting to Smaller Units Convert 41 centimeters to millimeters.

The centimeter is a larger unit than the millimeter. To convert centimeters to millimeters, [____________] by [____________].

$41 \times 10 = 41.0$ ←

To multiply by [____________], **move the decimal point** [__] **place(s) to the right.**

$41 \text{ cm} = $ [____________] mm

❷ Converting to Larger Units Convert each measurement.

a. 4,201 meters to kilometers

The meter is a smaller unit than the kilometer. To convert meters to kilometers, [____________] by [____________].

$4{,}201 \div 1{,}000 = 4.201$ ←

To divide by [____________], **move the decimal point** [__] **place(s) to the left.**

$4{,}201 \text{ m} = $ [____________] km

b. 195 centimeters to meters

The centimeter is a smaller unit than the meter. To convert centimeters to meters, [____________] by [____________].

$195 \div 100 = 1.95$ ←

To divide by [____________], **move the decimal point** [__] **place(s) to the left.**

$195 \text{ cm} = $ [____________] m

Course 1 Daily Notetaking Guide

Name_______________________________ Class_______________________________ Date _______________

Example

❸ Converting Units of Mass or Capacity Complete each statement.

a. 125 g = ▨ kg

To convert grams to kilograms, divide by [ ].

$125 \div 1,000 = 0.125$ ←   To divide by [ ], move the decimal point [ ] place(s) to the left.

125 g = [ ] kg

b. 8.4 L = ▨ mL

To convert liters to milliliters, multiply by [ ].

$8.4 \times 1,000 = 8,400$ ←   To multiply by [ ], move the decimal point [ ] place(s) to the right.

8.4 L = [ ] mL

Check Understanding

1. Convert each measurement.

   a. 15 centimeters to millimeters

   b. 837 kilometers to meters

   c. Number Sense Which measurement is greater: 500 millimeters or 5 meters? Explain.

2. Convert each measurement.

   a. 0.5 centimeters to meters

   b. 75 millimeters to centimeters

   c. Sports A sprinter runs 60,000 meters each week to train for a 400-meter race. How many kilometers does the sprinter run each week?

3. Complete each statement.

   a. 15 mg = [ ] g

   b. 386 L = [ ] kL

   c. 8.2 cg = [ ] g

Course 1 Daily Notetaking Guide

Lesson 9-3 *(pp. 440–445)*

Perimeters and Areas of Rectangles

Lesson Objectives	NAEP 2005 Strand: Measurement
▼ Estimate areas of irregular shapes by using squares ▼ Find perimeters and areas of rectangles	Topic: Measuring Physical Attributes Local Standards: ____________________

Vocabulary and Key Concepts

Perimeter and Area of a Rectangle

$P = 2\left(\boxed{} + \boxed{}\right)$

$A = \boxed{} \times \boxed{}$

Perimeter and Area of a Square

$P = \boxed{}\,s$

$A = s^{\boxed{}}$

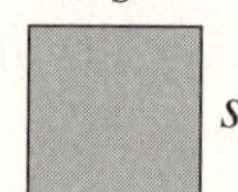

Area is ____

Perimeter is ____

Example

❶ **Estimating the Area of an Irregular Shape** Estimate the area of the pond at the right. Each square represents 8 square yards. Count the squares that are full, almost full, about half full, and almost empty.

$\boxed{}$ ← $\boxed{}$ squares are full.

$\boxed{}$ ← $\boxed{}$ squares are almost full, and $\boxed{}$ are almost empty.

$\boxed{} \times \frac{1}{2} = \boxed{}$ ← $\boxed{}$ squares are about half full.

$\boxed{}$ ← Total number of squares.

About $\boxed{}$ squares are covered. Each square represents $\boxed{}$ square yards.

The area of the pond is about $\boxed{} \times \boxed{}$, or about $\boxed{}$ square yards.

Check Understanding

1. Estimate the area of the lake. Each square represents 9 square miles.

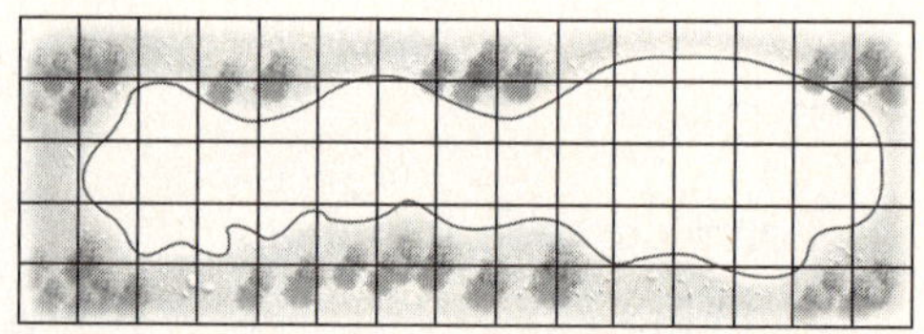

Examples

❷ Finding Perimeter and Area To renovate their bedroom, the Novaks are carpeting the floor and pasting a wallpaper border along the top of each wall. Find the perimeter and area of their bedroom.

14 ft | bedroom

12 ft

The length is ☐ ft. The width is ☐ ft. →

$P =$ ☐ ← **Use the formula for perimeter.**

  $= 2(12 + 14)$ ← **Substitute** ☐ **for ℓ and** ☐ **for w.**

  $= 2 \times$ ☐ ← **Add.**

  $=$ ☐ ← **Multiply.**

$A =$ ☐ ← **Use the formula for area.**

  $= 12 \times 14$ ← **Substitute** ☐ **for ℓ and** ☐ **for w.**

  $=$ ☐ ← **Multiply.**

The perimeter is ☐ feet. The area is ☐ square feet.

❸ Finding the Area of a Square The perimeter of a square is 28 meters. Find its area.

Use the perimeter formula.

$P = 4s$

☐ $= 4s$

$\dfrac{☐}{☐} = \dfrac{4s}{☐}$

☐ $= s$

Use the area formula.

$A = s^2$

  $= ☐^2$

  $= ☐$

The area of the square is ☐ square centimeters or ☐ .

Check Understanding

2. Find the perimeter and area of a rectangle with a length of 8 feet and a width of 5 feet.

3. Find the area of each square given the side s or the perimeter P.

  a. $s = 7$ inches

  b. $P = 24$ feet

Lesson 9-4 *(pp. 446–450)*   ## Areas of Parallelograms and Triangles

Lesson Objectives	**NAEP 2005 Strand:** Measurement
▼ Find the area of parallelograms and triangles	**Topic:** Measuring Physical Attributes
❷ Find the areas of complex figures	**Local Standards:** _______________________

Vocabulary and Key Concepts

Area of a Parallelogram

$A = \boxed{} \times \boxed{}$

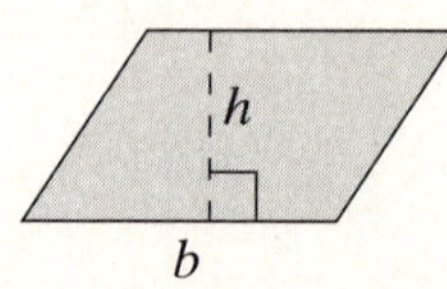
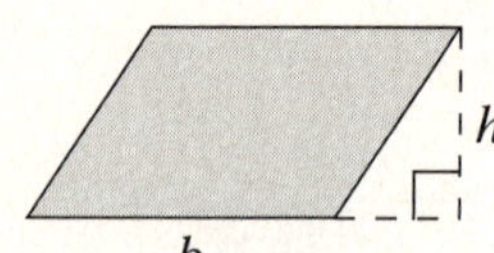

Area of a Triangle

$A = \frac{1}{2}\boxed{} \times \boxed{}$

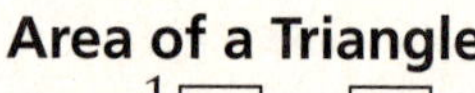
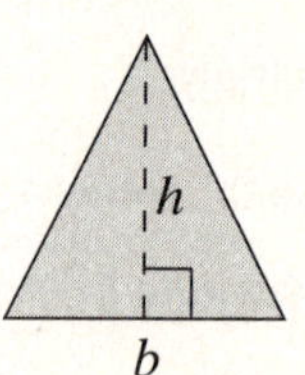
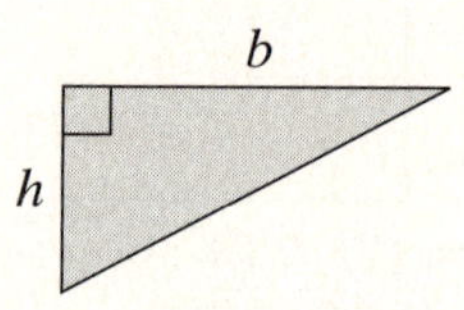

The $\boxed{}$ of a parallelogram can be any side of a parallelogram.

The height of a parallelogram is ___________________________________

Any side can be the $\boxed{}$ of a triangle.

The height of a triangle is ___________________________________

____

Example

❶ **Finding the Area of a Parallelogram** Find the area of the parallelogram.

$A = \boxed{} \times \boxed{}$ **Use the formula for the area of a parallelogram.**

$= \boxed{} \times \boxed{}$ **Substitute** $\boxed{}$ **for b and** $\boxed{}$ **for h.**

$= \boxed{}$ **Simplify.**

The area of the parallelogram is $\boxed{}$ square inches.

Check Understanding

1. Find the area of each parallelogram given the base b and height h.

  a. $b = 14$ m, $h = 5$ m   **b.** $b = 30$ ft, $h = 17.3$ ft

$\boxed{}$ $\boxed{}$

Examples

❷ Finding the Area of a Triangle A park is a triangular plot of land. The triangle has a base of 214 m and a height of 70 m. Find its area.

$A = \frac{1}{2} \,\boxed{} \times \boxed{}$ ← **Use the formula for the area of a triangle.**

$\quad = \frac{1}{2} \times \boxed{} \times \boxed{}$ ← **Substitute** $\boxed{}$ **for** *b* **and** $\boxed{}$ **for** *h*.

$\quad = \boxed{}$ ← **Simplify.**

The area of the triangle is $\boxed{}$ square meters.

❸ Finding the Area of a Complex Figure Find the area of the figure.

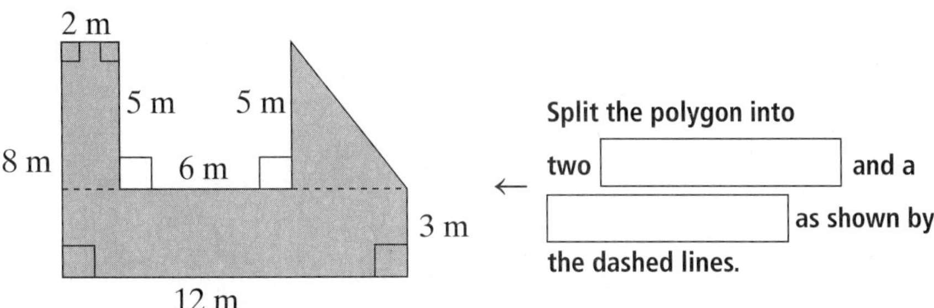

Split the polygon into

two $\boxed{}$ and a

$\boxed{}$ as shown by

the dashed lines.

Area of the smaller rectangle: $\boxed{} \times \boxed{} = \boxed{}$, or $\boxed{}$ m^2

Area of the larger rectangle: $\boxed{} \times \boxed{} = \boxed{}$, or $\boxed{}$ m^2 ← **Find the area of each polygon.**

Area of the triangle: $\frac{1}{2}\left(\boxed{} \times \boxed{}\right) = \frac{1}{2}\left(\boxed{}\right)$, or $\boxed{}$ m^2

The total area is $\boxed{} + \boxed{} + \boxed{}$, or $\boxed{}$ square meters.

Check Understanding

2. a. A triangle has a base of 30 meters and a height of 17.3 meters. Find its area.

b. Number Sense Suppose the base of the triangular plot of land in Example 2 were doubled. How would the area change?

3. Find the area of the complex figure below.

Name_______________________ Class_______________________ Date___________

Lesson 9-5 *(pp. 452–455)*   Circles and Circumference

Lesson Objectives	**NAEP 2005 Strand:** Measurement
▼ Identify parts of a circle ▼ Find circumference	**Topic:** Measuring Physical Attributes **Local Standards:** _______________

Vocabulary and Key Concepts

Circumference of a Circle

$C = \pi d$

$C = 2\pi r$

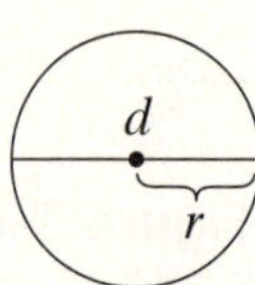

A circle is _______________________

____

____

A radius is _______________________

____

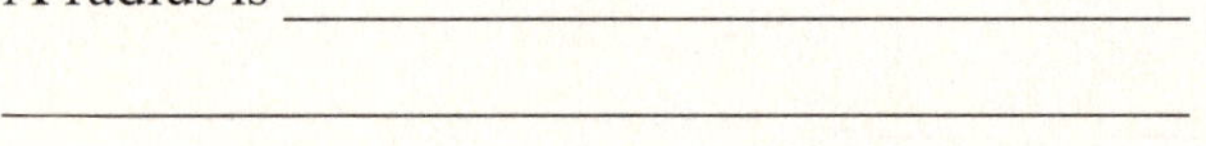

A chord is _______________________

____

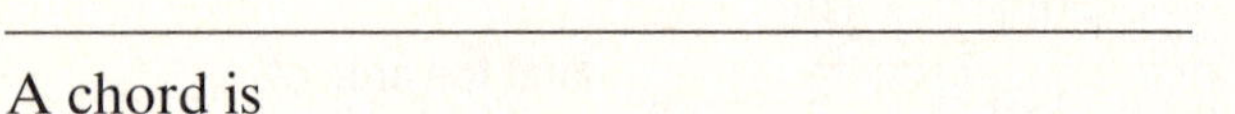

A diameter is _____________________

____

Circumference is __________________

____

Example

❶ Identifying Parts of a Circle

a. List the radii shown in circle R.

The radii are [＿＿＿] , [＿＿＿] , and [＿＿＿] .

b. List the chords shown in circle R.

The chords are [＿＿＿] , [＿＿＿] , and [＿＿＿] .

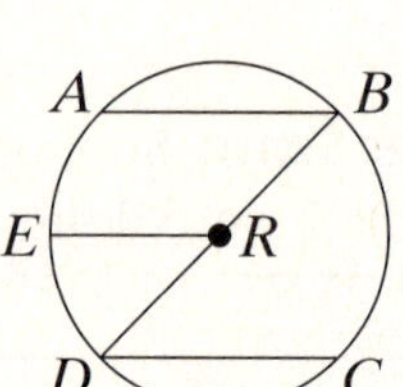

Check Understanding

1. List the diameter shown in circle R. [＿＿＿]

Examples

❷ Finding Radius and Diameter On July 22, 2002, the world's largest wooden nickel was unveiled in San Antonio, Texas. The radius of the wooden nickel is 80 inches. What is its diameter?

$d = $ [   ]   ← **The diameter is** [   ] **the radius.**

$= $ [   ] × [   ]   ← **Substitute.**

$= $ [   ]   ← **Simplify.**

The diameter is [   ] inches.

❸ Finding the Circumference of a Circle The surface of one type of trampoline is bounded by a circular frame with a 7-foot radius. Find the circumference of the frame to the nearest foot.

$C = \pi d$ ← **Use the formula for the circumference of a circle.**

$\approx$ [   ] × [   ]   ← **Substitute** [ ] × [ ] **for d and** [   ] **for π.**

$= $ [   ]   ← **Multiply.**

The circumference of the trampoline frame is about [   ] feet.

Check Understanding

2. Find the unknown length for a circle with the given dimension.

a. $d = 8$ cm, $r = ?$

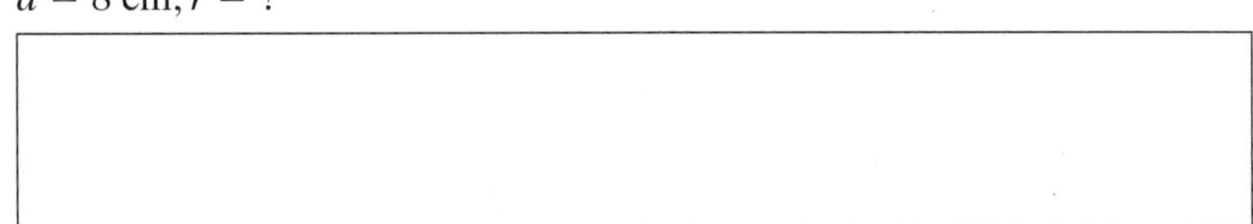

b. $r = 10$ in., $d = ?$

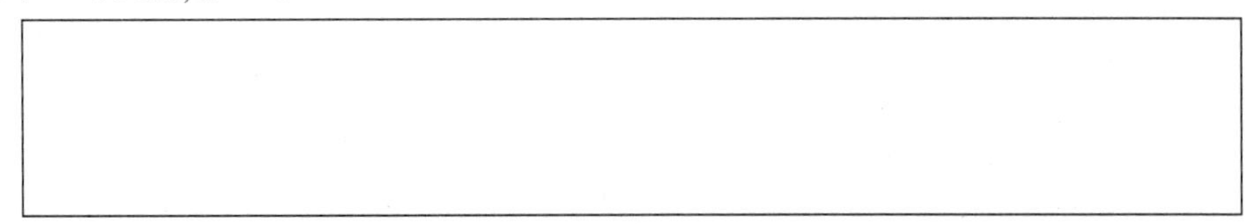

3. Find the circumference of a circle with a diameter of 5.8 centimeters. Round to the nearest centimeter.

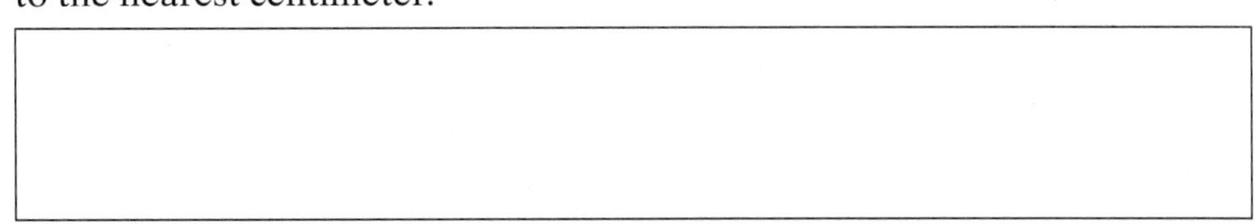

Lesson 9-6 *(pp. 456–459)*

Area of a Circle

Lesson Objective	**NAEP 2005 Strand:** Measurement
▼ Find the area of a circle	**Topic:** Measuring Physical Attributes
	Local Standards: ____________________

Key Concepts

Area of a Circle

$A = \pi r^2$

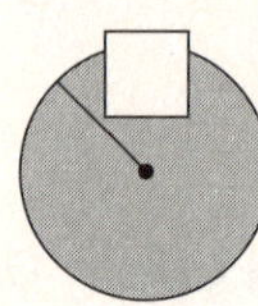

Example

❶ **Finding the Area of a Circle** Find the area of a circle with diameter 18 inches. Round to the nearest tenth.

The radius is [____] the diameter, or [____] inches.

Estimate Use 3 for π. So, $A \approx 3 \times$ [____], or [____] square inches.

$A = \pi r^2$ ← **Use the formula for the area of a circle.**

$\approx$ [____] $\times$ [__]^2 ← **Substitute** [__] **for r and** [____] **for π.**

$=$ [____]   ← **Multiply.**

The area is about [____] square inches.

Check Understanding

1. Find the area of each circle. Use 3.14 for π.

a.

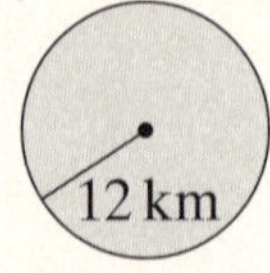

b.

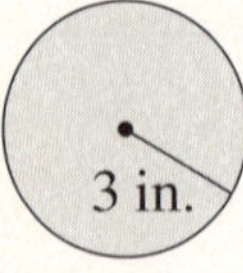

c.

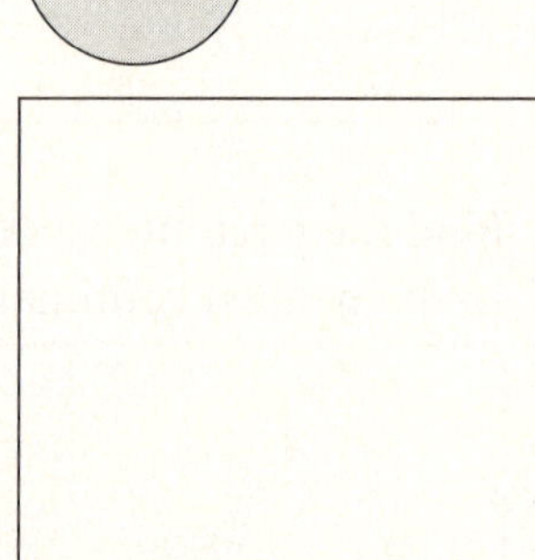

Name_________________________________ Class_________________________________ Date _______________

Example

❷ **Gardening** Find the area of a circular flower bed with radius 7 feet. Use $\frac{22}{7}$ for π.

$A = \pi r^2$ ← **Use the formula for the area of a circle.**

$\approx \dfrac{\boxed{}}{\boxed{}} \times \boxed{}^2$ ← **Use** $\dfrac{\boxed{}}{\boxed{}}$ **for** π **and** $\boxed{}$ **for** r.

$= \dfrac{22}{7}^{\boxed{}} \times 49^{}_{\boxed{}}$ ← **Divide 7 and 49 by their GCF,** $\boxed{}$.

$= \boxed{}$ ← **Multiply.**

The area of the flower bed is about $\boxed{}$ square feet.

Check Understanding

2. Find the area of each circle. Use $\frac{22}{7}$ for π.

a. 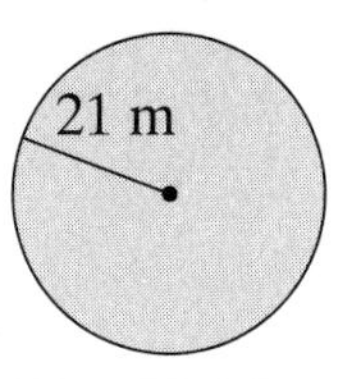

b. 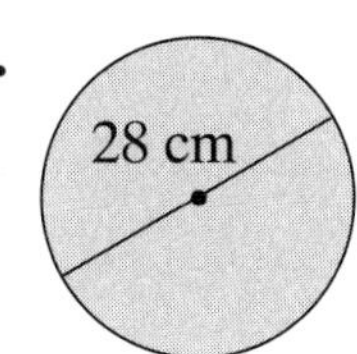

c. 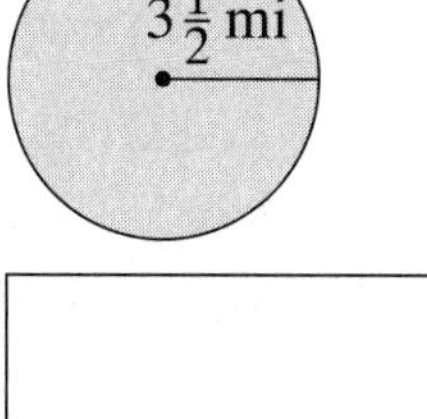

d. Find the area of a 14-inch large pizza.

Lesson 9-7 *(pp. 462–466)*

Three-Dimensional Figures
and Spatial Reasoning

Lesson Objective	**NAEP 2005 Strand:** Geometry
▼ Identify three-dimensional figures	**Topic:** Dimension and Shape
	Local Standards: _____________________

Vocabulary

A three-dimensional figure is ____

____

A prism is ____

____

A cube is ____

____

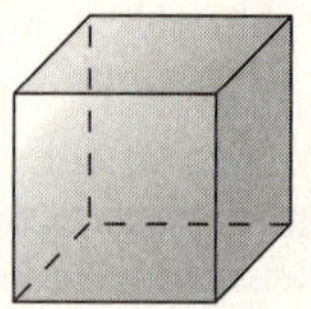

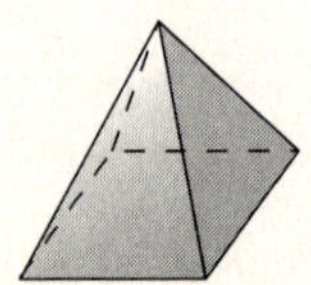

A pyramid is ____

____

A cylinder is ____

____

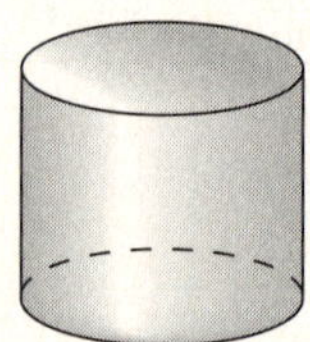

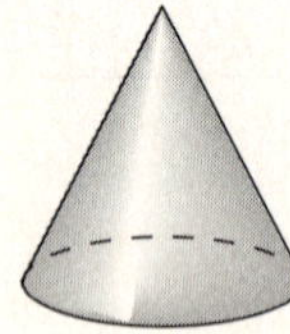

A cone is ____

____

A sphere is ____

____

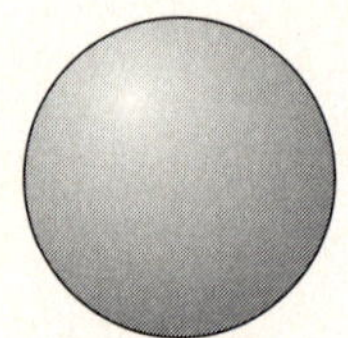

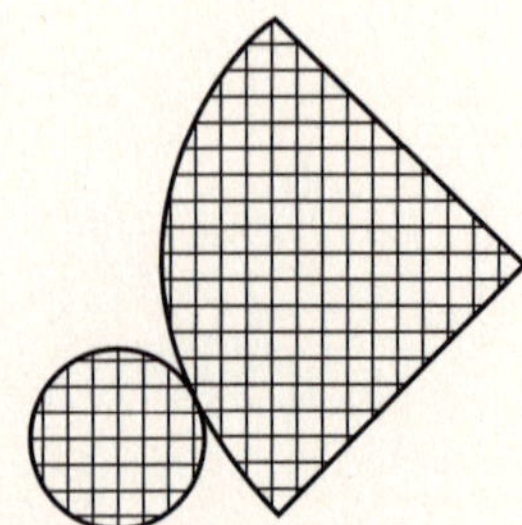

A net is ____

____

Name_____________________________ Class_____________________________ Date _____________

Examples

❶ Naming Prisms Name the prism.

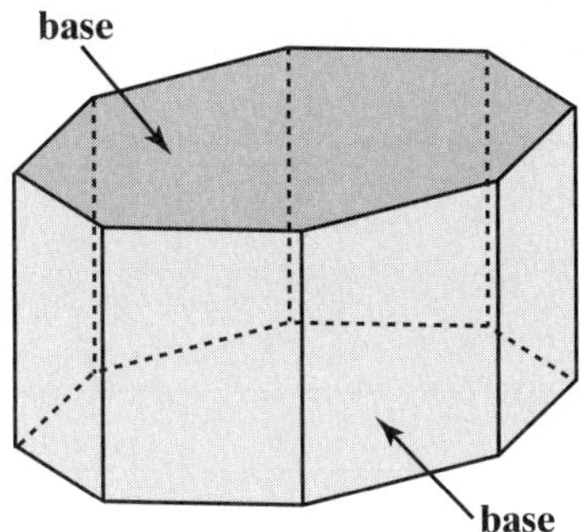

Each base is an [_____________]. The figure is an [_____________] prism.

❷ Identifying Three-Dimensional Figures Name the three-dimensional figure shown.

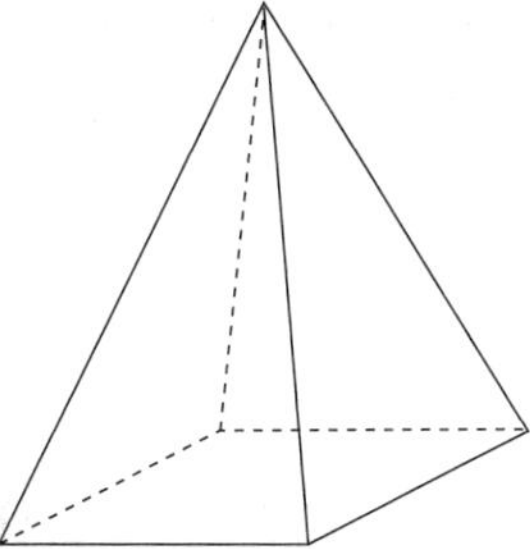

The figure is a [_____________] with a [_____________]

for a base. The figure is a [_____________].

Check Understanding

1. Name each prism.

a. 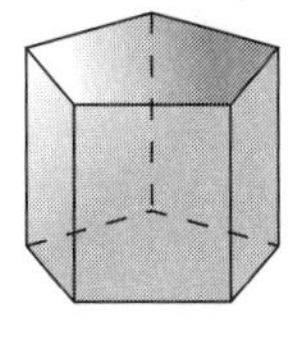   **b.** 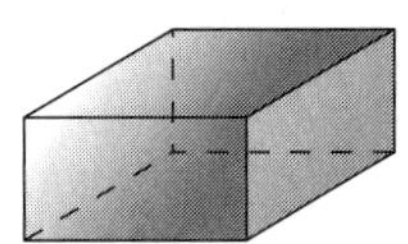   **c.** 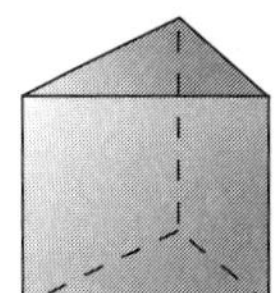

d. Reasoning In these prisms, what shape is any face that is not a base?

2. How are a cylinder and a cone alike? How are they different?

Lesson 9-8 *(pp. 467–471)*   **Surface Areas of Prisms and Cylinders**

Lesson Objectives	**NAEP 2005 Strand:** Measurement
▼ Find the surface area of a prism	**Topic:** Measuring Physical Attributes
▼ Find the surface area of a cylinder	**Local Standards:** ______________________

Vocabulary

Surface area is ____

____

Example

1 **Finding the Surface Area of a Prism** Find the surface area of the pizza box.

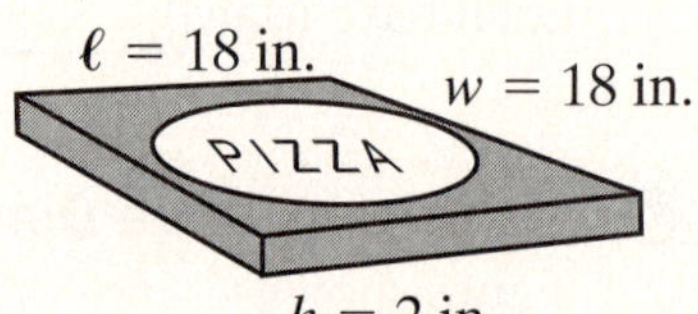

Step 1 Draw and label a net for the prism.

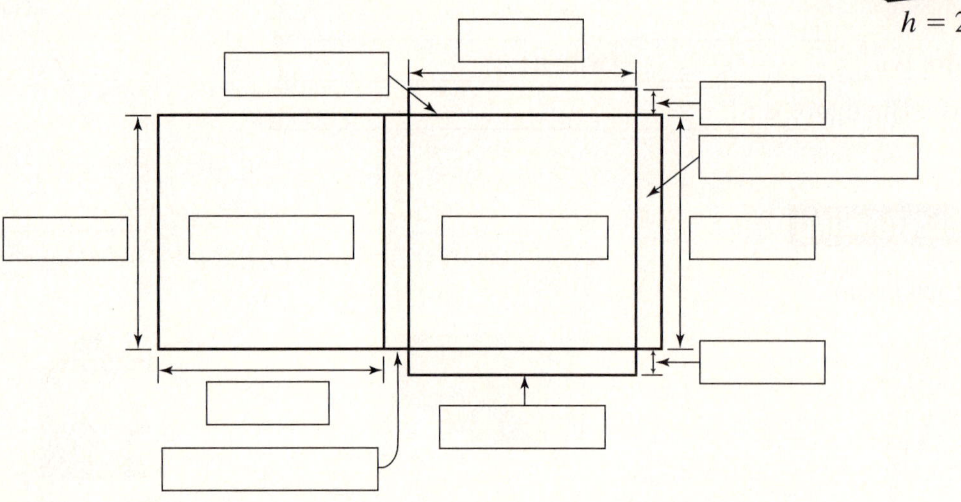

Step 2 Find and add the areas of all the rectangles.

Back	Top	Left	Bottom	Right	Front

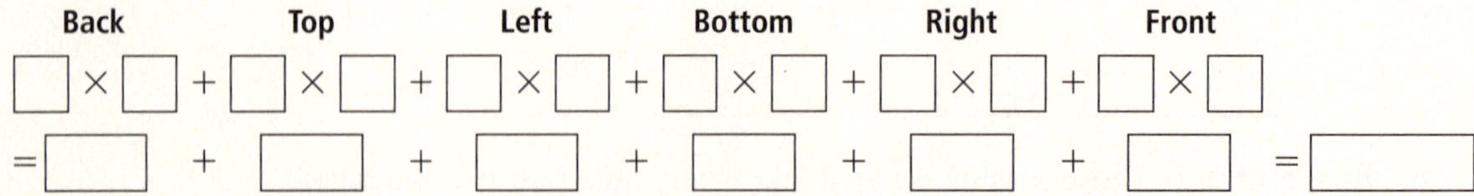

The surface area of the pizza box is [   ] square inches.

Check Understanding

1. Find the surface area of each prism.

a. 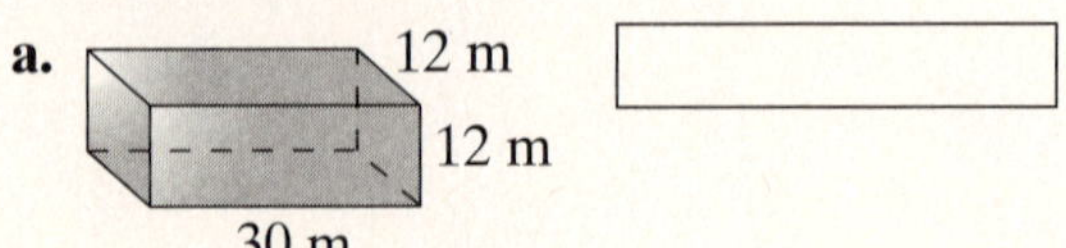

[   ]

b. 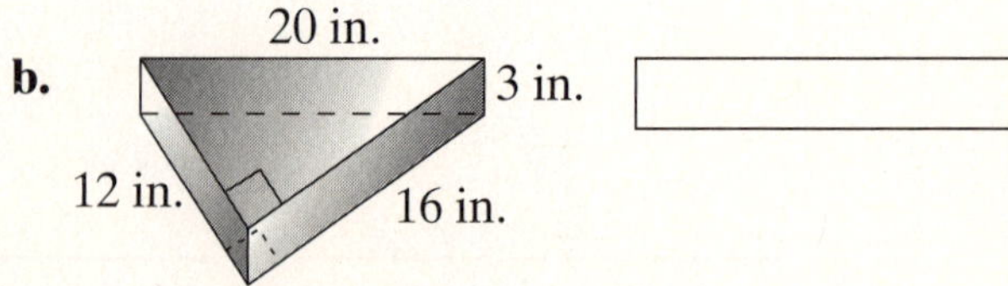

[   ]

❷ Finding the Surface Area of a Cylinder Find the surface area of the cylinder. Round to the nearest tenth.

Step 1 Draw and label a net for the cylinder.

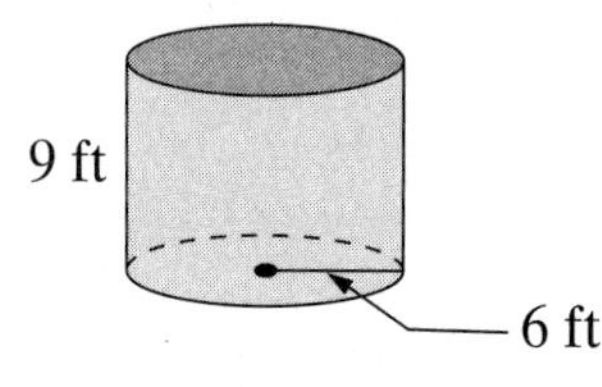

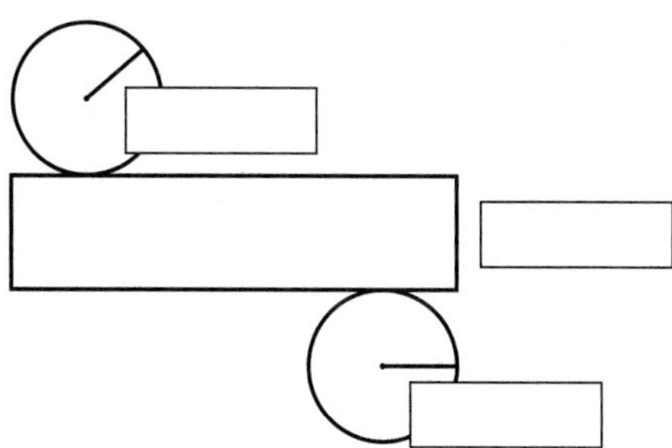

Step 2 Find the area of one circle.

$A = \pi r^2$ ← Use the formula for the area of a circle.

$\approx$ ☐ $\times$ ☐^{2} ← Substitute ☐ for *r* and ☐ for π.

$=$ ☐   ← Multiply.

$=$ ☐   ← Round to the nearest tenth.

Step 3 Find the area of the rectangle.

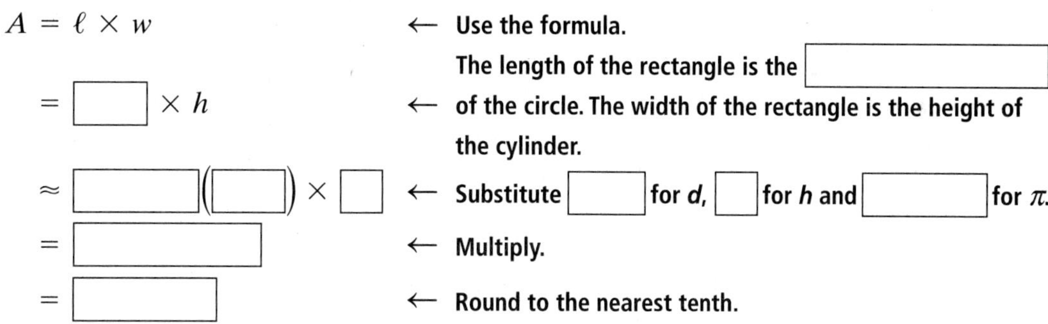

$A = \ell \times w$ ← Use the formula.

The length of the rectangle is the ☐

$=$ ☐ $\times h$ ← of the circle. The width of the rectangle is the height of the cylinder.

$\approx$ ☐ (☐) $\times$ ☐   ← Substitute ☐ for *d,* ☐ for *h* and ☐ for π.

$=$ ☐   ← Multiply.

$=$ ☐   ← Round to the nearest tenth.

Step 4 Add the areas of the rectangle and the two circles.

☐ $+$ ☐ $+$ ☐ $=$ ☐

The surface area of the cylinder is about ☐ square feet.

Check Understanding

2. Reasoning Explain how you can use the formula S.A. $= 2\pi r^2 + C \times h$ to find the surface area of a cylinder.

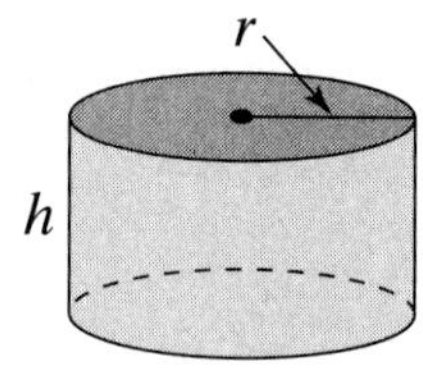

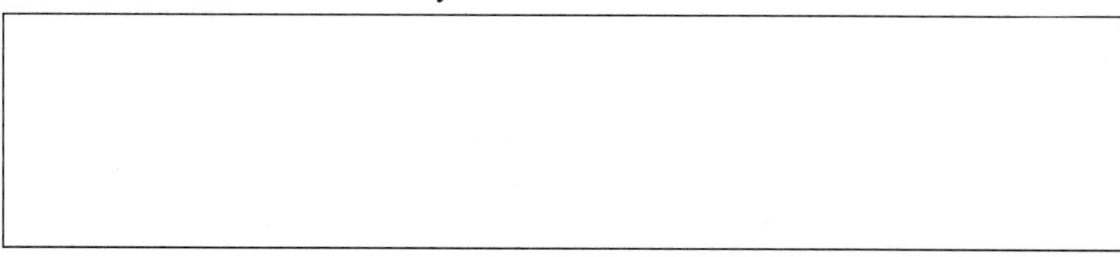

Lesson 9-9 *(pp. 472–476)*　　　　Volumes of Rectangular Prisms and Cylinders

Lesson Objectives	**NAEP 2005 Strand:** Measurement
▼ Find the volume of a rectangular prism	**Topic:** Measuring Physical Attributes
▼ Find the volume of a cylinder	**Local Standards:** ____________________

Vocabulary and Key Concepts

Volume of a Prism

Volume = Area of Base × Height

$V = \boxed{} \times \boxed{}$

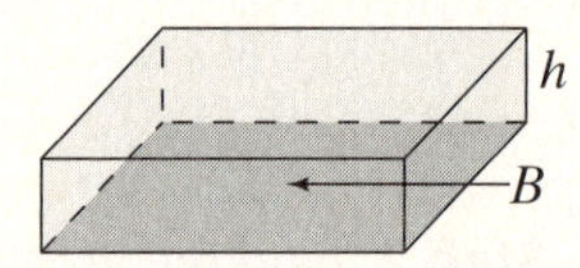

Volume is ____

____

A cubic unit is ____

____

Example

❶ **Counting Cubes to Find Volume** Find the volume of the rectangular prism shown.

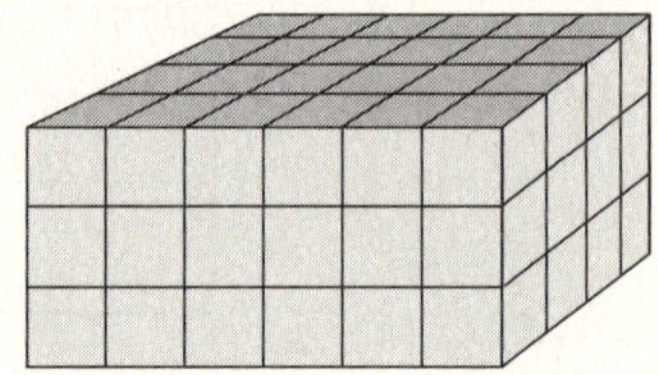

Each layer of the prism is $\boxed{}$ cubes by $\boxed{}$ cubes. This equals $\boxed{} \times \boxed{}$, or $\boxed{}$ cubes. The prism is $\boxed{}$ layers tall. The prism has a total of $\boxed{} \times \boxed{}$, or $\boxed{}$ cubes.

The volume of the prism is $\boxed{}$ cubic units.

Check Understanding

1. Use the rectangular prism at the right.

   a. What is the volume of one horizontal layer?

   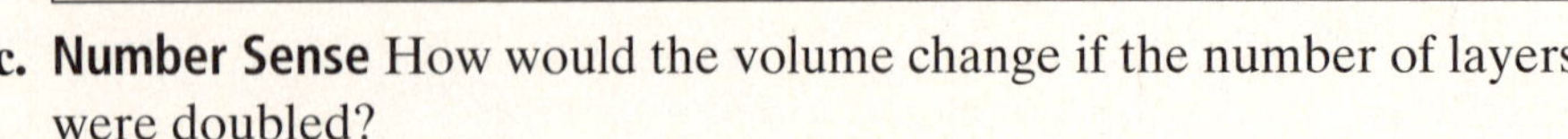

   b. What is the volume of the entire prism?

   c. **Number Sense** How would the volume change if the number of layers were doubled?

Name________________________________ Class________________________________ Date ______________

Examples

❷ Finding the Volume of a Prism Find the volume of the storage container shown.

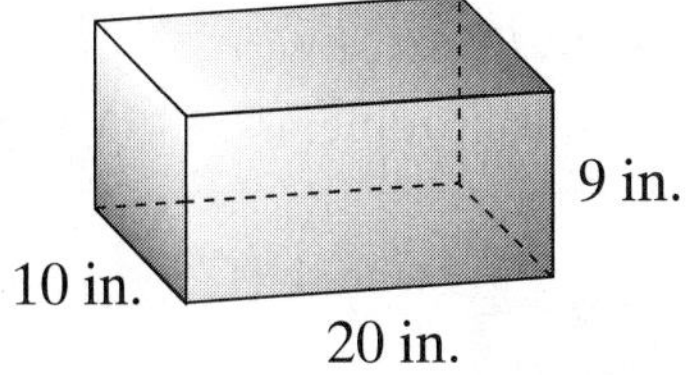

$A = \ell \times w \times h$ ← Use the formula for the volume of a rectangular prism.

= ☐ × ☐ × ☐ ← Substitute ☐ for ℓ, ☐ for w, and ☐ for h.

= ☐ ← Multiply.

The volume is about ☐ cubic inches, or ☐ in.^{3}

❸ Finding the Volume of a Cylinder Find the volume of the can of tuna. Round to the nearest tenth.

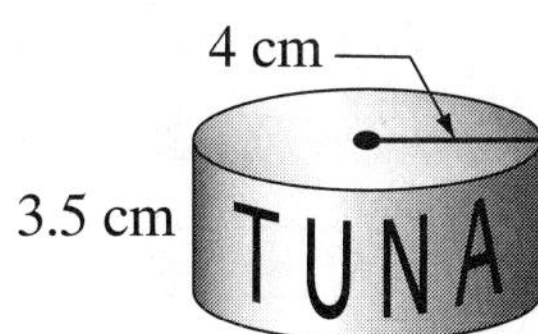

Step 1 Find the area of the base.

Area of Base $= \pi \times r^2$

≈ ☐ × ☐^{2} ← Substitute ☐ for r and ☐ for π.

= ☐ ← Multiply.

Step 2 Find the volume.

Volume $= B \times h$

≈ ☐ × ☐ ← Substitute ☐ for B and ☐ for h.

≈ ☐ ← Multiply.

The volume is about ☐ cubic centimeters, or ☐ cm^3.

Check Understanding

2. Find the volume of a rectangular prism with a length of 8 meters, a width of 7 meters, and a height of 10 meters.

3. Find the volume of a cylinder with a radius of 4 inches and a height of 9 inches. Round to the nearest cubic inch.

Lesson 9-10 *(pp. 477–480)*

Work Backward

Lesson Objective	Local Standards: _______________________
▼ Solve problems by working backward	

Example

❶ **Baking** Ali baked some cookies. She gave a dozen to her friend. She gave half the remaining cookies to her mother, and she kept the rest. The next day, she ate four of the cookies that she kept. A dozen cookies were left. How many cookies did Ali bake?

Read and Understand

You know how many cookies Ali had at the end. You know how many she gave away or ate. You want to know ⬚.

Plan and Solve

To find the number Ali baked, begin with the number she had at the end. Then work backward.

To undo the amounts she gave away or ate, add.

$$12 \leftarrow \text{Ali had 12 cookies left at the end.}$$

$12 + \boxed{} = \boxed{} \leftarrow$ She ate $\boxed{}$. Add.

$\boxed{} + \boxed{} = \boxed{} \leftarrow$ She gave $\boxed{}$ to her mother. Add.

$\boxed{} + \boxed{} = \boxed{} \leftarrow$ She gave a $\boxed{}$ to her friend. Add.

Ali started with $\boxed{}$ cookies.

Look Back and Check

Read the problem again. Start with $\boxed{}$ cookies. Subtract the amounts as she eats or gives away cookies.

$\boxed{} - \boxed{} = \boxed{}$

$\boxed{} \div \boxed{} = \boxed{}$

$\boxed{} - \boxed{} = \boxed{}$

The answer checks. ✔

Name_______________________________ Class_______________________________ Date _______________

Check Understanding

1. A teacher lends 7 pencils to her students in the morning, collects 5 before lunch, and gives out 3 after lunch. At the end of the day, she has 16 pencils. How many pencils did the teacher have at the start of the day?

Name_____________________________ Class_____________________________ Date_____________

Lesson 10-1 *(pp. 491–495)*   **Using a Number Line**

Lesson Objectives	**NAEP 2005 Strand:** Number Properties and Operations
▼ Graph integers on a number line	**Topic:** Number Sense
▼ Compare and order integers	**Local Standards:** ____________________

Vocabulary

Two numbers are opposite if ____

____

Integers are ____

____

The absolute value of a number is __________________________________

____

Examples

❶ **Representing Situations With Integers** You are six spaces behind your opponent in a board game. What integer represents your situation?

[　　] ← **A integer less than 0 is represented as** [　　].

❷ **Identifying Opposites** Name the opposite of 5.

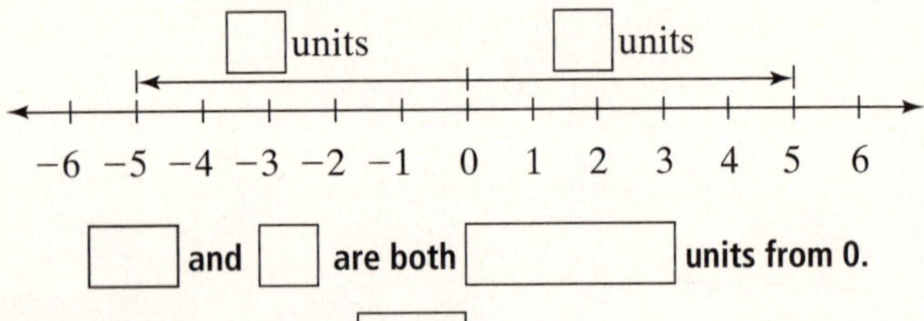

[　] units   [　] units

$$-6 \quad -5 \quad -4 \quad -3 \quad -2 \quad -1 \quad 0 \quad 1 \quad 2 \quad 3 \quad 4 \quad 5 \quad 6$$

[　] and [　] are both [　　] units from 0.

The opposite of 5 is [　].

Check Understanding

1. The altitude of New Orleans, Louisiana, is 8 feet below sea level. Use an integer to represent this altitude.

2. Name the opposite of −3.

    Course 1 Daily Notetaking Guide

Examples

❸ Finding Absolute Values Find the value of $|-19|$.

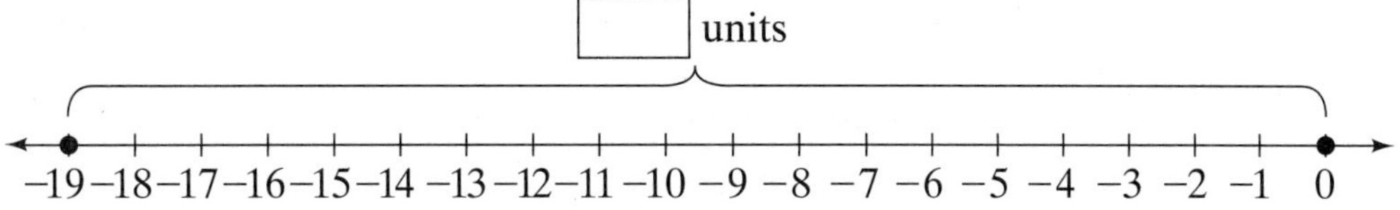

Since -19 is ⬚ units from 0, $|-19| = 19$.

❹ Comparing Integers Compare -12 and -10.

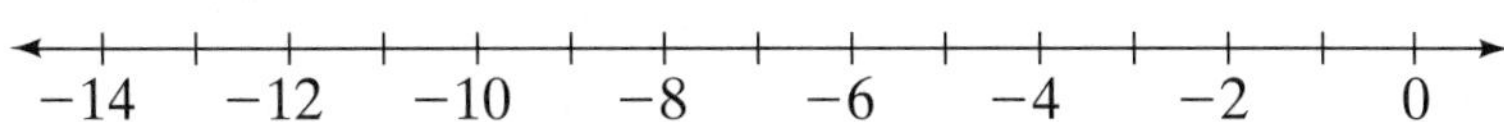

Since -12 is to the ⬚ of -10 on a number line, -12 ⬚ -10.

❺ Ordering Integers Order from least to greatest: $16, -2, -35, 68, -10$.

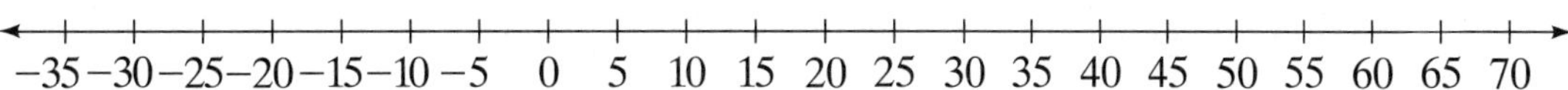

In order from least to greatest, the numbers are ⬚, ⬚,
⬚, ⬚, ⬚.

Check Understanding

3. a. Find $|-1|$.

⬚

b. Find $|7|$.

⬚

c. Find $|-9|$.

⬚

4. Compare using $<$ or $>$.

a. 5 ⬚ -3 **b.** -12 ⬚ 9

5. Order these numbers from least to greatest: $-25, 100, -50, 75$.

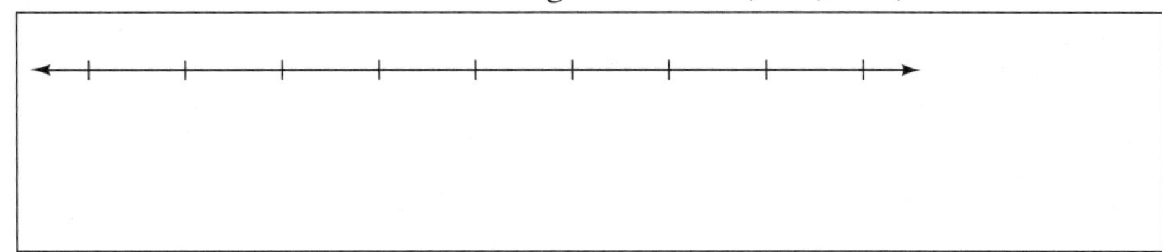

Lesson 10-2 *(pp. 497–501)*   **Adding Integers**

Lesson Objectives	**NAEP 2005 Strand:** Number Properties and Operations
▼ Add integers with the same sign ▼ Add integers with different signs	**Topic:** Number Operations **Local Standards:** ________________________________

Key Concepts

Adding Integers With the Same Sign The sum of two positive integers
is [ ]. The sum of two negative integers is [ ].

Examples: $2 + 3 =$ [ ] $-2 + (-3) =$ [ ]

Adding Integers With Different Signs To add integers with different signs,
first find the [ ] of each number. Then, subtract the
[ ] absolute value from the [ ]. The sum has the
[ ] sign of the integer with the [ ] absolute value.

Examples: $2 + (-3) =$ [ ] $-2 + 3 =$ [ ]

Examples

❶ Using a Number Line Use a number line to find the sum $-3 + (-5)$.

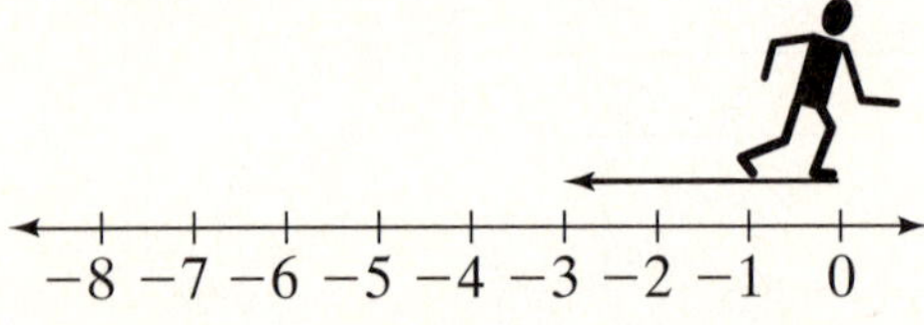

Start at [ ]. Face the positive direction.

Move [ ] 3 units for -3.

Then move [ ] 5 units for [ ].

You stop at [ ].

So, $-3 + (-5) =$ [ ].

❷ Adding Integers With the Same Sign Find each sum.

a. $9 + 9$

$9 + 9 =$ [ ]

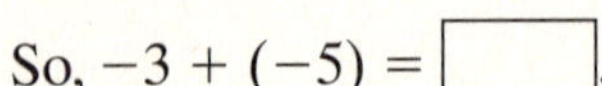

The sum of two positive integers is [ ].

b. $-6 + (-10)$

$-6 + (-10) =$ [ ]

The sum of two negative integers is [ ].

❸ Using a Number Line Find $-4 + 7$. Use a number line.

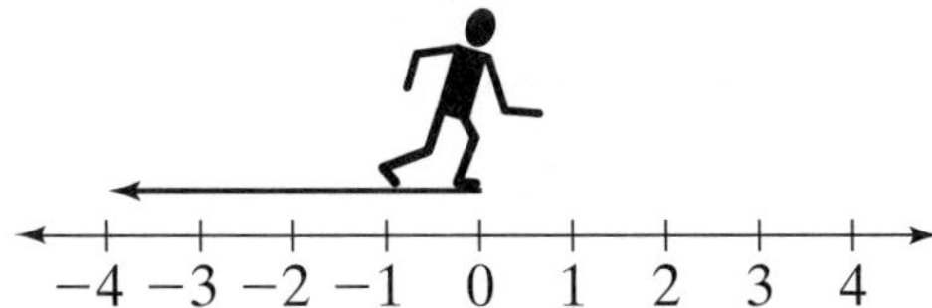

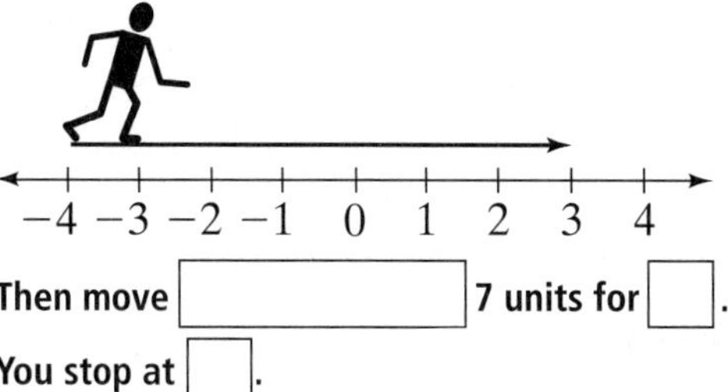

Start at ☐ , and face the positive direction.

Move backward ☐ units for -4.

So, $-4 + 7 = $ ☐ .

Then move ☐ 7 units for ☐ .

You stop at ☐ .

❹ Adding Integers With Different Signs Find each sum.

a. $8 + (-10)$

$|8| = $ ☐

$|-10| = $ ☐

$10 - 8 = $ ☐

$8 + (-10) = $ ☐

← Find the absolute values of the integers. →

← Subtract the absolute values. →

← The sum has the sign of the integer with the greater absolute value. →

b. $-4 + 16$

$|-4| = $ ☐

$|16| = $ ☐

$16 - 4 = $ ☐

$-4 + 16 = $ ☐

Check Understanding

1. Find each sum. Use a number line.

a. $-1 + (-3)$

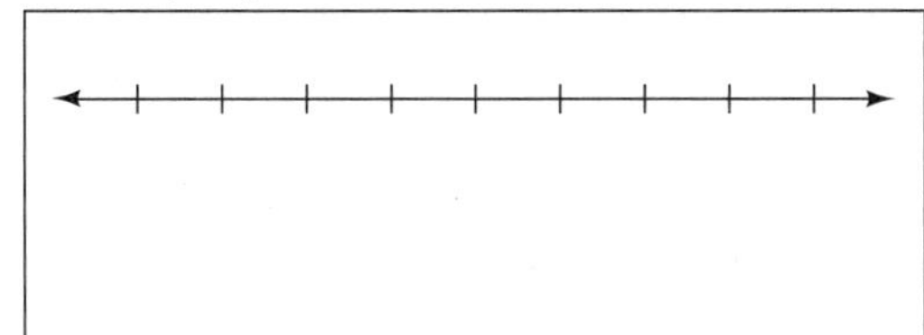

b. $2 + 10$

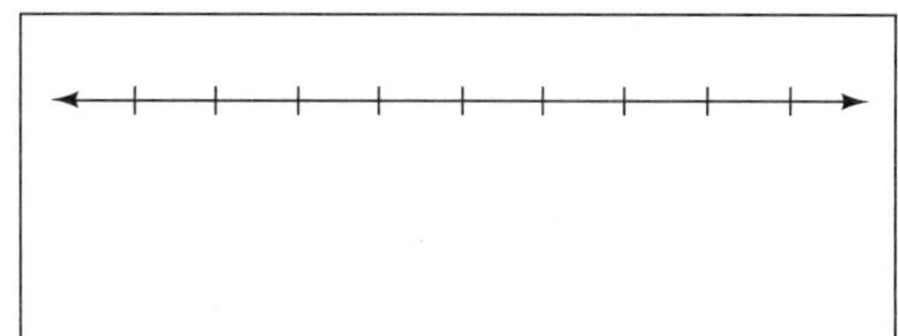

c. $4 + (-1)$

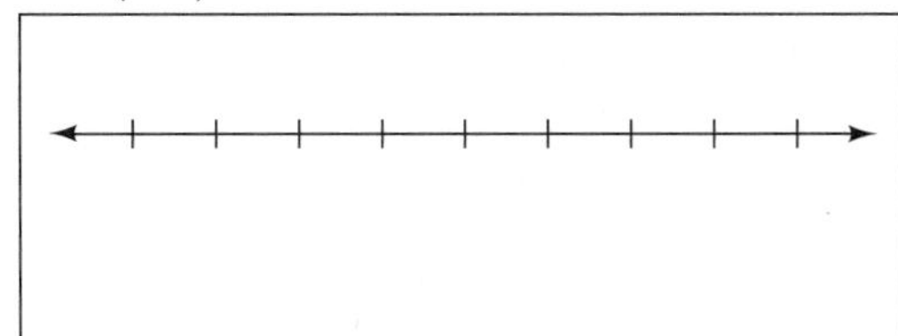

d. $-1 + 4$

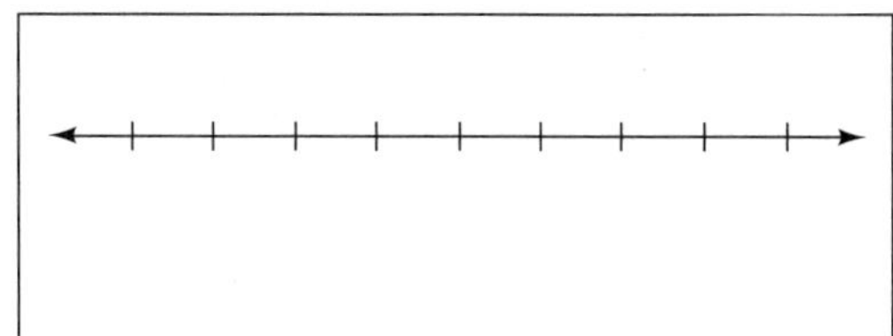

2. Find each sum.

a. $7 + 9$

b. $-9 + (-12)$

c. $7 + (-10)$

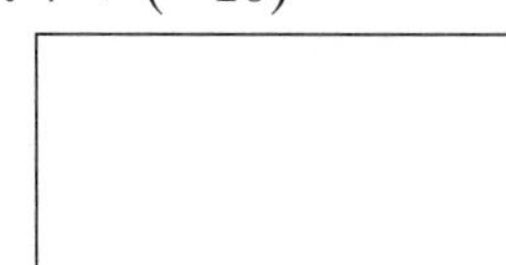

d. $-11 + 4$

3. Number Sense The sum of two negative integers is ☐ .

Lesson 10-3 *(pp. 503–508)*   Subtracting Integers

Lesson Objectives	**NAEP 2005 Strand:** Number Properties and Operations
▼ Subtract integers ❷ Solve problems with integers	**Topic:** Number Operations **Local Standards:** _____________________________

Key Concepts

Subtracting Integers You subtract an integer by adding its opposite.

Examples:

$10 - 6 = 10 +$ ☐ $10 - (-6) = 10 +$ ☐

$-10 - 6 = -10 +$ ☐ $-10 - (-6) = -10 +$ ☐

Examples

❶ Using a Number Line to Subtract Integers Use a number line to find $4 - (-4)$.

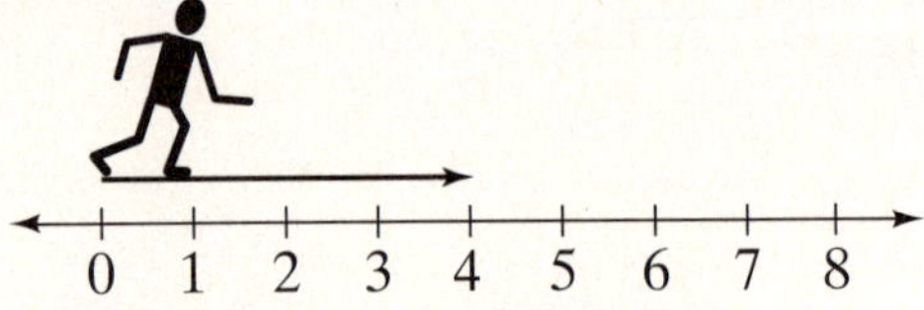

Start at 0. Face the positive direction.

Move forward ☐ units for 4.

So, $4 - (-4) =$ ☐.

For subtraction, turn around.

Then move ☐ 4 units

for −4. You stop at ☐.

❷ Subtracting Integers Find each difference.

a. $-5 - (-7)$ $-5 - (-7) = -5 +$ ☐   ← To subtract −7, add its opposite, ☐.

                                  $=$ ☐   ← Simplify.

b. $-9 - 6$ $-9 - 6 = -9 + ($ ☐ $)$ ← To subtract 6, add its opposite, ☐.

                                  $=$ ☐   ← Simplify.

Check Understanding

1. Use a number line for each subtraction.

a. $4 - 1$ **b.** $4 - (-1)$

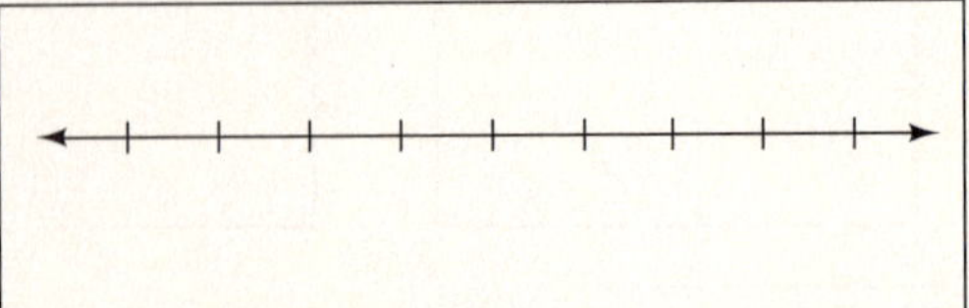

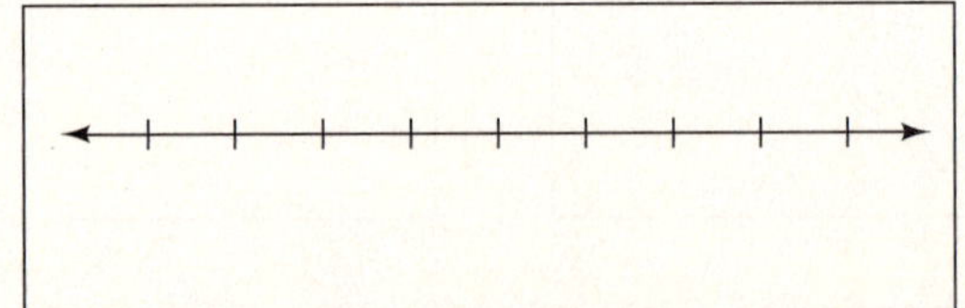

                    Course 1 Daily Notetaking Guide

Examples

❸ Juan owes his sister \$14. She told him to subtract \$8 of what he owes if he feeds the dog. Write an integer to show how much money Juan will owe if he feeds the dog.

Find $-14 - (-8)$. $-14 - (-8) = -14 + \boxed{}$ ← **To subtract −8, add its opposite.**

$ = \boxed{}$ ← **Simplify.**

The integer $\boxed{}$ shows that Juan will owe his sister $\boxed{}$.

❹ **Solving Equations With Integers**   Solve each equation.

a. $x + 8 = 5$ $x + 8 - \boxed{} = 5 - \boxed{}$ ← **Subtract** $\boxed{}$ **from each side.**

$x = 5 + \left(\boxed{}\right)$ ← **To subtract 8, add its opposite.**

$x = \boxed{}$ ← **Simplify.**

b. $y - 11 = -1$ $y - 11 + \boxed{} = -1 + \boxed{}$ ← **Add** $\boxed{}$ **to each side.**

$y = \boxed{}$ ← **Simplify.**

Check Understanding

2. Find each difference.

a. $9 - (-3)$ **b.** $-6 - (-2)$ **c.** $-3 - 5$

 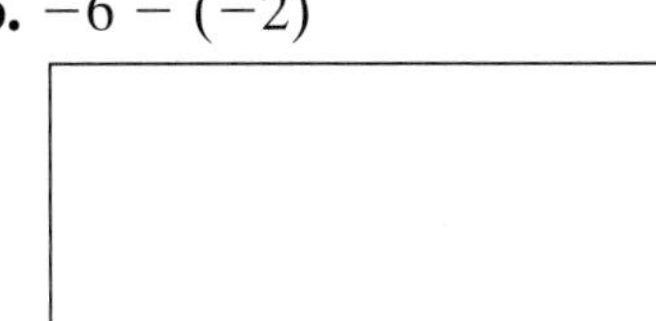 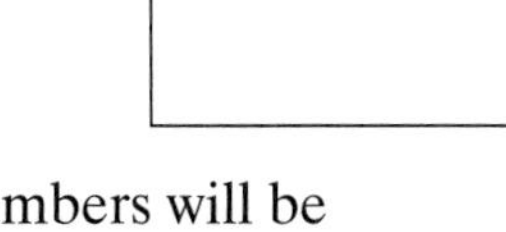

d. Number Sense How can you tell that the difference of two numbers will be positive or negative without doing the computation?

3. The research submarine *Alvin* was 1,872 feet below sea level ($-1,872$). It then moved to a position of 1,250 feet below sea level ($-1,250$). How many feet did it move?

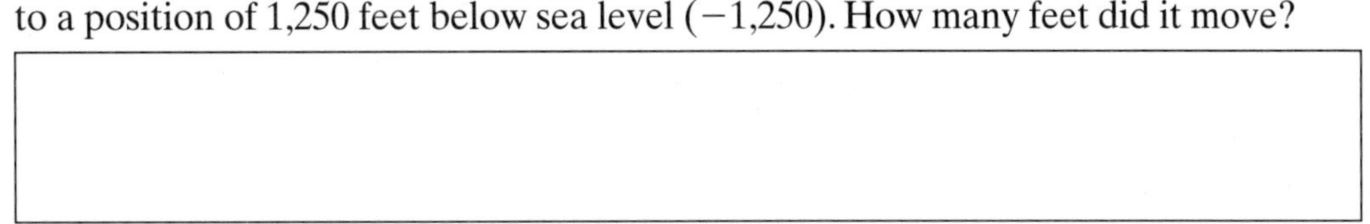

4. Solve each equation.

a. $b + 14 = 8$    **b.** $c - 15 = -5$ 

Lesson 10-4 *(pp. 509–512)* **Multiplying Integers**

Lesson Objective	**NAEP 2005 Strand:** Number Properties and Operations
▼ Multiply integers	**Topic:** Number Operations
	Local Standards: _____________________

Key Concepts

Multiplying Integers

The product of two integers with the *same* sign is ⬚.

The product of two integers with *different* signs is ⬚.

Examples:

$4 \times 5 = $ ⬚ $4 \times (-5) = $ ⬚

$-4 \times (-5) = $ ⬚ $-4 \times 5 = $ ⬚

Example

❶ **Using a Number Line to Multiply Integers** Use a number line to find $5 \times (-2)$.

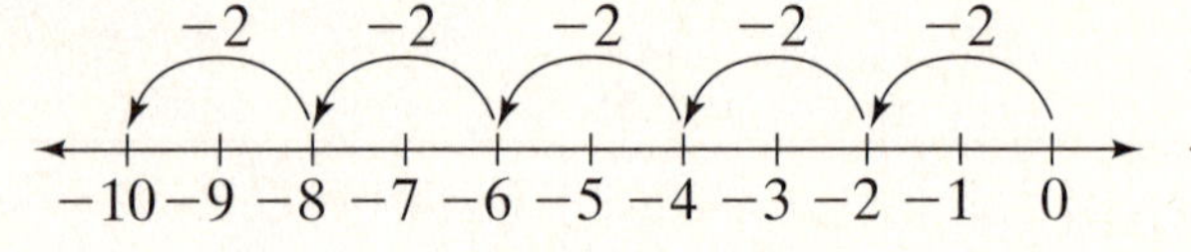

Start at ⬚.

Make ⬚ groups

of ⬚ on the number line.

The sum of 5 groups of -2 is ⬚. So, $5 \times (-2) = $ ⬚.

Check Understanding

1. Use a number line to find each product.

   a. $3 \times (-4) = $ ⬚

   b. $-3 \times (-4) = $ ⬚

   c. $-4 \times 3 = $ ⬚

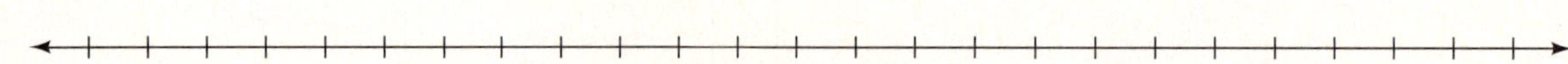

Name_________________________________ Class_________________________________ Date _______________

Examples

❷ Multiplying Integers Find each product.

a. $-2 \times (-6)$ $-2 \times (-6) = \boxed{}$ ← $\boxed{}$ **product**

same signs,

b. -7×2 $-7 \times 2 = \boxed{}$ ← $\boxed{}$ **product**

different signs,

❸ The value of a telephone calling card decreases 20¢ for each minute used. Write an integer to express the change in the card's value for a 4-minute call.

$\left(\boxed{}\right) \times 4 = \boxed{}$ ← **Use a** $\boxed{}$ **number to represent the card losing value.**

The amount, $\boxed{}$, expresses the change in the card's value.

Check Understanding

2. Find each product.

a. -6×7

b. $-9 \times (-3)$

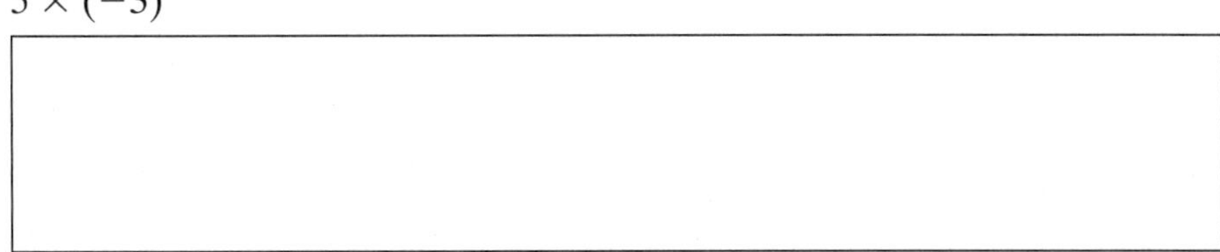

c. $5 \times (-3)$

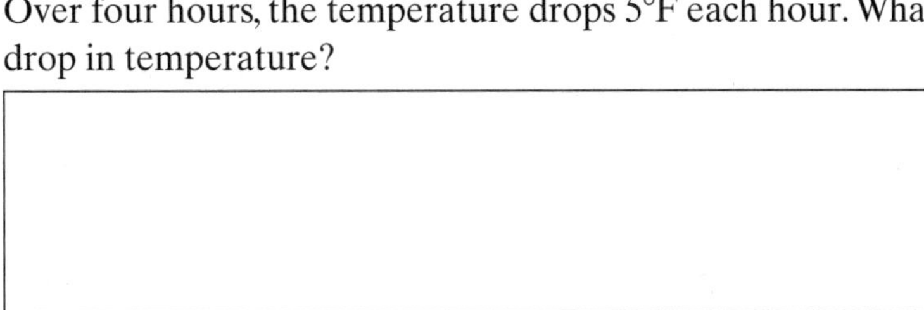

3. Over four hours, the temperature drops 5°F each hour. What is the total drop in temperature?

Lesson 10-5 *(pp. 513–516)*   Dividing Integers

Lesson Objectives	**NAEP 2005 Strand:** Number Properties and Operations
▼1 Divide integers	**Topic:** Number Operations
▼2 Solve equations	**Local Standards:** _______________________________

Key Concepts

Dividing Integers

The quotient of two integers with the *same* sign is [ ].

The quotient of two integers with *different* signs is [ ].

Examples:

$20 \div 4 = \boxed{}$ $20 \div (-4) = \boxed{}$

$-20 \div (-4) = \boxed{}$ $-20 \div 4 = \boxed{}$

Example

❶ Dividing Integers Find each quotient.

a. $-33 \div (-3)$ 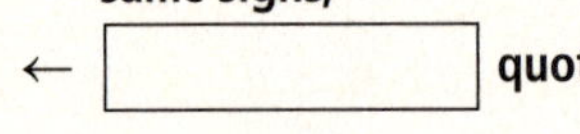 $-33 \div (-3) = \boxed{} \leftarrow \boxed{\text{same signs, }} \text{quotient}$

b. $24 \div (-6)$ $24 \div (-6) = \boxed{} \leftarrow \boxed{\text{different signs, }} \text{quotient}$

Check Understanding

1. Find each quotient.

a. $-24 \div 6$

b. $-36 \div (-2)$

Examples

❷ Solving Equations With Integers Solve each equation.

a. $\frac{x}{5} = -6$

$\boxed{} \times \frac{x}{5} = \boxed{} \times (-6)$ ← **Multiply each side by** $\boxed{}$.

$x = \boxed{}$ ← **Simplify.**

b. $-8y = 24$

$\dfrac{-8y}{\boxed{}} = \dfrac{24}{\boxed{}}$ ← **Divide each side by** $\boxed{}$.

$y = \boxed{}$ ← **Simplify.**

❸ Wind Speed In a 2-hour period, the wind speed decreased from 28 mi/h to 18 mi/h. If the speed decreased the same amount each hour, how much did the wind speed change each hour?

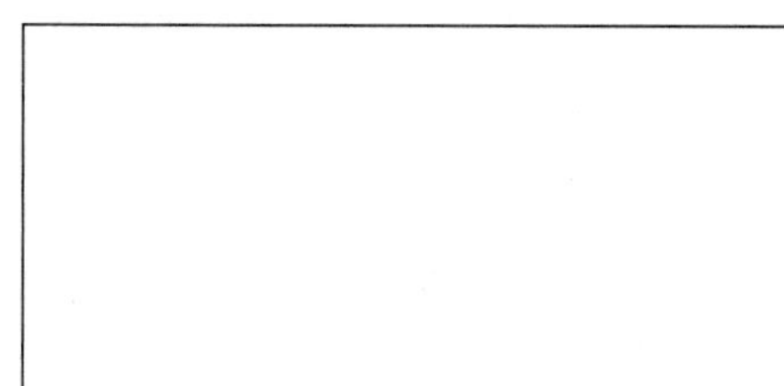

Words | total change | divided by | number of hours | equals | change per hour

Let $\boxed{r}$ = the average change per hour.

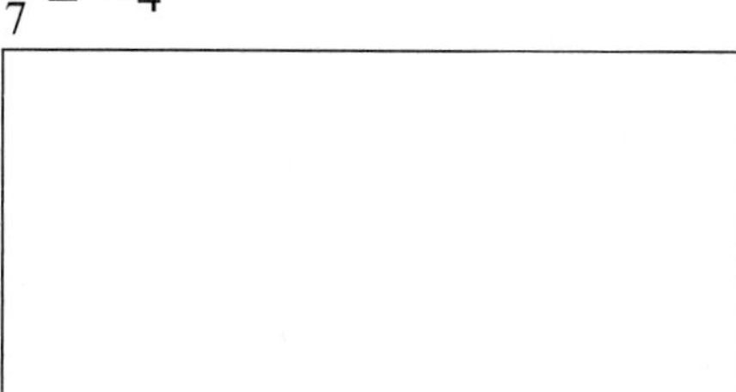

Equation $\boxed{}$ ÷ $\boxed{}$ = $\boxed{}$

$-10 \div 2 = r$

$\boxed{} = r$ ← **Simplify.**

The wind speed changed an average of $\boxed{}$ mi/h each hour.

Check Understanding

2. Solve each equation.

a. $-6z = 36$

b. $\frac{u}{7} = -4$

3. The value of a share of stock decreased $20 over the last 5 days. What integer represents the average decrease in stock value each day?

Lesson 10-6 *(pp. 518–521)*

Graphing on the Coordinate Plane

Lesson Objectives	NAEP 2005 Strand: Algebra
▼ Name coordinates ▼ Graph points on a coordinate plane	Topic: Algebraic Representations Local Standards: _______________________

Vocabulary

The coordinate plane is _______________________

____

The plane is divided into four regions,

called ☐.

The origin is _______________________

____

An ordered pair is _______________________

____

Quadrant ☐　　Quadrant ☐

☐-axis

☐-axis

Quadrant ☐　　Quadrant ☐

Example

❶ **Naming Coordinates** Find the coordinates of point A.

Point A is ☐ units to the ☐ of the y-axis.
The x-coordinate is ☐.

Point A is ☐ units below the x-axis. The y-coordinate
is ☐.

The coordinates of point A are ☐.

Check Understanding

1. Find the coordinates of each point in the coordinate plane.

a. C　☐

b. D　☐

c. E　☐

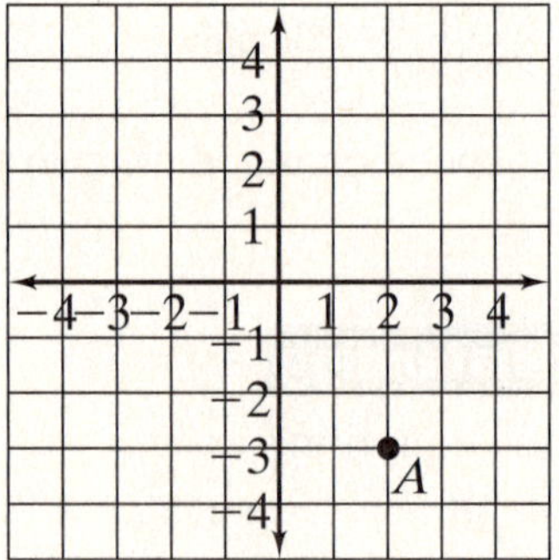

Examples

② **Graphing Ordered Pairs** Graph the point $X(-1, -3)$ in a coordinate plane.

Step 1

Start at the ______.

Step 2

Move ☐ unit to the ______.

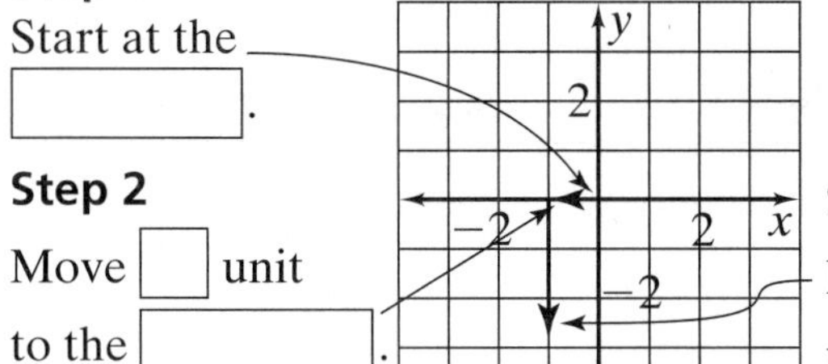

Step 3

Move ☐ units ______.

③ **Using Map Coordinates** Use the coordinate grid. If you travel 2 units down and 3 units right from B, what are the coordinates of your location?

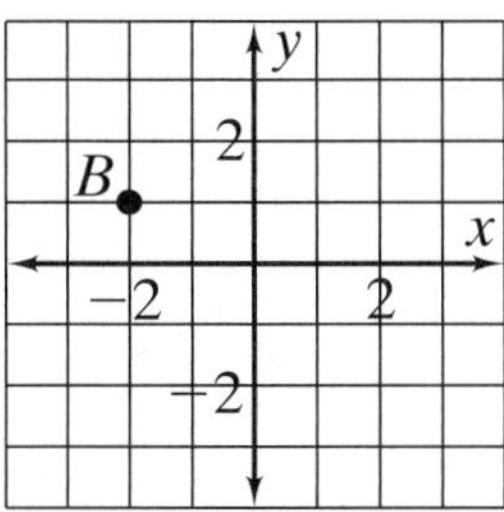

You are at ______.

Check Understanding

2. Graph these points on the coordinate plane: $A(-4, -4), B(-3, 2), C(1, -2)$.

3. Suppose you leave the library and walk 2 blocks south and then 5 blocks east.

a. At which building are you located?

b. What are the coordinates of the building?

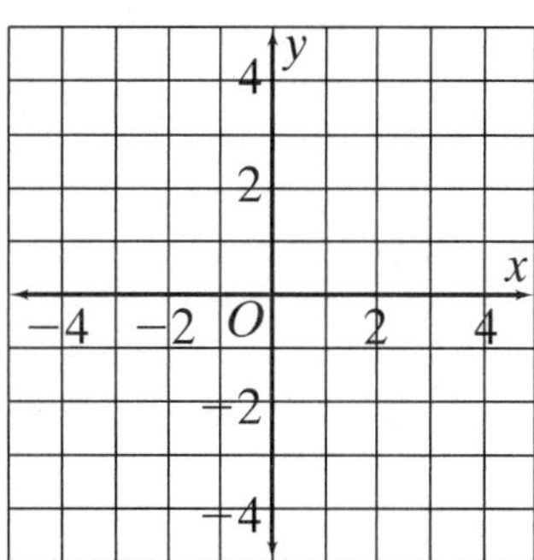

Lesson 10-7 *(pp. 523–526)*   Applications of Integers

Lesson Objectives	NAEP 2005 Strand: Algebra
▼ Find profit and loss	Topic: Algebraic Representations
▼ Draw and interpret graphs	Local Standards: _______________________

Example

❶ Finding Profit or Loss Find the profit or loss for each month.

Month	Income	Expenses
Sept.	$1,250	−$1,250
Oct.	$3,200	−$2,550
Nov.	$4,250	−$3,570
Dec.	$2,530	−$2,840

a. Sept.

$\boxed{} + \left(\boxed{}\right) = \boxed{}$ ← **Add income and expenses for September.**

There was no profit or loss for September.

b. Oct.

$\boxed{} + \left(\boxed{}\right) = \boxed{}$ ← **Add income and expenses for October.**

There was a $\boxed{}$ of $\boxed{}$ for October.

c. Nov.

$\boxed{} + \left(\boxed{}\right) = \boxed{}$ ← **Add income and expenses for November.**

There was a $\boxed{}$ of $\boxed{}$ for November.

d. Dec.

$\boxed{} + \left(\boxed{}\right) = \boxed{}$ ← **Add income and expenses for December.**

There was a $\boxed{}$ of $\boxed{}$ for December.

Name_____________________________ Class_____________________________ Date _____________

Check Understanding

❷ Drawing and Interpreting Graphs Draw a line graph based on your answers to Example 1a–d. In which month did the greatest profit occur?

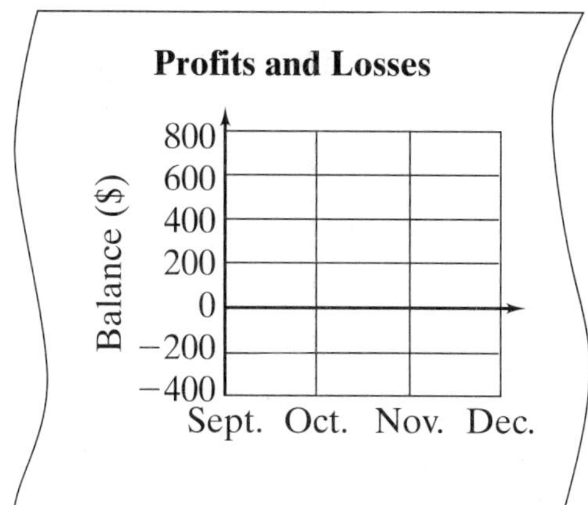

The balances vary from [   ] to [   ]. So, make a scale from −$400 to $800. Use intervals of $200.

The greatest profit was in [   ].

Check Understanding

1. Find the profit or loss for each period.

Income and Expenses for Flower Mania		
Month	**Income**	**Expenses**
Jan.	$11,917	−$14,803
Feb.	$12,739	−$9,482
Mar.	$11,775	−$10,954
Apr.	$13,620	−$15,149

a. January

b. March

c. April

d. January through April

2. Use the data from Example 1. In which month did the greatest loss occur?

Lesson 10-8 *(pp. 527–532)*

Graphing Functions

Lesson Objectives	**NAEP 2005 Strand:** Algebra
▼ Make a function table	**Topic:** Algebraic Representations
▼ Graph functions	**Local Standards:** ______________________

Vocabulary

A function is ____

____

Examples

❶ Completing a Function Table Complete the function table given the rule Output = Input ÷ (-3).

Input	Output
-9	
-3	
12	
15	

← Divide -9 by [ ] . Place [ ] in the Output column.

← Divide -3 by [ ] . Place [ ] in the Output column.

← Divide 12 by [ ] . Place [ ] in the Output column.

← Divide 15 by [ ] . Place [ ] in the Output column.

❷ Graphing a Function Make a table and graph the function $y = -2x$.

Input (*x*)	Output (*y*)
-2	
-1	
0	
1	
2	

❸ Henry receives \$8.00 per hour for babysitting two children. The function $e = 8h$ shows how the earnings e relate to the number of hours h that Henry babysits. Make a table and graph the function.

Hours	Earnings ($)
1	
2	
3	
4	

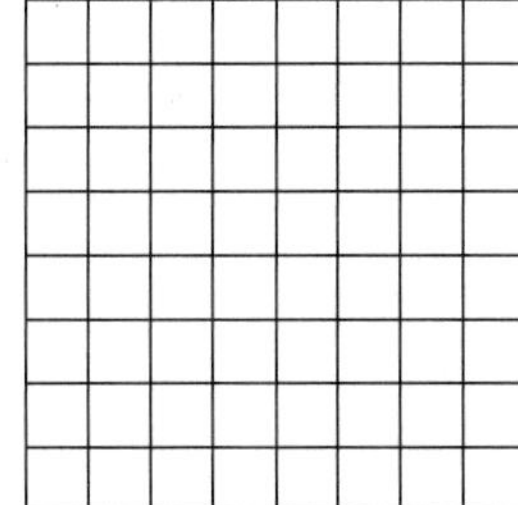

Check Understanding

1. Complete the function table given the rule.

a. Rule: Output = Input ÷ 4

Input	Output
16	
−24	
36	

b. Rule: Output = Input − 8

Input	Output
−6	
−1	
4	

2. Make a table and graph the function $y = x - 3$.

Input(x)	Output(y)
−2	
−1	
0	
1	
2	

3. Suppose a car is driven at a steady rate of 45 miles per hour. The function $d = 45t$ shows how time t relates to distance d. Make a table and graph the function.

Time (hours)	Distance (miles)
0	
1	
2	
3	
4	
5	

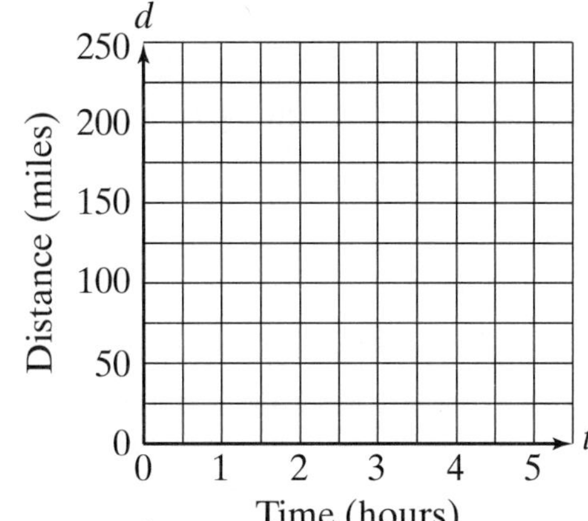

Lesson 10-9 *(pp. 533–535)*   Make a Graph

Lesson Objective	NAEP 2005 Strand: Algebra
▼ Make a graph	Topic: Algebraic Representations
	Local Standards: ______________________

Example

1 Making a Graph Marie weighed two objects in class. She found that a
1-lb object was 0.45 kg. A 4-lb object was 1.8 kg. Use a graph to find the
weight (mass) in kilograms of a 2.5-lb object.

Read and Understand

A 1-lb object has mass ⬚ kg. A 4-lb object has mass ⬚ kg.
You need to find ⬚ lb in kilograms.

Plan and Solve

To approximate 2.5 lb in kilograms, ***make a graph.*** You know two pairs
of equivalent weights. Write the ordered pairs as ⬚ and
⬚ .

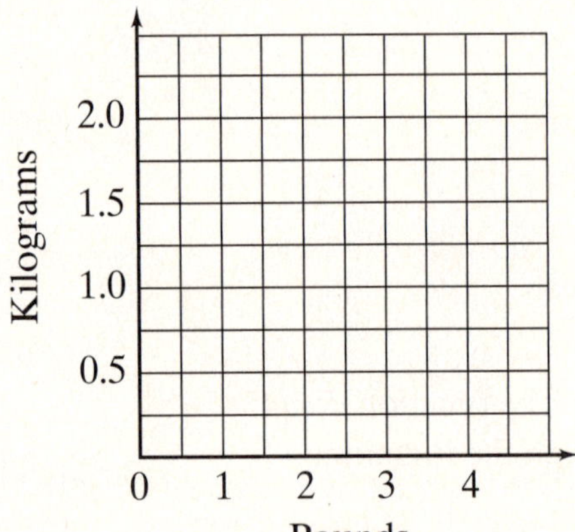

Connect the points with a line. The kilogram weight when the pound
weight is 2.5 is about ⬚ kg.

Look Back and Check

Using number sense, since 1.1 kg is about halfway between 0.45 kg
and 1.8 kg, and 2.5 lb is about halfway between 1 lb and 4 lb, the
answer is reasonable.

                          Course 1 Daily Notetaking Guide

Name_______________________________ Class_______________________________ Date _______________

1. Use the graph to estimate the mass of an object that weighs 3.5 lb.

Lesson 11-1 *(pp. 547–551)*   **Probability**

Lesson Objective	**NAEP 2005 Strand:** Data Analysis and Probability
▼ Find probability	**Topic:** Probability
	Local Standards: _________________________

Vocabulary and Key Concepts

Probability of an Event

When outcomes are equally likely,

the probability of an event = $\dfrac{\boxed{}}{\boxed{}}$.

Equally likely outcomes are ______________________________________

An event is ______________________________________

The probability of an event is ______________________________________

____

Examples

❶ Probability of an Event A spinner is divided into 8 equal sections numbered 1 through 8. Find each probability for one spin of the spinner.

a. $P(6)$

There is $\boxed{}$ outcome for the event "6" out of $\boxed{}$ equally likely outcomes.

$P(6) = \dfrac{\boxed{}}{\boxed{}}$ ← outcomes with event "6"
← total number of outcomes

The probability of spinning a 6 is $\dfrac{\boxed{}}{\boxed{}}$.

b. $P(2 \text{ or } 3)$

There is $\boxed{}$ outcome for the event "2" and $\boxed{}$ outcome for the event "3" out of $\boxed{}$ equally likely outcomes.

$P(2 \text{ or } 3) = \dfrac{\boxed{}}{\boxed{}}$ ← outcomes with event "2" or event "3"
← total number of outcomes

$= \dfrac{\boxed{}}{\boxed{}}$ ← Simplify.

    Course 1 Daily Notetaking Guide

Name_________________________ Class_________________________ Date _______________

❷ Finding Probability The 6th grade class made 73 of the 100 posters made by the school.

a. Find the probability that a randomly selected poster was made by the 6th grade class. Write your answer as a fraction, a decimal, and a percent.

$P(\text{6th grade poster}) = \dfrac{\boxed{}}{\boxed{}}$ ← **number of 6th grade posters**

← **total number of posters**

$= \boxed{}$, or $\boxed{}$ %

b. State whether the above event is *impossible, unlikely, equally likely, likely,* or *certain.*

The probability is between $\boxed{}$ and $\boxed{}$, so the event is $\boxed{}$.

Check Understanding

1. A number cube is rolled once. Find each probability.

a. $P(\text{odd}) = \dfrac{\boxed{}}{\boxed{}} = \dfrac{\boxed{}}{\boxed{}}$

b. $P(5) = \dfrac{\boxed{}}{\boxed{}} = \dfrac{\boxed{}}{\boxed{}}$

c. $P(2 \text{ or } 6) = \dfrac{\boxed{}}{\boxed{}} = \dfrac{\boxed{}}{\boxed{}}$

d. Reasoning Is $P(3)$ different from $P(4)$? Explain.

2. a. Reasoning How many posters would the 6th grade class have to make for there to be an equal chance that a randomly selected poster would be one of theirs?

b. In a bag of mixed nuts, 6 of 10 nuts are pecans. Find the probability of selecting a pecan at random. Write your answer as a fraction, a decimal, and a percent.

Course 1 Daily Notetaking Guide

Lesson 11-2 *(pp. 553–557)*   **Experimental Probability**

Lesson Objective	**NAEP 2005 Strand:** Data Analysis and Probability
▼ Find experimental probabilities	**Topic:** Probability
	Local Standards: _______________________________

Key Concepts

Experimental Probability

$$P(\text{event}) = \frac{\boxed{}}{\boxed{}}.$$

Example

❶ Experimental Probability In 30 times at bat, Jan struck out 14 times. What is the experimental probability that Jan will strike out at her next at-bat?

$$P(\text{strike-out}) = \frac{\boxed{}}{\boxed{}} \quad \leftarrow \textbf{ number of strike-outs}$$
$$\qquad\qquad\qquad\quad \leftarrow \textbf{ total number of at-bats}$$

$$= \frac{\boxed{}}{\boxed{}} \quad \leftarrow \textbf{ Simplify.}$$

The experimental probability of a strike-out is $\frac{\boxed{}}{\boxed{}}$.

Check Understanding

1. Franklin and Tommy play 30 matches. Franklin wins 12 matches. What is the experimental probability that Franklin wins a match?

$$P(\text{Franklin wins}) = \frac{\boxed{}}{\boxed{}} \quad \leftarrow \textbf{ number of wins}$$
$$\qquad\qquad\qquad\qquad \leftarrow \textbf{ number of matches}$$

$$= \frac{\boxed{}}{\boxed{}}$$

Name_________________________________ Class_________________________________ Date _______________

Example

❷ Analyzing Experimental Probability You and your friend want to play a game with a spinner. The table at right shows the results of 120 spins. Which of the following games seems fair? Explain.

Red	Yellow	Blue
58	23	39

a. You win with yellow and your friend wins with blue.

The experimental probability of spinning a yellow is $\dfrac{\boxed{}}{\boxed{}}$.

The experimental probability of spinning a blue is $\dfrac{\boxed{}}{\boxed{}}$.

Since the spinner favors blue, the game seems to be $\boxed{}$.

b. You win with red and your friend wins with blue or yellow.

$\boxed{} + \boxed{} = \boxed{}$ ← **Add to find the number of trials for blue or yellow.**

So $P(\text{red}) = \dfrac{\boxed{}}{\boxed{}}$ and $P(\text{blue or yellow}) = \dfrac{\boxed{}}{\boxed{}}$.

Since the probabilities are about $\boxed{}$, the game seems to be $\boxed{}$.

Check Understanding

2. In Example 2, suppose you win with red or blue and your friend wins with red or yellow. Does the game seem fair?

Lesson 11-3 *(pp. 558–562)*   **Making Predictions From Data**

Lesson Objectives	**NAEP 2005 Strand:** Data Analysis and Probability
▼ Make predictions from probabilities	**Topic:** Probability
▼ Make predictions based on sample	**Local Standards:** _______________________

Vocabulary

A population is ____

____

A sample is ____

____

Example

❶ **Making a Prediction From a Probability** Kiko bought 35 raffle tickets.
Each ticket has a 20% probability of winning a prize. How many prizes
should he expect to win?

number of tickets that win a prize	×	number of tickets	=	P(prize)

$$\frac{\square}{\square} \quad \times \quad \boxed{} \quad = \quad \boxed{} \quad \leftarrow \text{Write 20\% as } \frac{\square}{\square}.$$

Then multiply.

He can predict that about ☐ tickets will win a prize.

Check Understanding

1. At an arcade, Juanita plays a game 20 times. She has a 30% probability
   of winning each game. How many times should she expect to win?

                              Course 1 Daily Notetaking Guide

Name_______________________________ Class_______________________________ Date ______________

Example

❷ **Quality Control** A random sample shows that 6 wallets out of 400 are defective. Predict how many wallets out of 15,000 will be defective.

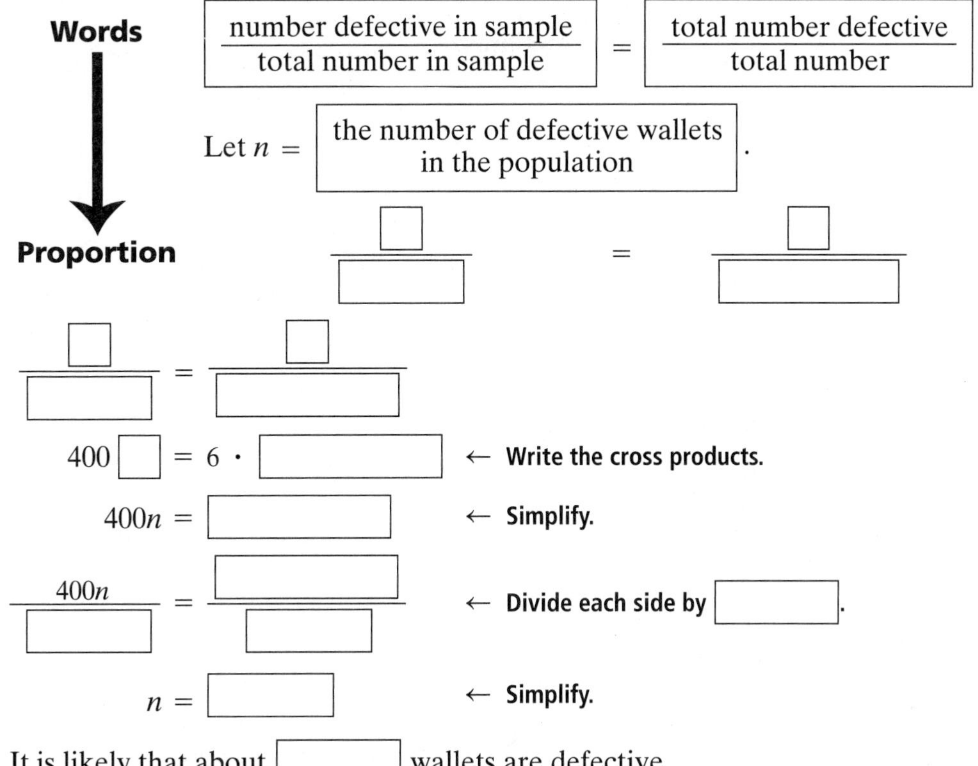

It is likely that about [   ] wallets are defective.

Check Understanding

2. Suppose 1,000 wallets are selected at random from 20,000 wallets, and 54 are defective. How many of the 20,000 wallets are likely to be defective?

Lesson 11-4 *(pp. 563–566)*   Simulate a Problem

Lesson Objective ▼ Solve problems by simulation	**NAEP 2005 Strand:** Data Analysis and Probability **Topic:** Probability **Local Standards:** ______________________

Vocabulary

A simulation is ____

____

Example

1 Solving a Problem by Simulation Yan runs a restaurant. His favorite customer leaves the restaurant each night between 8:00 P.M. and 9:00 P.M. His next-best customer comes to the restaurant every night between 8:45 P.M. and 9:45 P.M. What is the probability that these customers will dine in the restaurant at the same time? Use a simulation to solve the problem.

(Read and Understand)

The favorite customer leaves between [   ] and [   ]

The next-best customer arrives between [   ] and [   ]

You need to find the probability that the two customers will be in the restaurant at the same time.

(Plan and Solve)

You can't collect data from the customers, so simulate the problem with a [   ]. Assume each time is [   ] likely. Use two spinners like the ones below. One spinner will simulate a random time from 8:00 P.M. to 9:00 P.M. The other spinner will simulate a random time from 8:45 P.M. to 9:45 P.M.

Favorite Customer Leaves

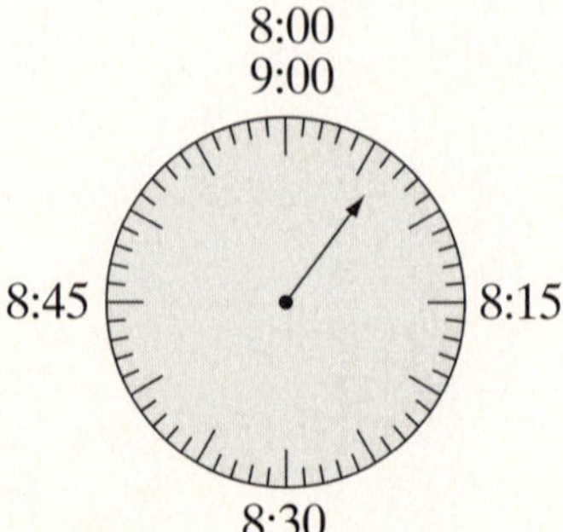

Next-Best Customer Arrives

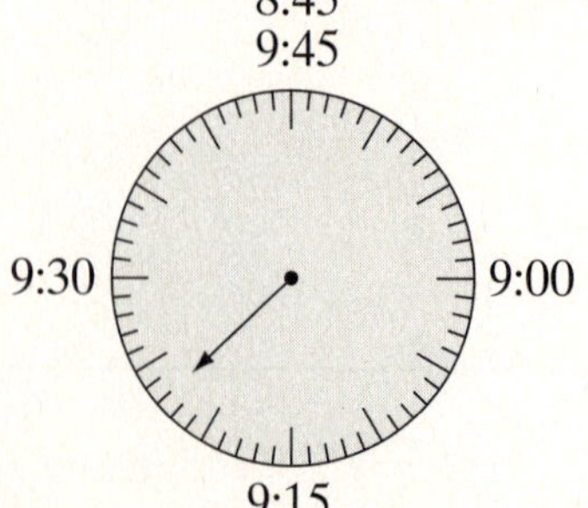

Name_________________________________ Class_________________________________ Date ______________

Spin each spinner once to simulate what may happen on a given day. The table below shows the results for 30 days. For each day, circle the earlier time. If Time 2 is circled, both customers will be in the restaurant at the same time.

| Time 1 = favorite customer leaves | | |
| Time 2 = next-best customer arrives | | |
Time 1, Time 2	Time 1, Time 2	Time 1, Time 2
8:30, 8:50	8:16, 9:23	8:11, 9:12
8:40, 8:45	8:04, 9:08	8:20, 9:43
8:52, 8:48	8:43, 9:36	8:27, 9:17
8:35, 9:16	8:09, 9:42	8:12, 9:31
8:42, 9:10	8:29, 9:14	8:52, 9:27
8:30, 9:15	8:16, 9:14	8:02, 9:03
8:41, 9:03	8:45, 9:07	8:10, 9:15
8:47, 9:20	8:28, 8:59	8:41, 8:45
8:23, 9:05	9:00, 8:50	8:50, 9:30
8:10, 9:38	8:18, 9:23	8:36, 9:11

In 30 simulations, Yan's favorite customer leaves after the next-best customer arrives ☐ times.

So, P(customers together) = $\dfrac{\boxed{}}{\boxed{}}$, or about ☐%.

(Look Back and Check) The table below summarizes the customers' times.

Favorite Customer Leaves	Next-Best Customer Arrives	Customers Together?
8:00 P.M. to 8:30 P.M.	8:45 P.M. to 9:15 P.M.	☐
8:30 P.M. to 9:00 P.M.	8:45 P.M. to 9:15 P.M.	☐
8:00 P.M. to 8:30 P.M.	9:15 P.M. to 9:45 P.M.	☐
8:30 P.M. to 9:00 P.M.	9:15 P.M. to 9:45 P.M.	☐

The table shows that it is ☐ that the two customers will be in the restaurant at the same time. Since P(customers together) is about ☐%, the answer is ☐.

Check Understanding

1. The forecast calls for a $\frac{2}{3}$ chance of rain in Detroit and a $\frac{1}{2}$ chance in Tampa. Find the experimental probability that it rains in both cities. Use two number cubes. Let 1, 2, 3, and 4 on one cube represent rain in Detroit. Let 1, 2, and 3 on the other cube represent Tampa.

Lesson 11-5 *(pp. 568–573)*

Tree Diagrams and the Counting Principle

Lesson Objectives	NAEP 2005 Strand: Data Analysis and Probability
▼ Use tree diagrams ▼ Use the counting principle	Topic: Probability Local Standards: ______________________

Vocabulary and Key Concepts

Counting Principle

Suppose there are m ways of making one choice and n ways of making a second choice. Then there are $\boxed{} \times \boxed{}$ ways to make the first choice followed by the second choice.

A tree diagram is ____

____

Example

❶ **Probabilities Using Tree Diagrams** Suppose you spin a spinner with 5 equal-sized sections numbered 1 through 5. You then toss a coin. What is the probability that you will get an even number and heads? Make a tree diagram to find all possible outcomes.

The diagram shows $\boxed{}$ equally likely outcomes. There are $\boxed{}$ outcomes where an even number is paired with heads.

So, $P(\text{even number, then heads}) = \dfrac{\boxed{}}{\boxed{}}$, or $\dfrac{\boxed{}}{\boxed{}}$.

Spinner	Coin	Outcome
1	H T	1H 1T
2	H T	2H 2T
3	H T	3H 3T
4	H T	4H 4T
5	H T	5H 5T

Check Understanding

1. Use the tree diagram from Example 1. Find the probability of spinning an odd number and getting a tails.

$\dfrac{\boxed{}}{\boxed{}}$

Examples

❷ Using the Counting Principle Flight attendants can wear one of four shirts, three pants, and two jackets. How many different combinations of uniforms are possible?

Use the counting principle to find the total number of uniforms.

Shirts   Pants   Jackets   Uniforms

$$\boxed{} \times \boxed{} \times \boxed{} = \boxed{}$$

There are $\boxed{}$ different uniform combinations.

❸ Finding a Probability A clothing manufacturer makes dress shirts in sizes and colors shown in the table. What is the probability that a randomly selected shirt will be a blue XL? Assume all possibilities are equally likely.

Sizes	S, M, L, XL, XXL
Colors	Blue, Green, Tan

Find the number of outcomes where the shirt is a blue XL, and find the total number of outcomes.

Size   **Color**   **Shirt Styles**

$\boxed{} \times \boxed{} = \boxed{}$ ← **number of blue XL outcomes**

$\boxed{} \times \boxed{} = \boxed{}$ ← **total number of outcomes**

$$P(\text{blue XL}) = \frac{\boxed{}}{\boxed{}}$$

The probability that a randomly selected shirt is a blue XL is $\dfrac{\boxed{}}{\boxed{}}$.

Check Understanding

2. Suppose the flight attendants in Example 2 can wear an additional shirt and pants. Find the new number of different uniforms.

3. Reasoning How can you use a tree diagram for Example 3? Explain.

Lesson 11-6 *(pp. 574–578)*   **Exploring Permutations**

Lesson Objectives	**NAEP 2005 Strand:** Data Analysis and Probability
▼ Find permutations ❷ Count permutations	**Topic:** Probability **Local Standards:** ______________________________

Vocabulary

A permutation is ____

____

Examples

❶ Using Organized Lists Make an organized list to find the permutations of the letters FOUR.

Make an organized list. Use each letter exactly once.

FOUR	OURF	URFO	RFOU

❷ Using a Tree Diagram Draw a tree diagram to find the 2-letter permutations of the letters JUMP.

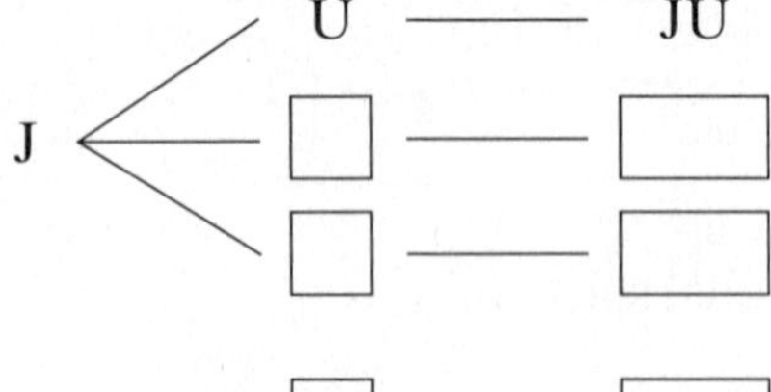

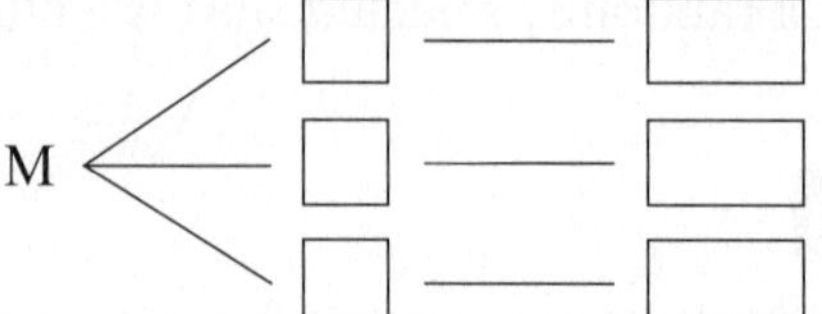

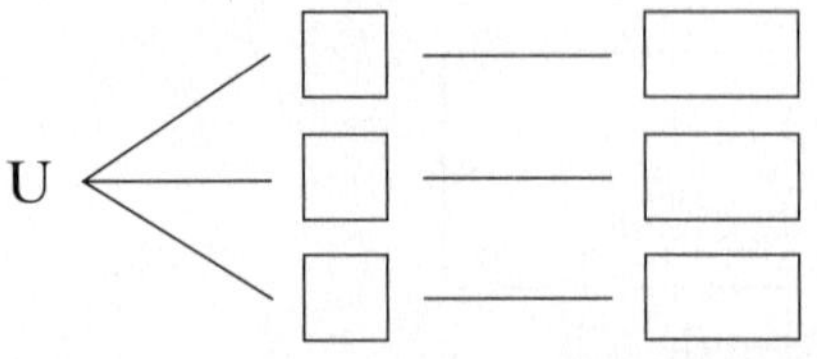

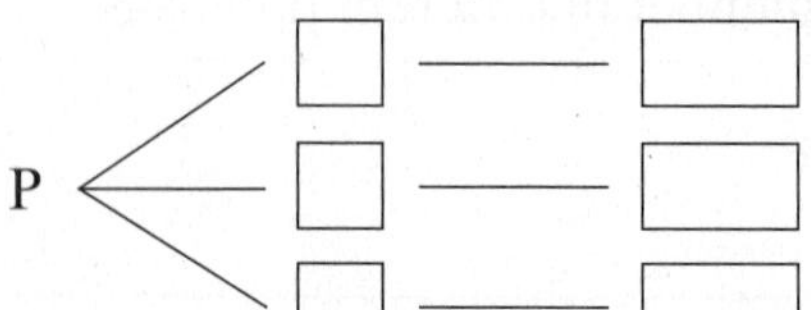

There are ☐ permutations.

Name________________________ Class________________________ Date ____________

Example

❸ **Applying the Counting Principle** Use the counting principle to find how many different ways you and 5 of your friends can sit on a bench at the bus stop.

Find the product of the number of outcomes for each seat on the bus.

choices for the first seat	choices for the second seat	choices for the third seat	choices for the fourth seat	choices for the fifth seat	choice for the sixth seat

☐ × ☐ × ☐ × ☐ × ☐ × ☐ = ☐

There are ☐ ways that you and 5 friends can sit on the bench.

Check Understanding

1. Make an organized list to find the permutations for the letters in CAT.

2. Draw a tree diagram to find the 3-letter permutations of the letters in PLAY. Here is how to start.

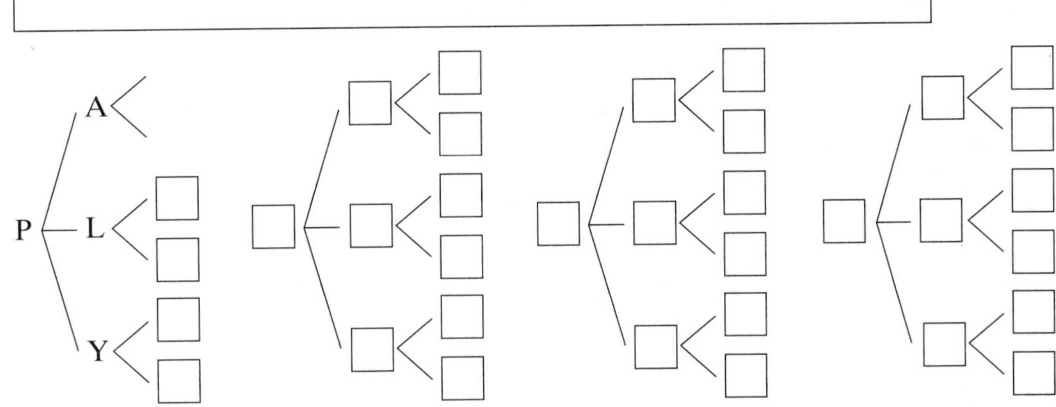

3. In Example 3, suppose a 6th friend joins you on the bench. In how many ways can all 7 of you sit on the bench?

Lesson 11-7 *(pp. 580–584)*

Independent Events

Lesson Objectives	**NAEP 2005 Strand:** Data Analysis and Probability
▼ Identify independent events ▼ Find probabilities of compound events	**Topic:** Probability **Local Standards:** _______________________

Vocabulary and Key Concepts

Probability of Independent Events

If A and B are independent events, then

$$P(A, \text{then } B) = \boxed{} \times \boxed{}$$

If the occurrence of one event does not affect the probability of another event, the two are $\boxed{}$.

$\boxed{}$ consists of two or more separate events.

Example

❶ Identifying Independent Events Decide whether or not events in each group are independent. Explain.

a. A card is drawn from a deck and replaced. A second card is then drawn from the deck.

$\boxed{}$: The first card has $\boxed{}$ on the selection of the second card.

b. A card is drawn from a deck. A second card is then drawn from the deck.

$\boxed{}$: After you draw the first card, there will be one less card in the deck. The first selection $\boxed{}$ the second selection.

Check Understanding

1. Decide whether the events are independent. Explain your answers.

a. You select a card from eight cards. Without replacing it, you select another card.

$\boxed{}$

b. You toss a coin and roll a number cube.

$\boxed{}$

Examples

❷ Probability of Independent Events There are six cubes in a bag. Four cubes are red and two cubes are blue. You draw a cube and put it back in the bag. You repeat this process two more times. Find the probability that you draw red cubes all three times.

The events are independent. The probability of drawing a red cube is

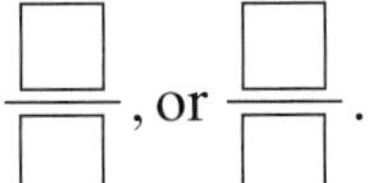 , or □/□ .

$P(\text{red, then red, then red})$ = 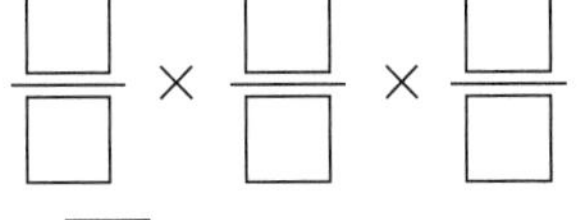 ← **Use the formula.**

= □/□ ← **Multiply.**

The probability of drawing three red cubes is □/□ .

❸ Alarm System Two neighbors have the same alarm system. Each alarm has 600 possible codes. What is the probability that the neighbors have the same code?

For each neighbor, the probability of having a specific code is □/□ .

$P(\text{2 neighbors with same code})$ = 

The probability of the two neighbors having the same code is □/□ .

Check Understanding

2. For the situation in Example 2, find $P(\text{red, then blue})$.

$P(\text{red, then blue})$ = 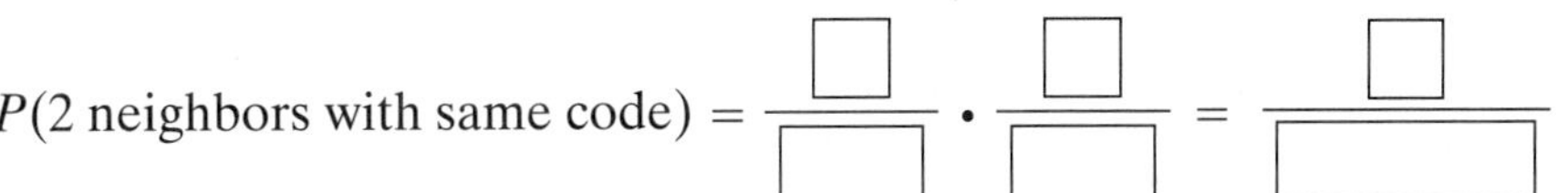

3. Reasoning Suppose in Example 3 three neighbors have the same alarm system. Would you multiply probabilities to find the probability that all three neighbors have the same alarm code? Explain your reasoning. Then find the probability.

Lesson 12-1 *(pp. 595–600)*   Solving Two-Step Equations

Lesson Objective ▼ Solve two-step equations	**NAEP 2005 Strand:** Algebra **Topic:** Equations and Inequalities **Local Standards:** __________________

Vocabulary

A two-step equation is ____

____

Example

1 **Solving a Two-Step Equation** Solve $6x - 14 = 16$. Check the solution.

$$6x - 14 = 16$$

$$6x - 14 + \boxed{} = 16 + \boxed{}$$ ← Add $\boxed{}$ to each side to undo the $\boxed{}$.

$$6x = 30$$ ← Simplify.

$$\frac{6x}{\boxed{}} = \frac{30}{\boxed{}}$$ ← Divide each side by $\boxed{}$ to undo the $\boxed{}$.

$$x = \boxed{}$$ ← Simplify.

Check $\quad 6x - 14 = 16$ ← Check your solution in the original equation.

$$6\left(\boxed{}\right) - 14 \stackrel{?}{=} 16$$ ← Substitute $\boxed{}$ for x.

$$\boxed{} = 16\checkmark$$ ← The solution checks.

Check Understanding

1. Solve each equation. Check the solution.

a. $5x + 3 = 18$ **b.** $3x - 4 = 23$

 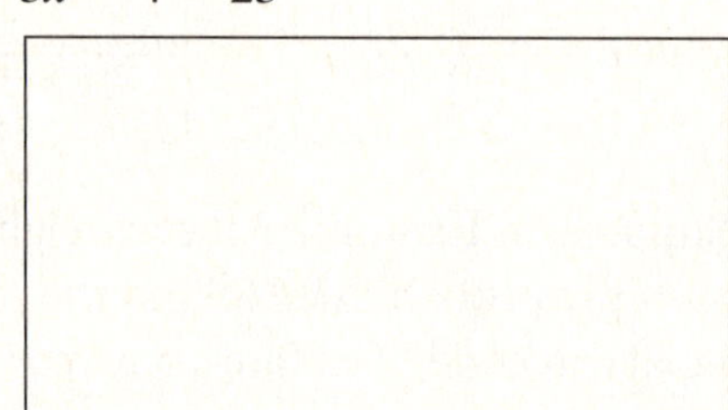

c. **Mental Math** What is the solution to $2a - 1 = 11$?

Example

❷ The Science Club sells birdfeeders for $4 each. The club spends $32 in building materials. The club's profit is $128. How many birdfeeders did the club sell? Use b to represent the number of birdfeeders. Use the equation $8b - 32 = 128$.

$$8b - 32 = 128$$

$$8b - 32 + \boxed{} = 128 + \boxed{}$$ ← **Add** $\boxed{}$ **to each side to undo the** $\boxed{}$.

$$8b = 160$$ ← **Simplify.**

$$\frac{8b}{\boxed{}} = \frac{160}{\boxed{}}$$ ← **Divide each side by** $\boxed{}$ **to undo the** $\boxed{}$.

$$b = \boxed{}$$ ← **Simplify.**

The club sold $\boxed{}$ birdfeeders.

Check Understanding

2. Solve $5p + 75 = 245$. Check the solution.

3. Jim and Scott agree to split the cost to rent a moped. Scott pays the entire bill, considers the $9 that he owes Jim, and tells Jim he now owes $12. How much was the total bill? Use m to represent the cost to rent the moped. Use the equation $\frac{m}{2} - 9 = 12$.

Lesson 12-2 *(pp. 601–605)*   Inequalities

Lesson Objectives	NAEP 2005 Strand: Algebra
☑ Write inequalities	Topic: Equations and Inequalities
☑ Identify solutions of inequalities	Local Standards: ____________________

Vocabulary

An inequality is ____

____

Symbol	Meaning
<	is [ ] than
>	is [ ] than
≥	is [ ] than or [ ] to
≤	is [ ] than or [ ] to
≠	is [ ] equal to

The graph of an inequality shows ____________________________________

____

A solution of an inequality is ______________________________________

____

Examples

❶ Writing an Inequality Write an inequality to express the situation.
Maria threw the softball more than 90 feet.

Words   [distance Maria threw the softball]   [is more than]   [90 feet]

Let [ ] = the distance Maria threw the softball.

Inequality   [ ]   [ ]   [ ]

The inequality is [ ].

❷ Writing Inequalities From Number Lines Write an inequality for the graph.

−2 −1 0 1 2

Since the circle is closed, use [ ] or [ ].

Since the graph shows values greater than −1, use [ ].

The inequality is [ ].

Name_____________________________ Class_____________________________ Date _____________

Examples

❸ Graphing Inequalities Write an inequality to represent the situation. Then graph the inequality. *Everyone in our class is 10 years old or older.*

If a = the age of a person in our class, a ⬚ 10.

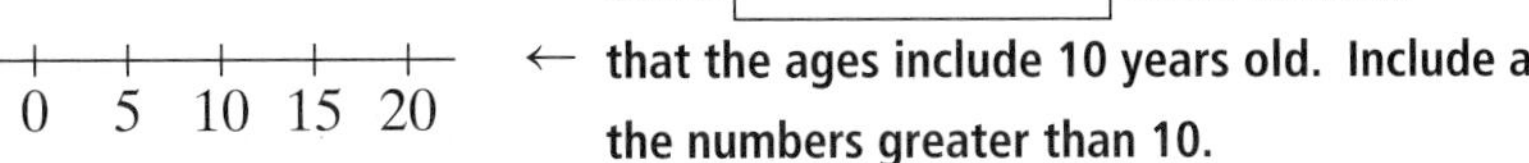

Use a ⬚ circle to show ← that the ages include 10 years old. Include all the numbers greater than 10.

Check Understanding

1. Most skydivers jump from an altitude of 14,500 feet or less. Write an inequality to express the altitude from which most skydivers jump.

2. Write an inequality for each graph.

a. 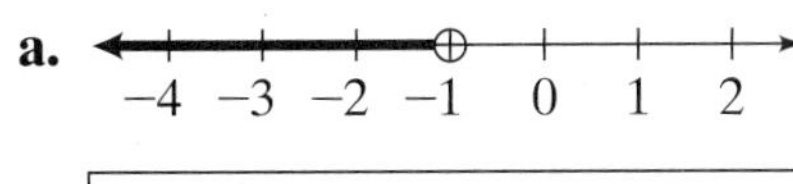

b. 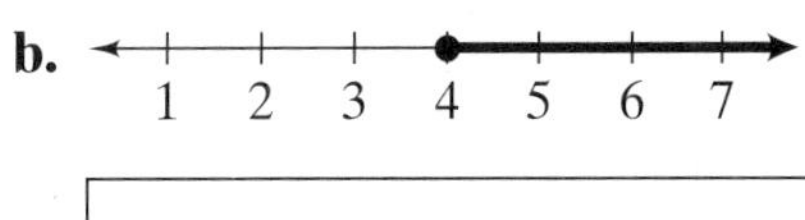

3. Write an inequality to represent the situation. Then graph the inequality. *Lisa spent at least 2 hours studying.*

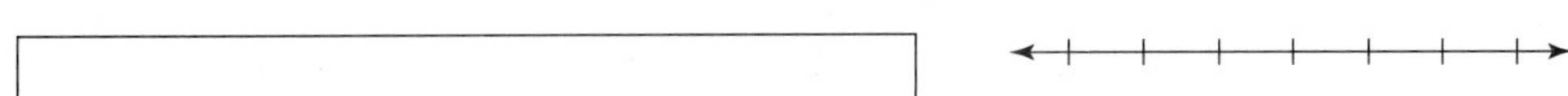

4. a. To be allowed into a certain jumping tent, you must be younger than 8 years old. Who of the following people can enter the jumping tent: Marissa (7 years, 11 months), Teagan (5 years), Ian (8 years, 3 months)?

b. Reasoning Are the solutions to $x < 3$ and $x \leq 3$ the same? Explain.

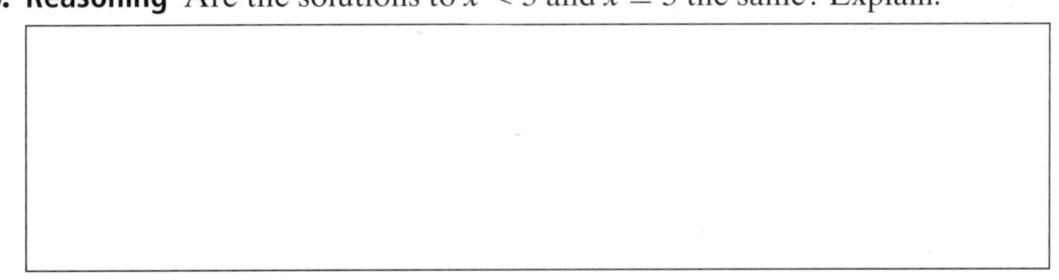

Name_______________________________ Class_______________________________ Date_____________

Lesson 12-3 *(pp. 606–609)*   **Solving One-Step Inequalities**

Lesson Objective	**NAEP 2005 Strand:** Algebra
▼ Solving inequalities by adding or subtracting	**Topic:** Equations and Inequalities
	Local Standards: _______________________________

Examples

❶ Solving an Inequality by Adding Solve $f - 4 \geq 8$.

$$f - 4 \geq 8$$

$$f - 4 + \boxed{} \geq 8 + \boxed{} \qquad \leftarrow \text{Add } \boxed{} \text{ to each side to undo the } \boxed{}.$$

$$f \geq \boxed{} \qquad \leftarrow \text{Simplify.}$$

❷ Saving Money Missy wants to save at least \$150 this month. She has saved \$112 so far. Write and solve an inequality to find how much more money she would like to save this month.

Words

amount saved	+	amount to save	is at least	\$150

Let $\boxed{}$ = the amount Missy still needs to save.

Inequality

$$\boxed{} \; + \; \boxed{} \quad \boxed{} \quad \boxed{}$$

$$112 + d \geq 150$$

$$112 - \boxed{} + d \geq 150 - \boxed{} \qquad \leftarrow \text{Subtract } \boxed{} \text{ from each side.}$$

$$d \geq \boxed{} \qquad \leftarrow \text{Simplify.}$$

Missy would like to save at least $\boxed{}$ more this month.

Name_______________________________ Class_______________________________ Date _______________

Check Understanding

1. Solve $u - 6 \leq 3$.

2. A restaurant can serve a maximum of 115 people. There are already 97 people dining in the restaurant. Write and solve an inequality to find how many more people the restaurant can serve.

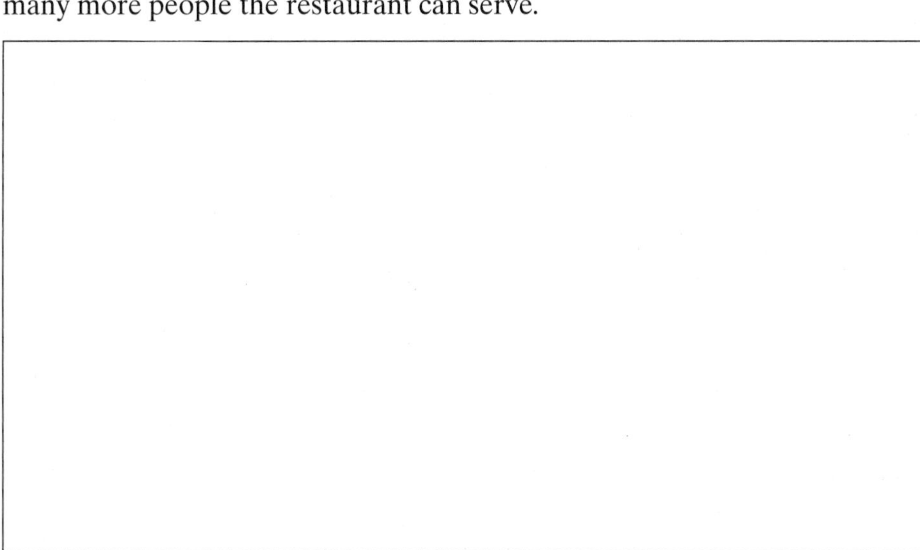

Lesson 12-4 *(pp. 611–614)*   **Comparing Strategies**

Lesson Objective	
▼ Solving a problem using two different methods	**Local Standards:** _______________________

Example

1 **Using Two Different Methods** Marcus is building a fenced rectangular enclosure for his turtles. He has 42 feet of fencing. Each short side will be 8 feet long. How long will each long side be?

Read and Understand

The short sides of the rectangular enclosure are

[ ] feet long. The fencing to go around the enclosure is [ ] feet long. The goal is to find the length of the [ ] sides of the enclosure.

Plan and Solve

Method 1

Since the fencing must go around the enclosure, draw a diagram of the

length of fencing and mark sections for each side. Mark two sections that

are [ ] feet long to represent the short sides. Divide the remaining length

into [ ] equal sections to represent the [ ] sides.

short	short	long	long
8 ft	8 ft	[ ] ft	[ ] ft

|← [ ] ft →|

Two sections of [ ] feet and two sections of [ ] feet can be made from the fencing. Each long side of the enclosure will be [ ] feet.

Method 2

Write and solve an equation.

Words | two short sides of rectangle | + | two long sides of rectangle | equals | perimeter of rectangle |

Let ☐ = the length of a long side.

Equation $2 \cdot$ ☐ $+$ $2 \cdot$ ☐ $=$ ☐

$16 +$ ☐ $= 42$ ← Multiply 2 and 8.

$16 -$ ☐ $+ 2r = 42 -$ ☐ ← Subtract ☐ from each side.

$2r =$ ☐ ← Simplify.

$\dfrac{2r}{☐} = \dfrac{☐}{☐}$ ← Divide each side by ☐.

$r =$ ☐ ← Simplify.

Since $r =$ ☐ , the long side of the enclosure will be ☐ feet.

[**Look Back and Check**] There are four sides of the enclosure measuring
☐ feet, ☐ feet, ☐ feet, and ☐ feet. The total used for the
enclosure is ☐ + ☐ + ☐ + ☐ , or ☐ feet. The answer
checks.

Check Understanding

1. a. Reasoning Look back at the two methods used to solve the example.
Which method would you use? Why?

b. The length of a board is 54 inches. You cut the board into two pieces.
One piece is 14 inches longer than the other. How long is each piece?

Lesson 12-5 *(pp. 616–620)*   Exploring Square Roots and Rational Numbers

Lesson Objectives	NAEP 2005 Strand: Number Properties and Operations
▼ Find square roots ▼ Classify numbers as rational	Topic: Estimation Local Standards: _______________________

Vocabulary

A square root of a given number is _______________________________________

____

A perfect square is ____

____

A rational number is ____

____

Examples

❶ **Finding Square Roots** Find $\sqrt{25}$.

Since ☐ × ☐ = 25, $\sqrt{25}$ = ☐.

❷ **Using a Calculator to Find a Square Root** Use a calculator to find $\sqrt{20}$
to the nearest tenth.

$\sqrt{20} \approx$ ⬚⬚⬚⬚⬚   ← On a calculator, press 2nd x^2 20 = .

$\approx$ ⬚   ← Round to the nearest tenth.

❸ A store is advertising its new square beach towels with an area of
64 square feet each. How long is each side of the towel?

The area of a square is found by ⬚⬚⬚⬚ a side. So, find the square root

of ⬚⬚ . Look for a number that is equal to ⬚⬚ when it is squared.

Since ☐^{2} = 64, $\sqrt{64}$ = ☐.

Each side of the towel is ☐ feet long.

Check Understanding

1. Find each square root.

a. $\sqrt{4}$ ⬚⬚⬚⬚⬚⬚⬚⬚   **b.** $\sqrt{100}$ ⬚⬚⬚⬚⬚⬚⬚⬚

Name_________________________________ Class_______________________________ Date _______________

Examples

❹ Approximating a Square Root Tell which two consecutive whole numbers $\sqrt{90}$ is between.

$\boxed{} < 90 < \boxed{}$ ← **Find the perfect squares close to 90.**

$\sqrt{\boxed{}} < \sqrt{90} < \sqrt{\boxed{}}$ ← **Write the square roots in order.**

$\boxed{} < \sqrt{90} < \boxed{}$ ← **Simplify.**

$\sqrt{90}$ is between $\boxed{}$ and $\boxed{}$.

❺ Identifying Rational Numbers Tell whether each number is rational.

a. 1.5   1.5 is a terminating decimal. It is $\boxed{}$.

b. 1.42443444...   This decimal does not repeat or terminate. It is $\boxed{}$.

❻ Classifying Square Roots of Whole Numbers Tell whether each number is rational.

a. $\sqrt{8}$ $\sqrt{8}$ is between $\boxed{}$ and $\boxed{}$. $\sqrt{8}$ is $\boxed{}$.

b. $\sqrt{169}$ 169 is a perfect $\boxed{}$. $\sqrt{169}$ is $\boxed{}$.

Check Understanding

2. Find each square root to the nearest tenth.

  a. $\sqrt{7}$ **b.** $\sqrt{10}$ **c.** $\sqrt{24}$ **d.** $\sqrt{86}$

3. How long is each side of a game board with an area of 81 square inches?

4. Tell which two consecutive numbers $\sqrt{8}$ is between.

5. Tell whether each number is *rational* or *not rational*.

  a. 0.232323   **b.** $\frac{3}{8}$ **c.** 1.112111211112...

  d. $\sqrt{7}$ **e.** $\sqrt{36}$ **f.** $\sqrt{121}$

Lesson 12-6 *(pp. 622–626)*   Introducing the Pythagorean Theorem

Lesson Objective	**NAEP 2005 Strand:** Geometry
▼ Use the Pythagorean Theorem	**Topics:** Relationships Between Geometric Figures
	Local Standards: _______________

Vocabulary and Key Concepts

Pythagorean Theorem

In any right triangle, the sum of the squares of the lengths of the ☐
(a and b) is equal to the square of the length of the ☐ (c).

Arithmetic

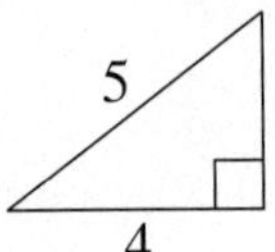

$3^2 + 4^2 = $ ☐

Algebra

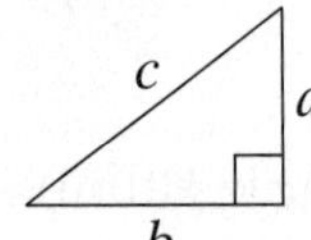

$a^2 + b^2 = $ ☐

The legs of a right triangle are _______________________________

____

The hypotenuse of a right triangle is _______________________________

____

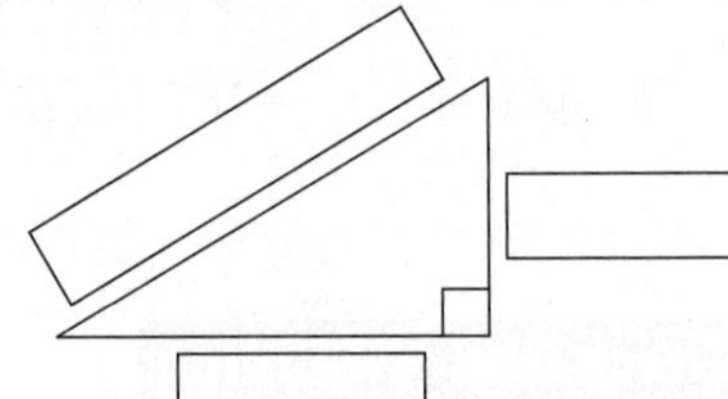

Examples

❶ Finding the Length of a Hypotenuse Two legs of a right triangle measure 20 and 21 units long. Find the length of the hypotenuse.

☐ ← Write the Pythagorean Theorem.

$20^2 + 21^2 = c^2$ ← Substitute 20 for ☐ and 21 for ☐.

☐ + ☐ $= c^2$ ← Square 20 and 21.

☐ $= c^2$ ← Add.

$\sqrt{☐} = \sqrt{☐}$ ← Find the square root of each side.

☐ $= c$ ← Simplify.

The length of the hypotenuse is ☐ units.

    Course 1 Daily Notetaking Guide

❷ Finding the Length of a Leg On a map, the towns of Shake, Rattle, and Roll form a right triangle. Shake is 5 miles due north of Rattle. Roll is directly east of Rattle. Shake and Roll are 15 miles apart. How far apart are Rattle and Roll?

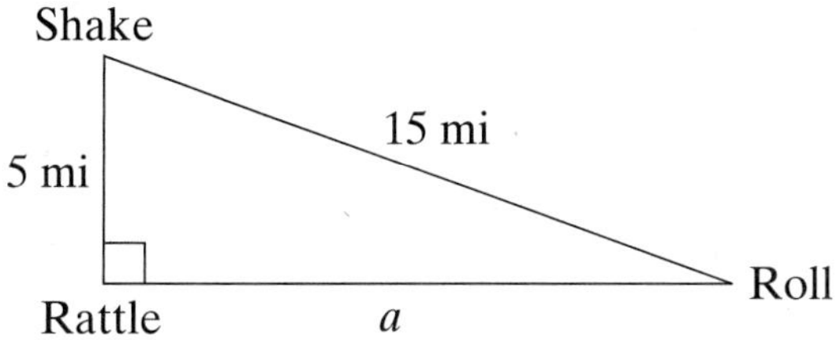

The three towns form a [____________] triangle. One leg has length [____] miles. The hypotenuse has length [____] miles.

$$[] \qquad \leftarrow \text{ Write the Pythagorean Theorem.}$$

$$a^2 + 5^2 = 15^2 \qquad \leftarrow \text{ Substitute 5 for } [\ ] \text{ and 15 for } [\ ].$$

$$a^2 + [\ ] = [\ ] \qquad \leftarrow \text{ Square 5 and 15.}$$

$$a^2 + [\ ] - [\ ] = [\ ] - [\ ] \qquad \leftarrow \text{ Subtract } [\ ] \text{ from each side.}$$

$$a^2 = [\ ] \qquad \leftarrow \text{ Simplify.}$$

$$\sqrt{[\ ]} = \sqrt{[\ ]} \qquad \leftarrow \text{ Find the square root of each side.}$$

$$a \approx [\ ] \qquad \leftarrow \text{ Simplify.}$$

Rattle is about [____] miles from Roll.

Check Understanding

1. a. Find the length of the hypotenuse of a triangle with legs of 12 inches and 16 inches.

b. Reasoning If both legs of a right triangle are under 12 inches, will its hypotenuse always be less than your answer to part (a)?

2. A ramp is attached to a rental truck forming a right triangle. The base of the triangle is 10 feet and the hypotenuse is 11 feet. How high is the top of the ramp? Round to the nearest tenth.